ETHICS AND INTERNATIONAL AFFAIRS

A philosopher and a specialist in international relations have combined in this book to analyze some of the major issues in present-day world politics. They apply to these a coherent ethical theory which gives a central place to conscience and moral principle, and stresses the need for the careful consideration of consequences.

The treatment of issues is realist throughout, in the sense that a conscious effort has been made to deal with problems as they would actually appear to statesmen; but, contrary to the "realists", it is maintained that a *combination* of prudential and moral considerations has played and should play a role in policy-making.

A philosophical exposure of the internal weaknesses of the "realist" position is backed up by a historical account of some particular decisions such as the Hiroshima bombing, and a discussion of some contemporary issues such as the nuclear deterrent, disarmament, the balance of power, intervention in the affairs of other states and world hunger.

J. E. Hare is Assistant Professor of Philosophy at Lehigh University, Pennsylvania. He was Visiting Fellow in the Humanities at the Medical College of Pennsylvania, American Philosophical Association Congressional Fellow and he has published articles in several journals of philosophy.

Carey B. Joynt is Monroe J. Rathbone Professor of International Relations at Lehigh University, Pennsylvania, where he has taught since 1951. He was Ford Foundation Fellow at Harvard and a Guggenheim Fellow at University College, London.

He is the author, with Percy E. Corbett, of *Theory and Reality in World Politics*, and has published articles in several journals of politics and philosophy.

ETHICS AND INTERNATIONAL AFFAIRS

J. E. Hare
and
Carey B. Joynt

St. Martin's Press   New York

For Terry and Catherine
and
For Anne and David

© J. E. Hare and Carey B. Joynt 1982

Printed in Hong Kong
First published in the United States of America in 1982

ISBN 0-312-26549-2

Library of Congress Cataloging in Publication Data

Hare, J. E., 1949–
    Ethics and international affairs.

    Includes bibliographical references and index.
    1. International relations – Moral and religious
aspects.   2. Ethics.   I. Joynt, Carey B., 1924–
II. Title.
JX1255.H37   1982   172'.4   81-14396
ISBN 0-312-26549-2   AACR2

Contents

Preface

The authors wish to thank the following for their many suggestions and helpful criticisms: R. M. Hare, White's Professor of Moral Philosophy, University of Oxford; Michael Howard, Regius Professor of Modern History, All Souls College, University of Oxford; F. H. Hinsley, Master of St. John's College, University of Cambridge; and Nicholas Rescher, University Professor of Philosophy, University of Pittsburgh.

These scholars took great trouble over the manuscript and between them saved us from many egregious errors. Those that remain are our own.

The authors and publishers would also like to thank George Kennan for permission to quote from his letters.

J.E.H.
C.B.J.

1 An Outline of Ethical Theory

WHAT IS A MORAL JUDGEMENT?

A chapter of this kind cannot give either a full or an original treatment of the topics it covers.[1] Its goal is rather to provide a framework of theory for the rest of the book. It seems sensible to start by saying something about the meanings of central moral terms like "ought" and "good", since these terms are going to play a large part in the argument of the book. The way to determine their meanings is to look at our usage of them, especially at the practices in which we engage in using them. This is largely a fact-finding investigation. We are not at this point recommending any usage, but trying to discover if there is any generally agreed way in which the words are used. Some people have accused this method of a bias towards conservatism, or of the tendency to maintain a practice just because it is the one we already have. But there is nothing to rule out our finding that we disapprove of some of the practices we discover, and therefore of the usages tied up with them. For there is a tie up. Some words with a moral content, like "gentleman" or "unAmerican", will no doubt seem to some people so bound up with disreputable moral views that they should not be used at all. The fact that a word is used in a certain way in our society does not force us to continue using it that way, or to continue to use it at all. It is necessary only that we make as clear as we can what the sense is in which we are using it.

One important practice in which we engage when using the moral words is that of advising. Advice can have a moral or a prudential character. We can advise or recommend to someone what we think is in his own interest, as when a stockbroker advises a client; or when a Secretary of State recommends to the President what he thinks is in the national interest. Or in the moral case, we can advise or recommend what we think is in the general interest. It is a feature of all these kinds of advice that when we advise someone we try to prescribe for his particular situation. And if the advice is sincere, he will be entitled to conclude that if we were in his situation ourselves, we would follow the advice we are giving him. Very often, to say "you ought to" is to say "if I were you, I would". At the risk of oversimplification, we can say that we very often use *moral* words when we want to give advice as to what we think it would be in the general interest for someone to do in a certain situation.

This account of our usage is full of pitfalls. But it has at least the virtue of highlighting the feature of moral judgements that has been called their *universalizability*. Moral judgements do have reference to the individual, but only as the individual is an example of a kind, namely the kind of individual like the one the judgement is about. It is often objected that individuals are unique, and that the same is true of individual situations. If individuals are unique, how can they be examples of a kind? We may reply that if there *were* to be a situation just like the one we are making our moral judgement about, we would be committed to making the same sort of judgement about it. And this is not an empty logical point. For in moral reasoning we have to consider the possible situation in which the roles of the individuals involved in our moral judgement are reversed.

It is not easy to find examples of moral thinking that are both manageably simple and realistic. As we shall see, it is characteristic of moral thinking that it can go on at different levels of complexity. For the time being we can choose a schoolboy example for the sake of its simplicity. If I am to judge that you ought to let me take the only two remaining biscuits on the plate, then I am committed to the judgement that if I were in your position and you in mine, including having each other's liking for biscuits, I should let you take both. I cannot judge that you ought to let me take both and that if the roles were reversed I ought not to let you take both. For the judgement, if universalizable, must prescribe the same action for the same situation, and therefore if you ought now to let me take both, it follows that I ought in your position to let you take both. The universalizability of moral judgements thus involves their *reversability*. It is a feature of our ordinary usage that we prescribe that others ought to do to us only what we prescribe that we should do to them if the roles were reversed.

There is another feature of moral judgements which is involved in this analysis, but it is harder to characterize. It is perhaps easiest to start with prudence, with the advice we might give to someone about what we think is in his best interest. Suppose the President recommends the imposition of import quotas on certain manufactured products. We would assume that he has taken into consideration what he thinks the nation most needs, perhaps the safeguarding of jobs in the face of serious competition from foreign products. There would be something fishy if he reached the conclusion that this would be the best policy for the country and then did not try to get the policy implemented. He might be influenced by moral concerns such as the need of other countries to earn foreign currency. But let us assume for the sake of the present example that he considers only the national interest. If he did not try to implement the policy, although he had apparently decided it was the best policy available, and if he was incapable of giving any reason for his inaction, we would be justified in doubting either his rationality or the sincerity of his original decision. Put simply, prudential judgements are usually taken as committing the person making the judgement to corresponding action, unless there are moral considerations which intervene.

It is very often true of moral judgements, as well as prudential ones, that when we make the judgement we are committing ourselves to act in a certain way in a certain type of situation. The difference is that in a moral judgement we are taking into consideration what prudence dictates not just for our own position, or the position of the person we are advising, but for the positions of all the parties affected by the decision.

One reason for hesitation here is that commitment to action does not seem to be *required* for the making of a moral judgement, whereas universalizability probably is necessary, though not sufficient. For it is certainly possible for a political leader to say that he knows that a certain policy is morally wrong and that he ought to stand up against it, but that the political pressures are too great to allow him to do this. All that is being claimed in the previous paragraph is that there is a central kind of moral judgement which does imply commitment to action in the way described. If this were not so, how could it be that we take a man's repeated failure to act in accordance with his own moral judgement as evidence against his sincerity?

To sum up, there are two consistency requirements that we tend to make of moral judgements, between what we say for others and what we say for ourselves, and between what we say and what we do.

INTUITIONS AND CONSEQUENCES

If the account is correct so far, how are we to select which moral judgements to make? Suppose a government official is deciding whether or not to resign from the government in wartime on a matter of conscience, and suppose that he wants very much to do the right thing, that is to say the morally right thing. How is he to decide what the right thing is? According to the above account, he has to decide what universalized prudence would dictate. But this of itself is not likely to get him very far in the absence of more substantive principles.

It may be that as soon as he starts thinking about it, his conscience speaks out loud and clear, telling him that the war is illegal and wrong, and that he must not selfishly put his own career ahead of the interests of the nationals of the invaded country or those in his own country whom he could alert by his resignation to the wrong being done. But how much weight should the voice of conscience be given? It is not clear that we can argue that what our consciences tell us must be right just because it is our consciences that tell us. For it seems likely that what our consciences tell us is at least partly dependent upon the way that we were brought up, and the influences from our early environment. Aristotle gives the analogy of a piece of wood being shaped by a carpenter. The wood is immersed in water, beaten and kept in a vice, until it takes on the desired shape. In the same way, a child is shaped, as we might say, by positive and negative reinforcement or by punishment, until it acquires a set of dispositions. In particular it acquires the dispositions to feel pleasure at the thought of some things and pain at the thought of others. The voice of conscience may be at times no more than the actualization of these previously acquired dispositions. We may decide then that the merit of what our consciences tell us depends at least partly on the merit of our early training. Perhaps the official in our example had an excessively legalistic father or perhaps he has developed from some early trauma an almost neurotic horror of violence. He might conclude that his early training was vitiated in exactly the respect that makes it unreliable as a guide for the present situation.[2] It may be that in the particular situation, he can do the most good by staying where he is and influencing the decision makers in what he thinks is a more acceptable direction.

But is it safe to conclude that the voice of conscience is dispensable, or that it should whenever possible be silenced altogether? We can call what conscience gives us "intuitions". It is true that these intuitions will not on many occasions be specific enough to take all the morally relevant factors into consideration. On many occasions they will conflict with one another. The intuition that one ought not to be party to a criminal policy and the intuition that one ought to be loyal to the government may not be in themselves mutually contradictory. But it may seem to the official in our example that as things are he cannot fulfill both at once. Moreover, it is likely to be the case sometimes that our intuitions can be shown to our satisfaction to be quite wrong. But the fact that our intuitions can fail us in these ways does not itself show that they are without value. What is important is to see where their value lies.

It is possible that there might be a higher ethical principle against which the worth of intuitions might be able to be measured. One candidate for this role is the principle that the rightness or wrongness of actions is determined by the goodness or badness of their consequences. We can call this "the consequentialist principle" and the appeal to it "the consequentialist method".[3] The debate over this principle, and its near relations, has been fierce and long. Some of this debate may be forestalled if it is recognized that this principle does not need to usurp the place of intuition. Tried and true general principles like the Ten Commandments, or like the principles "do not lie" or "do not break promises" can remain as the foundation of the character of the good man or woman. They will be principles that parents teach their children. And they will accordingly form dispositions in those children to feel pleasure at the thought of some things, like telling the truth, and pain at the thought of others. It will no doubt be the case that a good man should continue to feel pain at the thought of telling a lie even if it is his judgement, in the light of a consideration of the consequences, that on a particular occasion he should tell one. And he should no doubt feel pain at the thought of having told it, even if he is sure that that was the right thing to do in the circumstances. The point is that our intuitions do not give us "mere rules of thumb" (as is sometimes said by adherents of situation ethics), which we can break without compunction when the situation arises.

It will very often not be appropriate in moral thinking to appeal to the consequentialist principle at all. Our intuitions are not always incomplete or in conflict or wrong. They often tell us to do just what the consequentialist method would have told us. And even if they do sometimes fail, we can have supplementary intuitions to rectify them.

For example, the intuition that it is wrong to kill civilians in wartime may conflict with the intuition that it is wrong to take more lives than necessary to win the war. Suppose for example that killing these civilians will lead to a quick end to the war and thus save many more lives. Some moral thinkers have found convenient the principle of double effect, which we will discuss in more detail later. The principle says that unintended side effects are permissible, even if they are foreseen, as long as the intention is good in itself and the permitted evils are not disproportionate to the intended benefits. Certainly this principle was used in the Second World War to justify "withholding the intention and dropping the bomb".[4] This use was probably a misuse, but it illustrates how second-order intuitions can be used to supplement first-order ones. It might seem that the principle is too complex to be called an intuition. One could hardly learn it in this form at one's mother's knee. But those who support the principle claim that the formulation just given, or others like it, are expressions of a moral view that is implicit in a great deal of quite ordinary moral discussion.

It may be that much of the time we do not need to appeal to consequences. There is an analogy with the position of the United States Supreme Court, though it should not be pressed too far. Clearly the administration of justice would grind to a halt if every case had to be referred to the Supreme Court. There are accordingly intermediate courts to which appeal can be made, and although in principle every case could be appealed to the Supreme Court, very few in fact are.

Our intuitions give us rules which will very often tell us what to do without our having to question them. Unless we have a general reason for doubting our intuitions, we tend to proceed on the assumption that they are giving us the right answer until we discover incompleteness or conflict of the kind just described. Whether this assumption is right will depend on how good our early training was. The rules will be of many different kinds, as they have different roles to play. Some will have to be simple enough for us to verbalize to our children, like the principle, "it is wrong to cause physical injury to another person". Some will be more complex because they rank two or more duties, like the principle "it is wrong to cause physical injury to another person except in self-defence or the defence of another". It is easy to underestimate the complexity of principles that children can absorb. For they will observe and try to follow their parents' practice even if the parents do not verbalize the rules they are in fact complying with.

The usefulness of these rules does not disappear with childhood. For it may often be the case that as adults we are in situations that we recognize as precluding appeal to consequences. There are various sorts of situations like this. We may have too little time to think out the moral issue from scratch, and be compelled to rely on action-guiding rules that we have previously adopted. Or we may be under extraordinary stress, and recognize that the temptation to rationalize a wrong but expedient choice is likely to be too strong for us. Again it may be rational to stick to a rule which we have accepted as binding in previous less stressful circumstances. Or there may be no possibility, for one reason or another, of gathering the information that would be needed for making a decision based on consequences. Often the likely consequences of our actions are almost unknown to us, and our estimates, even when we feel surer, must always be liable to revision. Only an omniscient being, whose knowledge included future contingencies, would be immune from this sort of uncertainty.[5]

There will also be useful rules of procedure. Some will be simple, like the rule, "never make important decisions without sleeping on them first". Aristotle's principle that one should "lean against" one's dispositions as a result of early training. It is fairly simple itself and gives a way of ranking other more complex intuitions. It assumes that one knows oneself well enough to know the direction in which one characteristically goes wrong, and it then prescribes that one should choose what seems to one to go wrong equally in the opposite direction. If a person knows that he is slightly over-timid, he should do what seems to him slightly over-bold. On the national level, Aristotle's principle may be a useful recommendation to diplomats. A charitable interpretation of the "realists" like Hans Morgenthau and George Kennan is that they are advising American diplomats to err on the side of power politics because they have been too prone in the past to err on the side of a moralistic idealism. Intuitions which rank other intuitions can, on the other hand, be extremely complex. They are likely to get more complex as they get more specific, though this is not a necessary correlation. Thus the rule "it is wrong to cause physical injury to another person" is simpler and less specific than the rule "it is wrong to cause physical injury to another person except in self-defence or the defence of another". Clearly the second principle can itself be elaborated to include provisions for the killing of enemy soldiers in wartime, and so on. It is probably the case that both the simplicity-complexity scale and the generality-specificity scale have an infinite number of gradations.

But it may be that the official of our earlier example has gone as far as he can with his intuitions, and is still in great doubt. If his intuitions conflict, and he feels that his intuitions about how to rank them need themselves to be justified, he can still have recourse to the consequentialist method. Since he is not omniscient, he does not know for certain what will happen if he resigns or if he stays. But he does have some idea, based on his previous acquaintance and perhaps his reading, of what happens to junior cabinet ministers who resign; of how likely it is that they will ever get back into office; of how much effect their resignations have on national policy; of how much influence can be exerted by a dissident upon his colleagues in a war cabinet. If he chooses this sort of method of moral thinking, he will imagine himself in turn in the various possible roles he might be playing as a result of his decision, he will try to assess how much good he can do in each of them, and he will choose the best. Clearly this is going to be extremely complicated and difficult, and in the absence of omniscience, he is not going to achieve certainty. Since whatever he does, he may be breaking some rule which seems intuitively right, even what he finally chooses may seem merely the lesser evil, and he may feel remorse or even guilt about it. But it is not clear that the method is impossible, or that there is any alternative if his intuitions do not themselves provide a satisfactory answer.

We will sometimes use the terms "intuitive" and "critical" to describe the kinds of reasoning that moral agents go through. Intuitive reasoning is the use of intuitions to guide conduct directly. Critical reasoning is the appeal to the consequentialist method in order to settle disputes between intuitions, and to decide which intuitions it is right to encourage in oneself and in other people.

SPECIAL RELATIONS AND JUSTICE

The view that the consideration of consequences can be used as final court of appeal is full of difficulties. There is not space here even to mention, let alone deal with all the objections. But two objections in particular are relevant to the argument of the book. The first is that the consequentialist method cannot allow for so-called "special relations", and the second is that it cannot itself discriminate between just and unjust distributions. It is important that we should be able to provide an account of special relations since we are trying to deal with the relation of statesmen to their fellow-citizens. And it is important to see how justice fits into a theory of morality since it is often justice that is held to be normative for the relations between states.

The question about special relations is perhaps the easier one to answer. A familiar example is the following one. If you are taking your own child and your friend's child out in a boat, and they both fall in, and you can only save one, which do you save? It is claimed that a consequentialist cannot choose, if the total consequences are going to be equally bad either way, namely, the death of one child; whereas it is common sense that you ought to save your own child. This objection works only against a very simplistic form of consequentialism, a form that does not recognize the important place of intuition in moral thinking. On the account presented above, the father may be perfectly justified in saving his own child, as his intuitions will no doubt prompt him to do. When he thinks through the situation later, he may justify his action on the basis that it is best for parents to feel that they have to look after their own children first, since in the long run children will be better cared for if they do. Getting as close as he can to the knowledge of an omniscient and impartial observer, he may conclude that the intuition is one that parents should be encouraged to feel. The special relation between parent and child is in this way preserved. It is true that the intuition will in some cases justifiably be overridden. But this need not remove its general effectiveness. The same sort of thing can be said of a government deciding how much tax money to allocate to foreign aid. There is a strong argument on consequentialist grounds for saying that governments have the obligation in general to look after their own people first. But the argument can easily be taken too far. It would not justify the rulers of a prosperous nation guaranteeing to their own people a far higher standard of living by the outlay of its resources than could be achieved by the same resources in less prosperous countries elsewhere. Some of these problems will be tackled in the chapter on world order.

It is worth noting also that the form of consequentialism that we have just been presenting is not vulnerable to unusual examples like that of the drowning children, and this is precisely because they are unusual. The principles that we should internalize, and the intuitions that we should feel, on this view, are those which will result in the right action *most of the time*. It is not a proper objection that following the principles will in unusual cases produce a wrong action. The probabilities of a situation arising of a certain kind are thus of great relevance in the selection of principles. We may feel revulsion at the prescription which the consequentialist method comes up with in unusual cases, and our revulsion may be justified. To say this is admittedly ambiguous. For there is a sense in which the revulsion is not justified, namely that it rejects what is actually best by the consequentialist standard. But there is another sense in which it is justified, namely that there is nothing unreasonable about internalizing a prohibition on actions that in the large majority of cases produce unacceptable consequences. It is no doubt possible, for example, that in some unusual cases it would be right to bomb a city. But the fact that an ideal observer would in those cases prescribe it does not show that we would not be justified in finding such a prescription intuitively repellent.

It may be said that the danger of the sort of analysis we have given is that it is too easily abused; that it is too easy to find one's own situation exceptional, especially in wartime, and to appeal from the intuitive level to a consideration of consequences whenever one's intuitions tell one to do something inconvenient or risky. The reply is that this shows only that the consequentialist method needs to be used with caution. The estimate of how often it can be used to override an intuition will depend on a person's estimate of his capacity for objectivity. But if we argue that consequences should never be used to override an intuition, we must believe that any attempt to achieve an acceptable level of objectivity is doomed from the start.

The other objection to making the consideration of consequences a court of last appeal is that no consequentialist account can give its due place to the distinction between just and unjust distributions. One of the chief difficulties in discussing justice is that the term is so ambiguous. A full treatment of the subject would have to deal with formal justice, or impartiality, which can be said to make the requirement that in moral decisions each person count as one, and nobody as more than one; and it would have to analyze the broad sense in which justice is the same as righteousness,[6] and the narrower senses in which the term refers to the distribution of benefits and harms, or more narrowly still to the awarding of rewards and punishments.

This chapter is not the place to try to sort out all these senses, and the relations between them. All we will try to do is to reply to the objection about justice and the consequentialist method mentioned earlier. It is convenient to return to the example about the biscuits and to sacrifice realism for the sake of simplicity. It is claimed that the consequentialist cannot say whether it is better for each person to have one biscuit or for one of them to have both. If we measure consequences in terms of the satisfaction of desires, is not the amount of desire-satisfaction the same in both cases? Yet we would usually feel that it was unfair and therefore wrong for one person to get both biscuits.

To some extent the same response is appropriate to this objection as to the last one. An ideal observer might be in a position to make a judgement that the amount of desire-satisfaction would be exactly the same if one person had both biscuits and if each person had one. But it would be a highly *unusual* situation in which *we* were able to make that judgement. A person's satisfaction from the first biscuit would usually, for example, be greater than his satisfaction from the second; and there are likely to be enormous complications, even in a deliberately simplified case like this one, that arise from the effects of the alternative distributions on the parties' inter-personal relations. Envy may, for example, be promoted, or resentment. There is moreover a danger that the person who wants both biscuits may appeal to consequences in favour of his position illegitimately.

It may be claimed that what is required, if our distributions are to be just, is a strict adherence to the principle that unequal distribution is never justifiable. It is probably true that many people have egalitarian intuitions of this sort. But these intuitions are in many cases problematic. Suppose that there is one indivisible biscuit. Does justice dictate that neither person should have it because it is not the case that both can? It may be agreed that it is better that one person should have it than that neither should (though the issues are very complex, and one thinks of the distribution of scarce resources in high quality education or medical care). If so, unequal distribution will be justified in some cases. More straightforwardly, resources must to some extent be differentially distributed in accordance with different needs. Organists, for example, who have to slide a great deal on wooden benches, need more pairs of trousers than professional lifeguards. A welfare state would quite properly make an unequal distribution of trousers to accommodate the different needs of different professions. To take a more serious example, an unequal distribution of technologies between countries need not be in itself unjust if it corresponds to different domestic needs.

It may be held that there is a class of basic needs which all human beings have to the same extent. In Chapter 7 we will suggest that basic needs will include at least the necessities of life. But it does not seem that we can tell by asking what is *just* whether there are needs beyond the necessities of life which fall into this class. There have been varying intuitions through history as to what should be considered a just distribution. And if we ask *which* view of distributive justice we should accept, we are surely asking how much inequality it is proper to admit. The point is that we cannot appeal to distributive justice in order to settle which theory of distributive justice we should accept. Our criterion must therefore be one against which different theories can be measured. To go back to the biscuits, if we ask whether it is just that one person should have both, it may be that we are asking what our *present* conception of justice requires. The answer will then depend on what that conception is. But we may also be asking about that conception itself whether it can be justified. We may be asking what conception of justice it is right for us to have, and in particular whether it should be one that allows that degree of inequality. When answering *this* question (but not when answering the previous one) we need to get as close to the position of the ideal observer as we can, and see what the consequences would be for society at large of the general acceptance of the various rival theories of distributive justice we are considering. The failure to observe the distinction between these two sorts of questions may in part explain the popularity of the claim that the consequentialist method is inadequate to deal with justice.

How would an ideal observer decide which principles of justice to encourage? How much inequality would he allow? There are at least three factors which would tend to move him to prefer more equal distributions. First there is the fact that inequality tends to produce envy. This is to put the point negatively. We could also say that equality tends to encourage self-respect and mutuality. To give one person both biscuits not only deprives the other of some enjoyment, but also encourages in him bad feelings. To give each a biscuit encourages correspondingly good feelings (it is difficult to be more specific because of the poverty of the example). In international relations, the gap between richer and poorer nations is for this reason one of the chief threats to peace. Secondly, there is the fact of what is sometimes called "diminishing marginal utility". The millionaire gets less advantage from an extra hundred pounds than the subsistence farmer, and the same is true at a higher level with developed and subsistence economies. The distribution which maximizes happiness therefore will be the one that gives the resources to the less well-off, and this will tend to decrease inequality. Thirdly, there is the fact already mentioned that we tend to exaggerate the strength of our own desires, and the degree to which others are concerned that our needs be met. It will be safer therefore to "lean against" the assumption that peoples' desires for a thing are of an unequal strength.

The notion of "rights" is probably best seen as parasitic on the notion of justice. A person has a right to what it is just that he be given. Unfortunately the term is not an exact one. There are at least three ways of translating talk about "rights" into talk about correlative obligations. If I suggest that I have a right to a thing, I may mean simply that it is not wrong for me to have it, or that I should not be prevented from trying to get it, or that I should be given it.[7] Any discussion of 'human rights' needs to take account of which of these senses is involved. We will discuss some of these difficulties in the chapter on world order.

THE PLACE OF IDEALS

What is the place of ideals in moral thought? A consideration of this question will involve a discussion of egoism and altruism, and of the relations between morality and prudence. To talk about an ideal observer is already to talk about idealism in a sense. On the view we have been presenting, the ideal standard against which our decisions are to be measured is the standard set by the application of the consequentialist principle by someone who is both impartially benevolent and in possession of all the relevant information. It is because we are neither of these that we are often not in a position to apply the ideal standard directly. As was said earlier we have often, perhaps most of the time, to rely on principles or intuitions which we believe will recommend more often than not the decision that the ideal observer would have recommended.

It can be shown that we are not in fact ever in possession of all the relevant information. For on a consequentialist view all the future consequences of an action are relevant to evaluating it. We are never in a position to be completely certain in advance about any consequence, and even though we may be perfectly justified in predicting immediate consequences, the further they are removed in time, the less predictive power we have. Moreover we are limited in our power to assess the relevant probabilities. The probability of someone responding to our action in a certain way depends on the number of times he and people like him have responded in that way to actions like ours in the past. This information about the past, like the information about the future, we may not have. The probabilities will be especially unclear if the action being considered, for example nuclear attack, has very few precedents. That we are not impartially benevolent can be determined by a consideration of the number of times we prefer, individually and nationally, our own good to that of others, even when we know that the others' need is far greater than ours.

It is important to see, however, that the fact that the ideal may be unattainable does not make it irrelevant to our decisions. For it is of great theoretical and practical interest to know what the standard is at which we are aiming. As Aristotle would say, it helps an archer to shoot straight if he can see the target in front of him. The ideal standard shows us in which direction we should be moving, that of being less ignorant and less partial.

If we are to be impartially benevolent, we have to be able to want the good of others for its own sake. For to be impartial is to want the good whether it is ours or not. The contrary state of mind is to want a good only if it is going to be ours. One way, therefore, of asking the question about the place of ideals is by asking about the place of what have been called "the positive vicarious affects".[8] Vicarious affects are the feelings we have that are excited by the good or harm that happens to others. Malice, for example, is a negative vicarious affect, when we enjoy someone else's misfortune for its own sake. The desire for retribution against an enemy is a negative vicarious affect. Positive vicarious affects are when we rejoice at others' good and grieve at their misfortunes. We can ask the question, then, of how far an ideal observer would encourage the positive vicarious affects.

One merit of asking the question this way is that it shows the implausibility of saying that we simply do not have vicarious feelings at all. For we clearly have negative vicarious feelings. But why then should we not be capable of positive ones as well? There will undoubtedly always be alternative explanations in terms of self-interest. One famous case is the soldier who sacrifices his life to save the life of a comrade. It has been argued that what is really motivating him is the overwhelming desire for a brief moment of glory before the shell explodes, or the dread of the long years of remorse which would otherwise follow.[9] But what reason is there, other than prejudice, for denying what has usually been believed, that sometimes acts of heroism such as this are done primarily from regard for another person?

There is one reason often adduced which is not a good one. It is often said that we do what we do because we want to do it, and that *therefore* our motivations are always egoistic. The trouble with this argument is that it puts the cart before the horse.[10] The altruist does not help others because he wants to derive satisfaction from helping them. The only reason that he derives satisfaction from helping them is that he wants to help them. We might say that a person is altruistic if he wants the good of others. If he then works for that good, he will indeed be doing what he wants to do. But that will not show that his motivation is egoistic. It will show only that he has the strength of mind to carry out his purposes, and that those purposes are altruistic. If one is claiming that altruism is impossible, one has to show that altruistic desires or purposes are impossible. It is not enough to show that actions result from desires or purposes, for that is characteristic of all action, egoistic and altruistic alike.

Having said this, however, it must also be pointed out that positive vicarious affects may only occur in an unmixed condition extremely rarely. It may be the case that they mostly occur in combination with non-vicarious or egoistic affects. This is especially true at the national level. There were no doubt mixed motives behind the Marshall Aid Plan, and the gradual transition from British Empire to Commonwealth. The importance of maintaining that altruistic motives can nevertheless occur is that if they could not, it would be foolish to recommend them. An ideal observer would be unreasonable if he encouraged us to feel what it was psychologically impossible for us to feel. The possibility of mixed motives in politics will be illustrated in the chapter of this book which discusses the return of the Russian prisoners and the dropping of the first atomic bombs.

There are a number of prudential reasons that an ideal observer might give for recommending the positive vicarious affects. Any answer to the question "why should I want other people's good?" has to go beyond morality. For the answer "in order to be moral" is not likely to carry any weight. The justification of morality is exactly the issue. There can perhaps be religious answers to the question which go beyond morality, though this is controversial. But the obvious source for our answer is an appeal to prudence.

The first reason for thinking that it is prudent to encourage in oneself and others the positive vicarious affects is that they make possible mutual benefits which would not be possible without them. International cooperation is made much easier by genuine feelings of trust and goodwill. Some kinds of cooperative enterprise are impossible without these, even though both parties know in advance that the results of cooperation would be mutually beneficial. The second reason is that society is constructed in such a way as to reward the positive vicarious affects, or at least the appearance of them. Even self-sacrifice is honoured in our society (though it has not been in all, and our society also honours self-assertion). It is similarly true that the absence of concern for others for their own sake is generally condemned at the international level. Much national propaganda would not be effective in the absence of a general consensus that it is appropriate to praise and blame the behaviour of nations as well as individuals on moral grounds.[11]

It might be argued that the prudent person will therefore be careful to give the appearance of altruism, without actually suffering any of the disadvantages that would come from a genuine care for others. But people are not so easily deceived. Moreover, if we are to be altruistic on those occasions when it is to our advantage to be so, we need to encourage in ourselves a strong disposition to be so. Altruism is not a state of mind that can be put on and taken off like a false moustache. The only way to encourage the disposition is to practice it, and we may need therefore to practice it even on those occasions where it seems not to be to our advantage. Finally, if we do acquire the disposition, this will give us an additional prudential reason for acting in an altruistic way. For we will now feel painful remorse if we do not.

If we agree that there are these answers to the question "why should I want other people's good?", we can then ask how much vicarious feeling we should have. There is a lot to be said in favour of the suggestion that there is a decent minimum of regard for others which the members of a society must feel if the society is to be viable. The same would be true of any attempt to build an international society. We might say, then, that it is appropriate to praise someone for being more altruistic than is required by such a minimum standard, but that it is not appropriate to blame someone for not being so. The purpose of this suggestion is to allow us to say that some actions and dispositions are praiseworthy but not obligatory. And this seems true to our general practice. For we admire, for example, people who sell everything that they have and give to the poor, but we do not feel required thereby to follow their example.

It is sometimes said that America is prone to swing from idealism in international relations to cynicism and then back again.[12] A country might feel, at a moment of great national inspiration, that it could go a long way towards improving the world. But it might at the same time be true that there are certain underlying problems in the relationships of international power which are likely to defeat its best efforts. It is a delicate question how high a national goal can be set without leading in the long run to disenchantment. This may indeed not be in anyone's control, and even if it is, there may not be any helpful general answers to the question. But it is at least plausible to say that there is a decent minimum of good will and responsibility in international relations which can rightly be asked for, and that any idealism which leads in the long run to a cynical disregard for even this minimum is likely to do more harm than good.

It might be objected that even if we can reach a decent minimum standard by setting ourselves a relatively restricted goal, we are still letting ourselves off too lightly by doing so. For it is all too easy to think that although some people may be, so to speak, saint material, most of us are not. It is comforting to be able to leave the higher reaches of virtue to them, to use a mountaineering analogy, and confine our own aspirations to the lower slopes. But it is not clear that there is an unevenly distributed talent for doing what is right analogous for example to the talent for playing the violin. It may be the case that there is something in the natural endowment of some children that equips them for violin playing. If someone tries to play the instrument and fails miserably after a prolonged effort, he can reasonably say that he does not have the gift. But if someone tries to be altruistic and fails repeatedly, does he have *that* sort of excuse?

We can begin to answer this question by referring back to the standpoint of the ideal observer. Even if all human beings are born with the same capacities for doing what they think good, it will still be the case that some people find some things more difficult than other people do. Certain kinds of child neglect or child abuse, for example, create adults who are almost incapable of sympathy or of more than a brutal egoism. On the international level, the experience of losing millions of lives to a foreign invader may make it more difficult to trust that country even thirty years later in very different circumstances. An ideal observer would know for each person in each situation how difficult it would be to reach a particular goal and what the likelihood would be of eventual disenchantment. He would have the relevant information about every individual in a country and would therefore have enough information to make a judgement about how high a national goal it would be reasonable to set. If it is set either too low or too high, the long term result will be missed potential.

It is a different question whether or not we should try to approximate the judgement of the ideal observer. As with any direct appeal to the consequentialist principle, there is the issue of whether we are sufficiently knowledgeable and impartial to attempt it. In this case there is a special difficulty. It is easy for a person to try to excuse what he has done on the basis that he is simply the sort of person who tends to behave in this way. But this is not a good excuse for an individual or a country. It would not be a good excuse for the government of a country that is engaged in extending its "living room" to excuse this on the grounds of the natural tendency of its people towards expansion. It would not be a *good* excuse because this expansionist tendency was the focus of the original complaint. Moral complaints are characteristically lodged both at particular actions and at the dispositions which gave rise to them. If a poor country is complaining of the niggardliness of a richer one, it is not a good excuse that the citizens of the richer country are simply not very much interested in the plight of the rest of the world. For it is this lack of interest which is the focus of the initial complaint. It is a relevant excuse that a change of national disposition is very difficult to bring about. But this excuse is very easily abused for self-serving reasons. If it is possible to "lean against" this tendency to abuse it, and if genuine information is available about how much for example a country might be prepared to give to foreign aid if suitably encouraged, then it may be possible and desirable to try to approximate the judgement of the ideal observer. There are numerous problems here, and we will look at some of them in the final chapter.

There are a number of reasons that an ideal observer might have for prescribing a fairly restricted set of initial goals. The first is that if he did not, there would be a danger that not even a decent minimum standard would be reached. One way to illustrate this is by looking at the twentieth-century political realists. We will do this in more detail in the next chapter. Reinhold Niebuhr, placing himself in a long tradition including Kierkegaard and Nygren, wanted to insist on the tension between this-worldly and other-worldly values. He sometimes described this tension as that between justice and love, and articulated it as that between a standard which allows the claims of self-interest and one that allows only self-sacrifice. It is true that Niebuhr is not consistent about this, but at times he talks approvingly of a "frank dualism" between standards for individuals, where love can appropriately be striven for, and for groups, where it cannot be. His followers have not always been so devoted to the ideal of self-sacrifice. But they have inherited from him the frank dualism, which makes it inappropriate for groups to strive for self-sacrifice, especially national groups. The spheres of politics and international relations thus come to be declared out of bounds for the moralist. An attempt like Niebuhr's not to compromise the demand of the highest standard can be counterproductive. It can lead to less high standards actually being applied in politics than might have been if the initial demand had been more restricted.

The second reason for restricting the demand to a decent minimum is that it provides a reasonable incentive for societal action. The difficulty is to maintain the right balance between a standard which is too low and leads to unwarranted self-satisfaction, and one which is too high and leads to disillusion. To rule out self-sacrifice altogether as a proper demand in politics is to set the standard too low (though this is another long argument, and it needs to be shown that national groups *can* act sacrificially to some degree). But to demand unqualified self-sacrifice to the point of self-annihilation is to set the standard too high.

We could take the example of the redistribution of wealth through taxation, where the groups involved are not nations but social classes. A thorough-going application of the ethic of self-sacrifice might require that the rich allow themselves no use of their money until they have met all the needs of the poor that their money can meet (another long argument). Such a requirement is bound to be dismissed by most people as unrealistic. But to agree with this is not necessarily to agree that it is inappropriate to look for sacrifice at all from the wealthy classes.[13] It may be appropriate both for individuals and for groups to apply a standard that asks for somewhat more sacrifice than is licensed by self-interest, but not *very* much more. And it may result in a more just distribution than looking for either unlimited sacrifice or for only as much as can be justified by self-interest.

The third reason is that a decent minimum of regard for others, if generally adopted, would provide a kind of base camp (to go back to the mountaineering analogy), from which the higher slopes could be attempted. The possibilities of getting lost and isolated, or of running out of supplies, would be much less threatening if the base camp had been established. If a society shares some basic intuitions about how much altruism is reasonably to be asked for in certain situations, those who want to do more than that can make their efforts at least intelligible to a fair number of their contemporaries.

A major objection to this view of the decent minimum is that it has an inbuilt tendency towards conservatism. It may have been thought at some time that treating negroes as full human beings was above and beyond the call of duty. Some people did, and they were to be praised for it (as long as this did not encourage a rebellious spirit), but the large majority who did not were not to be blamed for not doing so. It might have been argued that to demand more of the white population was unrealistic, and that unrealistic demands tend to weaken the society's commitment to regard for others in general.

A partial reply to this objection is provided if we realize that the decent minimum standard is itself to be justified by reference as far as possible to the standpoint of the ideal observer. We might say now, looking back, that the ideal observer would not have approved putting freedom from racial prejudice of this sort *outside* the decent minimum. And it can be hoped that even then an insistence on impartial benevolence and sympathy and full information might have been at least as likely to produce social change as reliance upon intuitions or the authority of social habit. The earlier utilitarians in fact have rather a good record in this respect.

One final comment that may be worth making is that our society does seem to operate with a concept of a decent minimum. This is true in matters of prudence as in matters of morality. Thus we tend to recommend physical fitness, but to stigmatize as fanatical too devoted a pursuit of it. The standards of altruism in most societies *are* higher than self-interest would dictate, but they are not set unreachably high, except perhaps for major public offices. Thus admiration for those who give away all their possessions to help the poor is balanced by a sense that we have some obligations to ourselves, of self-respect and self-fulfillment. This fact does not show that the view is right, but it does suggest that our analysis is not hopelessly counter to common sense.

ACTS AND OMISSIONS AND THE PRINCIPLE OF DOUBLE EFFECT

We cannot end this chapter without mentioning two supplementary principles that have frequently been appealed to in the ethical analysis of international relations, the principle that commissions are worse than omissions and the principle of double effect. Both of these, we shall argue, have a legitimate place as intuitive principles, but not as absolutes.

The discussion of the first of these has centred most recently around examples in medical ethics, such as the removal of babies from the respirator in neonatal intensive care units. In these sorts of cases it may well be that a consequentialist can support the principle. For the options which the doctors *describe* as negative euthanasia, or allowing to die (as omissions) are often less harmful or probably less harmful than those that they *describe* as positive euthanasia, or killing (as commissions).[14] But if the choice is between an act of omission and an act of commission, and if the consequences of each are just as likely to be just as bad, it is hard to see how a consequentialist could find any morally significant difference. The distinction will only be morally useful if it is the case that the consequences of omission are *often* likely not to be as bad as those of the corresponding commission.

There are at least four reasons for thinking that this is the case. *First,* the moral distinction is already in current use. Killing is generally regarded as worse than allowing to die, for example, so that it occasions more remorse, or more resentment. *Second,* there would be a tremendous burden imposed by the need to find as good a justification for letting die as we now have to for killing. The time that a mother spends with her children could be spent raising famine relief money. She is no doubt letting someone die by not spending it in this way. But does she have to be able to say that she would be prepared morally to kill someone in order to have this time with her children? *Third,* it is sometimes the case that acts of omission are harder to avoid than corresponding acts of commission. Perhaps most of the things a person might do when he sees a child drowning might result in the child's death. He might walk away, or read a book, or admire the view. Only jumping in will save the child's life. Since the omission is thus harder to avoid, it can be argued that it is easier to excuse. In general this is true of our practice of allowing as an excuse, for example in a motor crash, an appeal to the difficulty of avoidance. *Fourth,* it may be the case that commissions tend to affect people we know, or can at least identify, whereas omissions often do not. When reading this sentence, there is perhaps an infinite number of things I am omitting to do. Most of these things would probably affect total strangers, such as the person in whose field the balloon lands which I might now be releasing, or the person receiving the bowl of rice purchased by the money I might now be sending to World Vision. It is this lack of personal contact which has led some relief organizations to establish personalized relations between donors and recipients with the aid of photographs and correspondence. It seems that people feel more responsibility to those who need help whom they know, and this may be justifiable on consequentialist grounds.

But none of these reasons is sufficient to allow us to conclude that there is an absolute rule that acts of commission are worse than the corresponding acts of omission. There may well be situations in which the direct consequences of a commission and an omission are the same, but the indirect consequences of the omission are worse. If we could find out when this is the case, we would be justified in preferring the commission.

Secondly, the principle of double effect. A consequentialist could agree that this is a "practical formula which synthesizes an immense amount of moral experience".[15] The principle relies initially on a distinction between two sorts of consequences, one which is intended, while the other is "beside" the intention. A direct intention of saving one's life may involve the foreseen side effect of causing the death of an assailant. Saint Thomas might not have approved of this, but his theological descendants were prepared to sanction self-defence on the grounds that "moral acts take their species according to what is intended, and not according to what is beside the intention".[16] The provisos were added that the permitted evil must not be seen as, and must not be, a means to the intended good, and that the permitted evil must not be disproportionate to the intended good.

Put this way, the principle of double effect is full of obscurities. The principle is often used in order to make more acceptable an absolute ban on certain kinds of intention, such as the intention to kill non-combatants in wartime. According to the principle, there are occasions when such killing may be permitted, but it may never be intended. The first difficulty is in identifying, except perhaps on theological grounds, which intentions are absolutely prohibited. This difficulty is not, however, peculiar to the principle of double effect. A second difficulty is that of distinguishing in particular cases between intended means and foreseen consequences. A third is in knowing what counts as disproportionate permitted evil. A fourth is that the distinction between acts and their consequences is in many cases a tenuous one.[17] It often depends on how the acts themselves are described (e.g. raising the arm, pulling the lever, dropping the bomb, hitting a centre of wartime production, or killing 10,000 civilians).

It may be that these obscurities in the principle can be clarified. The central intuition is a good one, that we judge the moral character of a person more by his direct intentions than by the side effects, even the foreseen side effects, of what he does. Most of the traditional theodicies, for example, tell us to judge the character of God by what He intends, and not by what He permits. But as with the principle about acts of omission and commission, this intuition cannot provide an absolute prohibition. Thus the principle is often appealed to to justify the view that it is never right to intend directly the death of the innocent. But there may be situations in which even such a direct intention is the lesser of two evils. If we can know that we are in such a situation, we may be able to justify the intention. But as with all intuitions with some general acceptance utility, we may be justified in feeling initially that it is always wrong to break them.

2 The Political Realists

THE REALIST TRADITION

In this chapter we are going to look at the views of three American theorists who have expounded a kind of political realism in international relations. These theorists, Reinhold Niebuhr, Hans Morgenthau and George Kennan, are not realists in the classical sense, but they share a number of theses with the founders of the realist tradition. We will look very briefly at this tradition, and then concentrate on its contemporary manifestation.

The figures who stand out most clearly from the ancient world as proponents of political realism are two sophists who appear in Plato's dialogues, Thrasymachus and Callicles, and the Athenian generals who spoke in the Melian dialogue recorded in Thucydides's *History*. The debate between Thrasymachus and Socrates is biased against the realist position in Plato's presentation.[1] Thrasymachus is made to seem not only a boor but a fool. His view is that "justice is nothing else than the interest of the stronger".[2] But during the course of the discussion with Socrates, he comes to use the terms "just" and "unjust" more conventionally, so that "injustice" implies the unbridled pursuit of self-interest. He says that for him "the best and most perfectly unjust state" will be the state most likely to be "unjustly attempting to enslave other states" or to have "already enslaved them, and be holding them in subjection".[3] For Thrasymachus, injustice of this consummate kind is the highest wisdom and excellence of a state, and there is no valid moral claim against a state which pursues its own interest to the total exclusion of the interests of others.

The Athenian generals acted on this policy in the course of their war with Sparta. It has often been pointed out how close their language is to that of the sophists. Melos, a small island and a colony of Sparta, had refused to submit to the naval might of Athens. Thucydides records a dialogue between the Athenians and the Melian ambassadors, in which the latter make an appeal to the principle that it would be *unjust* for the Athenians to take by force a Spartan colony. The generals reply that such a principle does not operate in the relations between states, or for that matter between individuals. It is rather by the necessity of nature that the strong rule. This is true of animals, of men and of gods. The Melians therefore, since they are weaker, must either yield or be destroyed. Thucydides tells us that they did not yield, and that "the Athenians ... slew all the men of military age, and made slaves of the women and children".[4]

What Thucydides himself thought of the dialogue and its consequences he does not tell us. But it is probable that he is charting the moral course of the great war just as he charted the physical course of the great plague.[5] In both cases his aim was therapeutic, to recount the symptoms so that the disease could be recognized before it was too late. It would be misleading to call Thucydides himself a "realist".[6]

In the *Republic*, Thrasymachus is defeated by the introduction of a number of highly debatable premises.[7] But one of Socrates's arguments that does have force is that there has to be a certain amount of "justice" even between criminals, if they are to succeed in their enterprises. There has to be "honour among thieves". A state that was *perfectly* unjust would not be able to cooperate with any other in the pursuit of goals which it could not attain single-handed. Thrasymachus could have replied that he did not mean to be taken so strictly; that the sort of unjust state he had in mind would not seek the destruction of any other state whose existence might be useful. But the argument might continue that there is in fact a very considerable overlap between the interests of states, and that the need for relations of trust and cooperation between nations grows together with the development of the technology of large scale destruction. Clearly this is the sort of argument that a political realist has to face in the twentieth century.[8]

There is another sophist whom Socrates is made by Plato to encounter, who holds a position similar to that of Thrasymachus. Callicles, in the *Gorgias*, rejects the conventional notion of justice, and claims that it is an invention of the weak majority to control the strong. Callicles adds a point about language which is an important part of the realist tradition. Talk about justice, in the conventional sense is a powerful weapon even if it does not correspond to reality, or as Callicles would say, "to nature". Moral words can be used to convince people of an obligation even where no obligation exists. He complains that "we take the best and strongest from their youth upwards, and tame them like young lions – charming them with the sound of the voice, and saying to them that with equality they must be content, and that the equal is the honorable and the just".[9]

Again echoing the sophists, Thucydides reflects in his History upon the way the war changed the meanings of the moral words. He writes, in an excursus on the evil effects of the civil war in Corcyra, and elsewhere in Greece, "words had to change their ordinary meaning and take that which was now given them. Reckless audacity came to be considered the courage of a loyal ally; prudent hesitation, specious cowardice ... the cause of all these evils was the lust for power arising from greed and ambition ... the leaders in the cities, each provided with the fairest professions, on the one side with the cry of political equality of the peoples, on the other of a moderate aristocracy, sought prizes for themselves in those public interests which they pretended to cherish ... But the use of fair phrases to arrive at guilty ends was in high reputation."[10] The ideologies have changed, but not the role of ideology itself, as this is seen by Niebuhr and Morgenthau.

Machiavelli is often invoked as the father of modern realism, especially by the opponents of the tradition. Indeed, the adjectival form of his name, "Machiavellian", is defined as an insult.[11] Morgenthau and Kennan both disclaim the label "Machiavellian". This is not the place to try to evaluate his thought in detail. But he is more subtle than Thrasymachus and Callicles, and more perceptive than his detractors usually allow. His main difference from the two sophists is that he maintains an important place for social morality, and for the private morality that grows out of it. Honesty, justice, devotion to duty, loyalty, and patriotism are, for him, necessary attributes of the good citizen; and a nation will not prosper unless, like the Swiss, its citizens have a high sense of duty to their neighbours as well as to their country.[12] It is true that he thought that this morality has on occasion to be overridden. He says, "You must know that there are two ways of contesting, the one by law, the other by force; the first method is proper to man, the second to beasts. But because the first is frequently not sufficient, it is necessary to have recourse to the second."[13] But he is recognizing here that the naked struggle for power through armed force, although sometimes necessary, is in a sense less than human. In this respect he resembles the modern rather than the ancient realists. He is unlike the moderns in that he does not seem to find this situation tragic. He wants, like Thucydides, to be of use to the student of political morality. But he conceives his usefulness to lie not in warning against the decline of morals that accompanies war, but in showing how best to exploit it. "It is necessary", he says, "for a prince wishing to hold his own to know how to do wrong."[14]

The name of Hobbes is often coupled with that of Machiavelli and the two thinkers are in many ways similar. But Hobbes is a systematic theorist, while Machiavelli is concerned more with practice. Machiavelli gives the impression that he writes books only because he cannot for the time being engage in serious politics. The relationship here is somewhat like that between the sophists and the generals at Athens, or between Morgenthau and Kennan in our century. But to say this is partly misleading because Hobbes was born about 60 years after Machiavelli's death. Hobbes brings to the tradition a theory of psychological egoism.[15] Felicity, for him, is continual success in getting what one wants, will is not different from desire but is the "last appetite in deliberating", pity and benevolence arise from self-love, as do all other appetites, and reason is the slave of the passions.[16] This last assertion is one which Morgenthau makes also. "Reason", he says, "is driven toward its goals by the irrational forces the ends of which it serves."[17] It is also an assertion that would have been acceptable to Callicles, the sophist, who encourages Socrates to stop doing philosophy because it makes him ignorant of "the pleasures and desires of mankind and of human character in general", and makes him vulnerable to anyone who might take him to court and, as it were, "box his ears with impunity".[18] Hobbes's views about felicity, will and benevolence are also accepted by Morgenthau, but only at the level of the state. For at the level of private morality, all three twentieth century realists want to accept the centrality of the demand for self-sacrifice. Hence, as they see it, the tragedy. Any politically active nation is, for Morgenthau, by definition engaged in the competition for power;[19] success in diplomacy consists entirely in maintaining or increasing national power. There is thus an unbridgeable gap, for him, between politics, which requires a sacrifice of others to self, and ethics, which requires a sacrifice of self to others.[20]

REINHOLD NIEBUHR

The first figure we shall consider in any detail is Reinhold Niebuhr.

Niebuhr was born in 1892, the son of a Lutheran minister. His work is a combination of theology and social commentary, and it has had a profound influence. He taught for most of his life at Union Seminary in New York. But his influence was not restricted to seminarians. Rather, he provided an articulate voice for those who had lived through the First World War and were disillusioned with Wilsonian liberalism. Niebuhr's position was a "Christian Realism" which was supposed to steer a course between optimistic illusion on the one hand and cynical despair on the other.

Our task in this book is not a theological one. But it is not possible to separate Niebuhr's views on international politics and ethics from his theology. He placed himself in the tradition of those Protestant theologians who wanted to make acute the tension between this-worldly and other-worldly values. Thus Soren Kierkegaard distinguished between *agape* and all other kinds of love (notably friendship and erotic love) on the basis that the other kinds were all alterable, preferential, and ultimately reducible to self-love. For him, the essence of *agape* is self-renunciation. "Wherever Christianity is, there is also self-renunciation, which is Christianity."[21] *Agape* is therefore as incompatible with the other kinds of love as self-renunciation is with self-love.

Similarly Anders Nygren, in *Agape and Eros*, characterizes *agape* as "a lost love" (the phrase comes from Luther, "*eine verlorene Liebe*"). Nygren says, "Christian love is, by its very nature, a lost love. It is the direct opposite of rational calculation. Even though again and again it finds itself deceived, that is no reason why it should become hesitant and reserved. 'For it is of the nature of love to suffer betrayal.' "[22] In the last clause he is again quoting Luther, who went on, "since it is exposed to all the uses and abuses of men, the general servant of good and bad, faithful and unfaithful, true and false alike".[23] Nygren dismisses all natural human loves as self-love, as Kierkegaard had done. He says, "The fact is that the resources of natural human life are exhausted in and with egocentric love."

Niebuhr follows the view that the essential characteristic of *agape* is self-sacrifice.[24] He concludes that it cannot be manifested in its full purity by any group or even any individual. He thinks, for reasons to be discussed presently, that it is reasonable to expect it in a tainted form from individuals in some contexts; but that it is never reasonable to expect if from groups. He sees the appropriate morality for groups as one not of self-sacrifice but of justice; for justice is the ethical principle "which typically admits the claims of self-interest".[25]

But the relations between love and justice, as Niebuhr sees them, are rather obscure. This obscurity is partly due to the fact that he tends to see and express objections to his own views without trying to sort out the resultant contradictions. Another difficulty is that he uses "justice" often, though not always, in a very broad sense; for him justice is sometimes the goal of all "rational" ethics.[26] He sees at least five differences between justice in this sense and *agape*. First, love "presupposes the resolution of the conflict of life with life";[27] justice does not. Second, love demands self-sacrifice; justice does not (though Niebuhr is not consistent about this). Since justice demands impartiality between the self and others, it will often be opposed to love. For love, on Niebuhr's view, is a kind of reverse discrimination against the self, and is thus unjust (though love may require justice in a choice between the conflicting interests of others). Third, love rules out the calculation of comparative interest ("the nicely calculated more and less"); justice requires it. Fourth, love does not take merit into account when serving others, though justice may (depending on one's view of justice). Fifth, the consideration that love gives to others is free, whereas that which justice gives will often be compelled.

It seems clear that for Niebuhr an ethics of *agape* is the only *pure* ethics. "Love meets the needs of the neighbour, without carefully weighing and comparing his needs with those of the self. It is therefore ethically purer than the justice which is prompted by reason."[28] *Agape* is the measure of the purity of any social ethics, and by that measure any social ethics is bound to be found wanting. Justice is seen as an inevitably tainted approximation to love. Thus Gandhi, in achieving justice in the relations between India and Britain, is said by Niebuhr to have had to "sacrifice a degree of moral purity". Together with this view about justice goes a view that politics are in themselves *amoral*. "(Love) will prevent the ideal of justice, which is a political-ethical ideal, *from becoming a purely political one* with the ethical element washed out", (emphasis added). Niebuhr is not entirely consistent in his language here. But the point seems to be that there are two conceptually autonomous spheres, politics and ethics. Pure politics is amoral, just as pure ethics is apolitical. Niebuhr can say, therefore, that there is a conflict between ethics and politics. "A realistic analysis of the problems of human society reveals a constant and seemingly irreconcilable conflict between the needs of society and the imperatives of a sensitive conscience. This conflict, which could be most briefly defined as the conflict between ethics and politics, is made inevitable by the double focus of the moral life."

He none the less insists that the statesman should be "under the influence of the foolishness of the moral seer".[29] He seems to think that although this influence is indispensable in the fight against injustice, it is dangerous and dependent upon an illusion. The illusion is that the moral ideal is realizable in society, and the harm the illusion causes is that it gives rise to fanaticism. But he thinks that to put the illusion "under the control of reason" is in the end to destroy it. He seems to be saying both that we ought to commit ourselves to the ideal in order that we might be motivated to fight for justice, and that we ought not to commit ourselves because the ideal cannot be rationally justified, and in the absence of reason we will become fanatics. If the illusion is to do its necessary work, it must not be doubted. But a large part of Niebuhr's book is devoted to showing the falsity of the illusion, and thus to fostering our doubt about it. Thus the belief in the possibility of a moral society in this world is condemned as a "romantic overestimate of human virtue and moral capacity" and as "politically unrealistic and confused".

It is not clear whether there is a consistent view that can be reconstructed. Niebuhr is a political realist. He also believes that God is working his purpose out as year succeeds to year, and that love will in the end win.[30] But he does not seem to allow that the approach of this victory gives practical guidance to statesmen. He says, "Whenever religious idealism brings forth its purest fruits and places the strongest check upon selfish desire, it results in policies which, from the political perspective, are quite impossible.... It would therefore seem better to accept a frank dualism in morals than to attempt a harmony between the two methods which threatens the effectiveness of both."[31] This is perfectly consistent with his political realism; but it is not clear how, if we accept the frank dualism, we are to bring the wisdom of the statesman under the influence of the foolishness of the moral seer.

What lies behind the view that politics and ethics are in tension is a doctrine of human nature.[32] Niebuhr is espousing for the most part a kind of psychological egoism of groups. But he has not tried to answer some of the well-known objections to psychological egoism in the philosophical literature. He needs to distinguish between the strong thesis that all actions of all groups arise solely out of self-love, and a number of weaker theses, such as that all actions of all groups arise partly out of self-love or that some actions of all groups arise solely out of self-love. The weakest thesis in this series, that some actions of some groups arise partly out of self-love is not controversial. Niebuhr claims, against the Marxists, that "there can never be a perfect mutuality of interest between individuals who perform different functions in society". It would seem to be true *a fortiori* that there could never be perfect mutuality between social groups with different social functions. But this tends to imply only the weakest thesis given above. If Niebuhr wanted to deny *any* place to ethics in politics, he would have to assert the strongest thesis of the series, that all actions of all groups arise solely out of self-love. But it is not clear what reason he could give for this. It would surely not be plausible to argue that the needs of different groups are never capable of simultaneous satisfaction. But if two groups, even two national groups, are both benefiting from a cooperative policy, and if there is no history of distrust and hostility between them, what is to stop them being glad for the sake of both parties that the cooperation is working? Moreover, if Niebuhr did want to hold the strongest thesis of the series, it would be inconsistent of him to tell the statesman not to insist "on the interests of his group when they are obviously in unjust relation to the total interests of the community of mankind", and to sacrifice immediate advantages for his group "for the sake of mutual advantages". Why should it not be possible to foster cooperativeness between groups rather than just balancing competing interests?

There are a number of explanations that Niebuhr gives for the greater selfishness of groups than individuals. First, if there are more selfish individuals than unselfish ones, it is likely that groups will be selfish under the influence of the majority of their members.[33] Second, groups are likely to be more remote from each other than individuals within groups, and there is therefore likely to be less information shared between groups and correspondingly less chance of imaginative identification.[34] Third, social groups are held together by emotion rather than reason, and are therefore less likely to feel moral constraints since these cannot operate in the absence of a high level of rationality. Fourth, unselfishness is impossible without self-criticism, but any criticism of a social group is bound to be construed as disloyalty, as was Socrates's criticism of Athens. Fifth, even altruism on the part of the individual is "slewed into nationalism", since what is outside the nation is "too vague to inspire devotion".[35] Sixth, ordinary (therefore selfish) people "project their egos" upon the nation, and are more devoted to the quest for national power the more their own "lusts for power and prestige" are thwarted by their individual circumstances.[36]

Many of these explanations are good ones, although it is not clear that moral constraints cannot operate "emotionally"; or that individuals cannot identify with any unit larger than a nation; or that individuals cannot project their frustrated altruistic desires upon the nation as well as their frustrated egoistic ones; or that some nations do not occasionally tolerate internal criticism. But the main point is that none of the reasons given above shows that morals do not belong in international politics. All they could show, if they were sound, is that morality between nations is likely to be harder to achieve than between individuals.

There is another point which is worth making about Niebuhr's characterization of *agape* as self-sacrifice.[37] The command to love one's neighbour as oneself seems to permit, if not encourage, some form of self-love.[38] As Niebuhr states it, *agape* seems to demand that one open oneself to continual exploitation. But it may be better to include some place for self-respect and even for self-fulfillment in one's highest ethical principle. Moreover there is something almost masochistic about the continual insistence on the suffering and tragedy that will inevitably accompany attempts to love. In Niebuhr's analysis, the stress is on the self, and the pain it will have to go through, rather than on the good that can be done for the other. But self-sacrifice is surely not an end in itself. It is justifiable only instrumentally, as the permitted by-product of an attempt to help others. Finally, the sort of judgements which Niebuhr wants to count as purely loving can probably not be universalized, as they require that the well-being of the person making the judgement not be considered. It may be that they will not therefore count as moral. For universalizability is probably a necessary condition for a judgement's being a moral one, and it requires that no one, not even the agent, be ignored in the assessment of benefits to be derived from an action.

To sum up, it seems that Niebuhr has fallen into the trap which he himself recognizes, "the tendency of religion to obscure the shades and shadows of moral life, by painting only the contrast between the white radiance of divine holiness and the darkness of the world".[39] Niebuhr wants to allow that it may be "responsible" to do the lesser evil on occasion. But it is still fair to characterize his view as Paul Ramsey does, that we are to go about "responsibly doing the greatest good possible, and gaining a general sense of guiltiness by calling it the lesser evil".[40] Niebuhr has impoverished our notion of "justice". His paradigm of justice assumes that a just consideration of the needs of others will be compelled. If, for example, an industrialist freely decides to give the workers a fair wage, he will be showing, for Niebuhr, not more justice but something more *than* justice. But his account here is neither desirable nor consistent with ordinary usage. It seems better to say that there is a set of moral principles which gives a decent minimum standard for international relations, and that it is possible for individual nations to go beyond these.[41] On this view self-sacrifice will be in many circumstances supererogatory — which is to say that we can be praised for displaying it but not blamed for not doing so. Complying with such a decent minimum need not be any less genuinely ethical than going above it, or any less genuinely political than going below it.

Niebuhr allows that some thinkers, notably the utilitarians, have proposed what he calls a "rational morality, which gives egoism equality of moral standing with altruism, provided both are reasonably expressed and observe the 'law of measure' ".[42] He condemns such a view on the grounds that it is less "realistic" than politics because it ignores the human tendency to compromise with selfishness, when it claims that the needs of self and others can be "nicely and equally balanced". He thinks it less realistic than religion because it ignores the "inner needs of the human spirit", and the fact that "in the sanctuary of their souls, selfish men know that they ought not to be selfish, and venerate what they feel they ought to be and cannot be".[43]

Both these criticisms are unfair. Niebuhr takes Aristotle as the father of "rational morality", and Aristotle was aware that we need to "lean against" our prevailing weaknesses. Rational morality can justify self-sacrifice as a counter-weight to a prevailing egoism, and thus as leading to impartiality in the long run. If we prescribe self-sacrifice, we are more likely to achieve the right balance between the interests of self and others (the mean). A utilitarian can also provide a place in his system for supererogatory action. The difference is that unlike Niebuhr he will not conclude that ordinary everyday morality is somehow morally impure. He will also not see the contrast between ethics and politics in the same way. Niebuhr's views about the appropriateness of making ethical demands on groups, especially national groups, and his rejection of "rational morality", are both derived from his analysis of *agape* as self-sacrifice. We can take the opposing view that justice in the broad sense, or what has been called "universalized prudence" is a proper part of *agape*. And we can go on to find a more significant place for ethics in international affairs.

HANS MORGENTHAU

Morgenthau attended Niebuhr's lectures at Harvard, and called him the greatest political thinker of his generation. But Morgenthau's interest is not theological and any dependence on Niebuhr tends to be implicit, rather than explicit. Morgenthau's most important book, *Politics Among Nations*, has had a large impact on the theory and practice of international relations. But the philosophical position which underlies this book receives its most sustained treatment in an earlier book, *Scientific Man and Power Politics*. It is in this earlier book that he is closest to Niebuhr. He supposes, as Niebuhr had done, that there is a tragic and uncloseable gap between ethics and politics. His interest is not theological, and he refers to the gap as one between justice and power, rather than love and power. But the effect on his evaluation of politics is the same. Ethics requires the sacrifice of self for others, and politics the sacrifice of others for self.[44] Like Niebuhr, he pours scorn on the attempt to bridge this gap by means of a "rational ethics". Utilitarianism, he says, tries to assert the essentially ethical nature of politics. An equal mistake, on the other side of the same coin, is to assert as "the Machiavellians" do, the essentially political nature of ethics. The truth, as he sees it, is that the tension between the two aspirations, for power and for virtue, is an "irresolvable" tragedy.

In fact Morgenthau goes further. He claims that not only no political action, but no action at all, can ever be just. His reasons for this can be given briefly as follows.[45] Even the best of intentions can produce appalling results when acted upon. No action in performance of one moral duty can fail to be in conflict with another duty. There is no inter-personal measure of happiness. We cannot reach our moral ends without immoral means, and we cannot use the ends–means distinction as a justification. Morality characteristically demands complete self-sacrifice, and we can never achieve this because every individual is infected by the *animus dominandi*, the lust for power (Morgenthau quotes Luther here, just as Niebuhr had done). For man to live by rational ethics, he would have to be rational; but in fact his reason is the slave of his passions.

A number of these arguments have been touched on in the first chapter of this book. It is perhaps charitable to suppose that Morgenthau is not thinking of any particular utilitarian theorist, but rather of some indefinite "prevailing school of thought". But the conclusion that no action, and especially no political action, can be just is an important one for Morgenthau's position. It is therefore worth giving a brief critical look at the reasons he gives to support it. Firstly, the occurrence of unintended and disastrous results does not show that the agent's decision was unjust. The distinction needs to be drawn between the evaluation of agents and the evaluation of their actions.[46] An agent's intention can be just, if he has taken reasonable care to think out the probable consequences, even if his action produces disaster through no fault of his. Secondly, the existence of a conflict between two *prima facie* duties does not mean that choosing the higher duty is immoral. Lying to save a life may be right even though lying to save embarrassment may be wrong. Thirdly, the attempt to measure how much something will contribute to the happiness of different people is difficult, but not, by common agreement, hopeless. This sort of measurement is implicit whenever scarce resources are distributed between different people, and it is only in extreme cases that it should not be undertaken.[47] The premise, fourthly, that ends do not always justify means does not license the conclusion that they never do. Thus at the level of prudence, short-term pain can be justified for the sake of long-term health, and the same is true, at the level of morality, with the long-term and short-term harm and well-being of others. Fifthly, the fact, if it is a fact, that all our actions are partly motivated by self-interest does not mean that they are all immoral. For the golden rule does not forbid our doing what we want for ourselves unless this interferes unduly with our doing for others what they want for themselves.

Morgenthau concludes that the gap between ethics and politics cannot be closed. He illustrates this view with a number of historical examples. We shall mention three typical ones. He claims that the failure of American foreign policy to see the inevitable gap between ethics and politics played a large causal role in the horrors of the First World War, in the disaster at Pearl Harbor, and in the rise of Fascism. Thus, he says that Wilson tried to make the First World War moral by suggesting that it would make the world safe for democracy, and that this resulted in the prolongation of hostilities beyond the mere defeat of the enemy. But the historical judgement is doubtful. Waltzer argues that "Wilson's Fourteen Points made possible a German surrender on terms that fell far short of the war aims of Lloyd George and Clemenceau".[48] Morgenthau's point is that turning wars into crusades is dangerous, because it is difficult to fight limited wars for unlimited goals. But the horrors of the war can be attributed as easily to the combination of *traditional* power politics with twentieth century technology. Morgenthau's analysis does not allow for this possibility. Here as elsewhere, he is too eager to make his point. Secondly, the claim about Pearl Harbor needs a great deal of qualification. It is true that America, throughout the inter-war period, insisted on the importance of such measures as the Briand–Kellogg pact to put an end to war as an acceptable instrument of national policy. It is true that there was a liberal prejudice against aggressive war. But Morgenthau concludes that the high command was *therefore* unprepared for the possibility of "unprovoked" enemy attack at Pearl Harbor. Again history is unclear. Roosevelt and Hull *were* prepared for a Japanese act of aggression. They knew that an attack was coming "somewhere in Thailand, Malaya, the Dutch Indies, and 'possibly' the Philippines".[49] But they did not take seriously enough the technology available to the Japanese, and they failed to guess where the attack would come. It is not at all clear that their error was due to an absence of 'realism'.

Morgenthau's third historical point is that the use of moral terms to describe national policy tends to encourage false expectations. He says that when their (liberal) world view no longer fitted with experienced fact, "the Germans rejected, with rationalism and liberalism, the whole Western tradition, and embraced Fascism instead".[50] But the causes of the rise of Fascism are multifarious and endlessly debated. It is probably true that the racial and political theories of national socialism were themselves products of nineteenth-century rationalism, and not just, as Morgenthau suggests, reactions against it. In any case the most he has established is that *unrealistic* moral evaluation ends up in inappropriate cynicism. It is a long step to the conclusion that no moral evaluation is desirable in international politics. The inference requires an additional premise, that all such evaluation is inevitably unrealistic. But this is just what the realists need to prove.

The theoretical point behind all these examples is that it is both false and dangerous for morality to be imported into international relations.[51] It is dangerous, he thinks, because it will continue to lead, as it has in the past, to more harm than good. He thinks it false because the real nature of international politics is an unending struggle for survival and power.[52] In this respect he has a view rather like the one he ascribes to Thrasymachus, that "the political sphere was governed exclusively by the rules of the political art of which ethical evaluation was a mere ideological by-product". The difference between the two is that Morgenthau thinks that there are absolute ethical demands which are in tragic tension with the demands of power. He thinks that these ethical demands should not be made of states, because states cannot operate by them; the best they can do is to operate by the perverted reflection of them, namely by ideology. But Morgenthau relies on an argument *a fortiori*: if an individual cannot be moral, how much less can this be asked of a state? Given the weakness of his claim about the individual, we can turn this argument around: if an individual can act ethically, even if not perfectly, why should not a state?

Two answers are given to this question in *Politics Among Nations*, which though philosophically more circumspect, relies on the same basic foundation of thought as the earlier book. As before, he stresses the tension between ethics and politics. But he adds two main features to his analysis. The first is the claim that any attempt to bring ethics into international relations is bound to end up in ideology. The second is the historical thesis that the impossibility of states behaving ethically is the result of the rise of nationalism in the nineteenth century.

For Morgenthau, ideology is national interest disguised in moral terminology. Even if an agent or a nation believes it is acting for the common good, the moral claims will still count as ideology as long as the basic motivation is still one of self-interest. If, as Morgenthau believes, all national action is basically self-interested, then all the moral claims of nations are, in his usage, "ideological".[53] This means that whatever the leaders and spokesmen of a country say, they must always be judged as insincere unless they talk in terms of the struggle for power. On Morgenthau's view, we know *a priori* that they cannot otherwise mean what they say, for international politics is by *definition* the struggle for power. He thinks we can see this from an analysis of human nature, which is everywhere infected by the *animus dominandi*, and which thus infects all social relations and all levels of social organization.

Some of the weaknesses of this view we have already considered. But in addition it leads him into a strangely inflexible position.[54] We will look at just a few examples. No nation, he has to say, can voluntarily surrender power. If it appears to be doing so, it is only in order to regroup its forces for another attack. But is it not possible that a nation, such as Britain, might grow genuinely weary of the exercise of power, and decide to hand it over? No state will ever agree, he says, to an international military force that would diminish to any degree its national sovereignty. No gradual progress towards collective security is possible, in his view, because any attempt to achieve partial collective security will inevitably end in world war. The quantity and quality of shared education and culture across nations are irrelevant, in his opinion, to the possibility of a world community, because they do not of themselves affect the balance of power. The fact that poison gas was not used in the Second World War is, for him, only an apparent objection to the claim that "nations will never forgo the use of all the weapons which their technology is able to produce". For nations on both sides were ready to use it, and were prevented only by military considerations. He says that America and Russia were engaged in the nineteenth century in pushing their frontiers forward into "politically empty territory". The indigenous inhabitants presumably did not exist "politically" because they did not have enough power. Finally, he says that the individual cannot identify with anything larger than the state, such as a world community, because the desire for national power arises out of the inevitable frustration of the desire for individual power, and national power can only be gained at the expense of other nations.

What characterizes all these examples is what we might call an "all or nothing" approach. Morgenthau does not seem to allow that an individual might partially identify with the world community, or that a nation might allow a partial surrender of national sovereignty, or that education and culture might have a degree of success in mitigating international hostilities. Morgenthau might reply that we are taking him too literally. But the problem is deep in his philosophical assumptions. We can illustrate this by examining why he does not say that Wilson and others were wrong to introduce morals into politics. For on the principle "ought implies can", if politics cannot be moral, it is not the case that they ought to be moral, nor, for that matter, that they ought not to be.

Morgenthau therefore says that Wilson and the directors of American foreign policy between the wars were wrong to introduce *ideology* into international politics. But this is where his philosophical assumptions get in the way. For to say this is to rely on a black and white picture of human nature. People and nations are rarely moved by unmixed altruism or unmixed self-interest. For example, moral anxiety can create a climate in which one set of prudential concerns is acted on rather than another. This is what probably happened in Athens, when the Athenians "repented" of their decision to destroy Mytilene, after it revolted, and decided that it was "more useful for the preservation of the empire" not to put to death those whom it was "in their interest to keep alive", even though they deserved to die.[55] There are many ways in which morality and prudence, or morality and "ideology", can be mixed together. Morgenthau makes it true by definition that no action can be truly "moral" unless it is totally sacrificial; and that no action can be truly "political" unless it is motivated entirely by the struggle for power. But ordinary usage is not so restrictive. If we do restrict the words in these ways, we will simply have to invent new ones with more inclusive senses. Suppose, for example, that the state voluntarily forsakes its position of pre-eminence in the affairs of another state. Can this be said to be a "political" action? If we have to answer in the negative just because of the *definition* of "political", then we will have to say that some of the things states do in their relations with each other are not political, and that any comprehensive theory of international relations must account for them.

The other new feature of *Politics Among Nations* is the analysis of the rise of nationalism and its effects.[56] In the two periods 1648–1772 and 1815–1914 there was, he claims, "a consensus of common moral standards and a common civilization, as well as of common interests, which kept in check the limitless desire for power, potentially inherent, as we know, in all imperialism and prevented it from becoming a political actuality". The struggle for power was mitigated, though not eliminated, by a common ethics, mores, and law. Against this background, he says, the art of diplomacy could be cultivated without having by itself to bear the burden of conformity to moral principles, and it was accordingly remarkably successful in avoiding major wars. The emergence of the nation as the focus of loyalty is what has led, in his opinion, to total war. For the people, especially if conscripted, have to be convinced of the virtue of the cause for which they are fighting. The mere glory of their prince will not be enough. And in this way the war is turned into a crusade, with all its attendant horrors.

It is difficult to deny the correlation between the rise of nationalism and that of total war. But the question remains what lesson we should draw for the contemporary conduct of international relations. Morgenthau's lesson is that international peace has never in history been more urgent and never less likely of achievement, because of the present moral, social, and political condition of the world.[57] His conclusion is one of almost unrelieved gloom, but he does express the hope that we can learn from history the possibility of recultivating the art of diplomacy and of freeing it from ideological constraint. In the absence of a moral consensus between nations, this will not, he thinks, be sufficient to give us a reasonable hope of peace. But it might at least mitigate the political conflicts that will inevitably arise. Morgenthau's prescription is thus that we should try to recreate from the past the essentially amoral character of diplomacy as it was used to pursue the essentially amoral goals of political leaders. He wants to insist on what he thinks of as the amoral character of the successful diplomacy of the past, and his vocabulary is consistently what might be appropriate for the praise of a master of chess. He talks of diplomats as "brilliant" and as not "committing errors". He refers to diplomacy as the "brains of national power", and to Germany's success from 1933–1940 as the "victories of one man's mind". It is true that he makes passing mention of the need for moral qualities in diplomacy. But it is not clear, given the rest of his theory, what role these qualities are supposed to play and he leaves this quite mysterious.

He admits that the only thing that kept the struggle for power within bounds was the existence of a moral consensus. But he says that this no longer exists, and he despairs of recapturing it in an age of nationalism. This means that the only thing he *now* sees can restrain the struggle for power is skilful diplomacy. But if the diplomats themselves are to be released from moral constraints, then their only function can be to make the struggle for power by their own nation more efficient. In fact, it is probable that Morgenthau realizes that his prescription is paradoxical. For he tries to reduce the paradox by introducing his own values in his advice to modern American diplomats.[58] Thus he condemns those who consider international politics exclusively as a technique, without ethical significance, for the purpose of maintaining and gaining power, and who can accordingly, like the Athenians in the Peloponnesian War, use the elimination of populations as a legitimate strategy. But he himself has defined politics in general, and international politics in particular, as the seeking of power. Where is the force of the proscription on genocide supposed to come from? He says that no foreign policy may admit mass extermination, even if this is required by the national interest, and that this limitation derives "from an absolute moral principle, the violation of which no consideration of national advantage can justify". In the same sort of way, he says that the objective of foreign policy is to bend, not to break, the will of the other side as far as necessary in order to safeguard one's own vital interests without hurting those of the other side. But if national will or morale is an important part of national power, then why should not diplomacy seek to break the will of the enemy? It is clear that Morgenthau needs to bring in morality, as he does, if he is to offer the hope that diplomacy can limit the struggle for power. But it is equally clear that he cannot consistently bring it in and maintain a strict theory of psychological egoism for states and their leaders. There is a different lesson to be drawn from the same historical data that Morgenthau considers. It is that if diplomacy is to be effective in maintaining moral limitations on the practice of international politics it must be as the instrument of a moral foreign policy. It is true that an amoral diplomacy might be appropriate to, or might even be required by, an amoral foreign policy. But the converse is also true. A diplomacy that respects the claims of morality requires a foreign policy that does the same. In fact, there have been very few times in the last 250 years when diplomacy and foreign policy have not been influenced by moral concerns; although it is as difficult to demonstrate this as it is to demonstrate its contrary. The moral consensus which Morgenthau refers to was reflected in the agreed limitations of warfare, and these limitations were implicit in the conventions of diplomatic exchange. It is artificial to try to divorce diplomacy from the moral climate in which it takes its place. But this is what Morgenthau tries to do in holding up an amoral diplomacy as a model, and at the same time lamenting the death of the moral consensus that gave that diplomacy its context.

It is interesting to look at Burke in this regard. He is quoted with approval by Morgenthau more often than any other author. Yet his view of the connection between morality and international relations is quite different from Morgenthau's.[59] One of his dominant concerns was the analysis of the French Revolution, which was the one period of history before 1914 which Morgenthau allows to be parallel to our own in its tendency towards nationalism and total war. Like Morgenthau, Burke recognizes the tendency of national leaders to use ideology, or as he says, "pretext", rather than morality itself. But he also recognizes that this is a perversion, and that individual citizens and their leaders can and should avail themselves of the substance rather than the simulacrum. His view is that the diplomacy of the past has been dignified by "all which made power gentle", by the "sentiments which beautify and soften private society". The main failing of the Revolution was, for him, that it tried to eliminate these sentiments and to explode them "as a ridiculous, absurd and antiquated fashion". His view was that the more power an individual possessed, the more he needed the "yoke of moderation and virtue", and that "the true law giver ought to love and respect his kind". "It seems", he says, "as if it were the prevalent opinion in Paris that an unfeeling heart and an undoubting confidence are the sole qualifications for a perfect legislator".

Burke's prescription is not an increase in cynicism about the place of morals in politics, for this itself is a product of the Revolution. The only things that can save France, in his view, are a return to the church, to the·monarchy, and more important than either of these, to a respect for moderation and virtue.

GEORGE KENNAN

George Kennan is, unlike Niebuhr and Morgenthau, a diplomat. He is perhaps most famous as one of the authors of America's policy of "containment". But he is like the other two in that he recognizes the demands of morality in private life and concludes that tragically these demands are not appropriate to the conduct of foreign policy. In fact, the tension is more apparent in Kennan, for he speaks more often in a high moral tone, and yet he is at the same time more uncompromising in his rejection of morality as appropriate in international relations.

He takes the view, like Morgenthau, that what is needed is a recaptured art of diplomacy. He says that the chief obstacle over the past few years has been what he calls "the legalistic–moralistic approach to international problems",[60] which can be characterized as "the carrying over into the affairs of states of the concepts of right and wrong, the assumption that state behaviour is a fit subject for moral judgement". He qualifies this in a slightly later book by saying that it is the purposes of states, as distinct from their methods, that are not "fit subjects for measurements in moral terms". His position is clearly stated in two letters which he wrote to one of the authors of this book, and we do not think that their publication would be unwelcome to him. On 7 December 1954, he wrote that the motivation of the United States government was "governed by considerations wholly different from those which govern individual conduct". Further, "in the conduct of external relations a government is concerned primarily with other governments. I am not aware that it has any duty vis-à-vis these other governments". And again in a letter of 2 January 1955, he said, "as a government official in Washington ... I am certainly animated by a whole body of considerations that have nothing to do with my own individual ethics, for in this capacity I am acting only as an agent rather than a principal; I have no right to insert personal ethical preferences into my actions. Nor would they be relevant if I did; for the process of government is not comparable to the process of individual life; it does not pursue the same aims, it does not have the same responsibilities or the same possibilities. The popular will ... expressed through the regular processes of government is the only motivating impulse the government is capable of knowing and recognizing.... In the end policy is what the elected representatives of the people decide they want. The government official has no choice but to endeavour to faithfully execute that mandate. It is idle for him to inquire whether it is 'right' or 'wrong'.... If he does not wish to perform it, he does not belong in the disciplined process of government".

There are a number of points of interest in these passages. We will concentrate on his claim that morality is too high, too abstract and too rigid a standard for foreign policy. We have already seen in Niebuhr and Morgenthau the assimilation of ethics to self-sacrifice. Kennan is part of the same tradition. "A government", he says, "is an agent not a principal; and no more than any other agent may it attempt to be the conscience of its principal. In particular, it may not subject itself to those supreme laws of renunciation and self-sacrifice that represent the culmination of individual moral growth".[61] This is presumably why he says that states do not have moral duties to each other. He construes moral duties as duties of self-sacrifice, which are too high for foreign policy. "The process of government", he says, "is a practical exercise and not a moral one", and the reason is that it is not a process in which "such things as altruism and sacrifice can find any pure expression". We have considered elsewhere the objections to this view.

He holds, secondly, that morality is too rigid a standard for the infinite complexities of individual situations. He seems to think of moral principles as rather like legal ones, and he says that "the law is too abstract, too inflexible, too hard to adjust to the demands of the unpredictable and the unexpected."[62] Thus America's Far Eastern policy was characterized at the beginning of the century by adherence to two slogans, "the open door" and "the integrity of China". But no two-word phrase like "open door" could possibly "have had any plain and comprehensive (sic) meaning adequate as a criterion for international agreement"; and "the integrity of China" was a slogan which by the end of the nineteenth century could only be expected to elicit the response, "What's in a name? It depends on what you call integrity." In the same sort of way, Kennan has grave doubts about the principle that America "has a duty to encourage and support the growth of democratic institutions, or at least the assurance of human rights across the world." For it may be, he says, that in a particular situation the more diffuse forms of political authority will fail to improve the lot of most of the people, where a more authoritarian form will succeed. To insist on the principle is in his view to try to impose on the rest of the world a set of values that might be appropriate only to a very specific situation (that of North Western Europe and the areas originally settled or colonized by it).

Perhaps Kennan's criticism can be rephrased as a dilemma; either a principle is interpreted so widely as to be unhelpful or it is interpreted rigidly enough to give a definite answer, but the answer is often inappropriate. Kennan could say that moral principles when imported into international relations are either too abstract or too inflexible. The principle that democracy should be supported is a good example where both kinds of criticism have been made of its use, and we can take it as a paradigm case. Churchill, Roosevelt and Stalin all saw themselves, and were seen, as champions of democracy in the Second World War. Autocratic regimes from Augustus to Hitler have found for themselves names including the words "socialist", "democratic", "people's" and "republic". When Kennan is at his most forbearing and tolerant, he seems to suggest that different states have different concepts of what "democracy" means in practice and that "the ways by which people advance toward dignity and enlightenment in government are things that constitute the deepest and more intimate processes of national life."[63] This is presumably why he says that the purposes of governments should be immune to moral criticism. He seems to mean that terms like "democracy" and "dignity" are honorifics. They are defined as complimentary and are in this sense too vague to be useful. For no state will allow its form of government to be called "undemocratic", as this would be tantamount to allowing that it was not responsive to the fundamental needs of its people.

On the other hand, Kennan criticizes the use of "democracy" as a criterion in foreign policy because it is too inflexible. He seems to be thinking here of specific institutions like the ballot box or the separation of powers, and he quotes de Tocqueville with approval, "there is nothing absolute in the theoretic value of political institutions, and their efficiency depends almost always on the original circumstances and the social conditions of the people to whom they are applied". Kennan's position seems to be that there is a threshold below which the methods of a government can be morally condemned. A government may not "enslave its labour", "treat its people like children", or "promise men things it knows to be illusory, hold out short-term advantages as baits for a long-term enslavement, encite hatreds and fan suspicions and try to strike profits from the workings of bitterness and blind fury".[64] If the threshold here is a moral one, it is not clear how we can avoid evaluating all the behaviour of a state morally to see whether or not it falls below the threshold. But in any case, if there is a government that does not do this sort of thing, its purposes and practices should be tolerated in Kennan's view with equanimity, whether or not they are "democratic" in the narrow institutional sense.

But neither abstractness nor inflexibility are inherent in the nature of moral principles. It is useful to appeal here to the distinction between levels of moral thinking that was outlined in the first chapter. It is true that intuitive principles may for some purposes be extremely simple and general. But there are innumerable degrees of specificity in a principle. This can be seen by reflecting on the rules of etiquette, which range from the most general prescription of courtesy to the seating arrangements for marquesses and viscounts. A diplomat need not be restricted to the degree of complexity appropriate to a child in kindergarten. Moreover, every complex principle is going to include a number of clauses of exception. The more experienced someone is in moral reasoning, the more such clauses there are likely to be. This is what makes the principles flexible enough to cope with varying situations. It is one of the functions of the consequentialist method to help decide when to allow exceptions to a principle and when to disallow them. A diplomat may refuse to use the method and insist on persevering with the simplest intuitions even in the face of refractory experience. But if he does, it will not be because he is mistakenly applying morals to international relations. It will be because he is applying an inappropriate method of moral reasoning.[65]

In fact, Kennan does believe, at least some of the time, in the applicability of moral principles to international relations. He has a profound conviction that America and the West have something of real value to share with the rest of the world; that they can be a source of hope and inspiration; and that the main thing holding them back is a lack of confidence and energy at home. This is a note which he has often sounded.[66] The emphasis is different from Morgenthau's. For whereas Morgenthau sees the only trace of hope in a revived art of diplomacy, Kennan, the diplomat, sees that diplomacy can only be successful against the background of a strong moral and spiritual example at home. He has in mind such things as the need to halt the disintegration of the cities, the depletion of the environment and the decline of educational standards.[67] But is it important for Americans to receive a first-class education, but not important for the rest of the world? Does it matter whether or not the ecology of other nations is disrupted? He says that we all have an obligation "as a political society to our own national ideals, and *through these ideals* to the wider human community of which we are in ever increasing measure a part".[68] This suggests that the ideals in question do have application to the rest of the world. In passages like this, he sounds much more like Socrates than like Thrasymachus. For Thrasymachus would not talk of any obligations or duties between nations, and certainly not of the application of ideals to the community of mankind. The terms in which Kennan states his objection to the attacks on Hiroshima and Nagasaki put him in the tradition of just war theory.[69]

Kennan thinks of the struggle between communism and the West as at least as much a battle of the mind as a battle of arms. This has also been the expressed view of the Soviet Union. Khruschev said in March 1958, "Friendship is real and strong when people share the same views about events, about history, about life. If you do not share the philosophy of the communist party because you have your own principles and your own views, then it is possible to maintain good relations with communists, but it is difficult to achieve a deep friendship as we understand it."[70]

Kissinger said in 1960, "Even communism has made many more converts through the theological quality of marxism than through the materialistic aspect on which it prides itself." He continues by talking about "the intangible factors on which the future political relationships of the world may well depend. As we gain in compassion and understanding, there is every prospect that we can infuse the values of human dignity and freedom with enough vitality so that the younger generations all over the world will feel obliged to come to grips with them emotionally and intellectually. The argument that this kind of spiritual elan is beyond the capability of democracy is equivalent to saying that democracy is doomed."[71]

These are views with which Kennan, at least some of the time, agrees, and it is hard to square this with his studied aloofness elsewhere. Perhaps there is nothing unexpected about this. For his dilemma is that of any man of conviction in a pluralist society. The dilemma has merely been projected onto the larger screen of international relations.

WHY SHOULD STATES BE MORAL?

It is not our intention to say that there are no differences between the three writers we have just discussed. All of them share a distaste for 'idealism', but beyond that they diverge. One way to express the difference is to point out the different kinds of idealism that they find objectionable.[72] There is a "pretentious" idealism which does not see the hypocrisy in the nation's claims to be the defender of transcendent values, and there is a "perfectionist" idealism which sees nothing but hypocrisy in this. Morgenthau and Kennan attack the first of these. They insist that there is a pretentiousness to the moral claims of the best of nations. Niebuhr, on the other hand, attacks both at once. For he is aware of the danger of the foolish moralism of the seer, but he also condemns the statesman whose "realism" involves declaring morality out of bounds on the grounds that the goal of perfection is unrealizable. It is Niebuhr's recognition of *both* dangers that so often gives his work the appearance of paradox. The differences between Morgenthau and Kennan are more subtle. Morgenthau seems to allow, whereas Kennan seems to deny, that there are objective values which we can use to evaluate the purposes of other states. They both agree, however, that morality should not be used as a guide for national policy. Kennan's most recent statement of this is that "the governing of human beings is not a moral exercise. It is a practical function ..."[73]. As we have seen, however, Morgenthau and Kennan are both guilty of smuggling in their own moral evaluations under the guise of national interest.[74] This is no less an error than that of the pretentious idealist who smuggles in the national interest under the guise of morality.

What lies at the heart of the realist position is the view that the function of a nation's leaders is to seek the national interest. Morgenthau puts this very strongly. There is, he says, for the nation "but one guiding star, one standard for thought, one rule for action: the national interest".[75] But the concept of the national interest is not a straightforward one. It may be that all that can be said is that the phrase "is significant rather by what it denies than by what it asserts. A state is seeking (national interest) when it is not concerned with the interests of any groups outside its own jurisdiction, except to the extent that they may affect domestic interests."[76] But this account is probably too restrictive. The realists assert that there is an irreducible core to the concept, namely national self-preservation. Morgenthau quotes Hamilton with approval, "Self-preservation is the first duty of a nation."[77]

Suppose the national interest is defined in terms of national survival. There are three points that need to be made. Firstly, it has not been traditional in, for example, the United States to accept survival as the exclusive principle of foreign policy.[78] The realists would attribute this to ideology. Secondly, the concept of survival is itself problematic. For it seems beyond dispute that it is the survival of values and not simply of human beings that is held to be at stake. But the judgement that there is a threat to the survival of freedom, for example, will involve an answer to the question whether there would be likely to be an *acceptable* degree of freedom left if the worst came to the worst. Thus the claim that national survival is threatened is likely to be at least in part a moral judgement. Thirdly, whether or not it is a moral judgement that something is in the national interest, it is certainly a moral judgement that the national interest should be the exclusive goal of foreign policy. The point is the same at the individual and at the national level. To judge that it is in my interest to do something is to make a prudential judgement (unless there are moral values implicit in what I consider my interests). But to judge that the interests of someone in my position should take precedence over those of others is to make a moral judgement — one which is universalizable and that tends to commit the person making the judgement to action. In this sense I am making a moral judgement if I say that nations in general ought to put their own interests first, or that any nation should do so which is in the sort of position my nation is in.[79]

Prudence can be used to some extent as a foundation for national morality just as it can for individual morality. Our discussion here will be parallel to the discussion of the question "Why should I be moral?" in Chapter 1. If a nation belongs to a larger group of nations, perhaps the European Common Market or NATO, it may find itself conforming to a number of rules which are not obviously in its own interest. This is because the day-to-day running of the group has generated its own momentum. There are rules which will have developed which are necessary for the smooth functioning of the group, but which may not be directly related to the well-being of any particular member. If conforming to such a rule goes too far beyond the interests of a member state, that state may decide to abandon its membership. But the functioning of the group may itself be valuable enough to outweigh minor inconveniences or disutilities. For the rules to be effective, however, it is necessary that infractions be noticeable by others in the group, and that at some point they will bring retaliation or expulsion. De Gaulle, for example, was notorious for his penchant for sailing close to the wind, but his successors have retreated noticeably from his erratic behaviour. In a group of this sort, it is likely to be the case that cooperation makes benefits possible that would not be so otherwise, that it requires conformity to rules which do not contribute directly to the well-being of any particular member, and that this conformity develops a momentum of its own which stops each member asking on each occasion whether conformity is in its interest.

It is a very long step, however, to any conclusion about a world community. Even the two groups mentioned in the previous paragraph are not inevitably stable. Some of the scepticism of the realists about the possibility for the foreseeable future of a world community is probably justified. But it needs also to be said that there are common dangers to be avoided which no nation can avoid single-handed. This is conspicuously true of the dangers of a nuclear holocaust. But there are also the manifold dangers from pollution and from inadequate natural resources or their inadequate distribution. To the extent that cooperation in these areas is possible, it is also possible that prudence may prescribe for many nations the deliberate avoidance of the constant question, "How is my nation benefited?", when conformity to a practice or a set of guidelines is in the general interest. Prudence will prescribe this as a way of "leaning against" the tendency to consider only short-term interest. It is not likely to prescribe this in those cases where conformity to a practice would mean national suicide or even substantial long-term sacrifice.

3   Ethics and War

PACIFISM

This chapter will consider two questions: Can the recourse to war be morally justified, and can moral limitations effectively be put on the methods of warfare? This century has already seen more people killed and more physical destruction in wartime than any previous century. But the responses to these questions have tended to be similar only in the passionate conviction with which they have been put forward. War is, by common consent, an evil; but there is no consensus on when, if ever, it is a lesser evil. In accordance with the ethical theory outlined in the first chapter, we will take a broadly consequentialist approach to these questions. We will claim that a modified theory of just war is still a useful one, even in a nuclear age, but that it should be regarded as a set of *prima facie* rules rather than absolute restrictions. The consequentialist is sometimes accused of holding that no moral restrictions can be put on the practice of war because any such restrictions could on occasion be justifiably overridden by considerations of military necessity or the national interest. If, on the other hand, we insist that wars and the conduct of belligerents should be evaluated morally, we are likely to encounter the opposite objection; in George Kennan's terms, moral principles are either too abstract or too vague to be useful in this context. But the position we are taking is neither that of the moralist (to use Kennan's term again) nor that of the amoralist. The moralist finds in the principles of just war theory a set of moral absolutes. The amoralist denies that these principles have an application to the real world. What we want to say is that as people have thought about war, both theoreticians and practitioners, they have time and again come up with general guidelines as to what is all right and what is not; and that in our reflections we have discovered, somewhat to our surprise, rather similar principles emerging. We did not set out to write a justification of just war theory. What we do *not* want to say is that these principles cannot be overridden. To use the language of the first chapter, they belong at the intuitive not at the critical level of moral thinking. But this does not remove their usefulness or indeed their urgency.

Some people have held that war is, like death, an inevitable part of the human condition, and that it is not properly subject to moral evaluation. Others have thought that all wars are justifiable and others again that none of them are. All these divergent views share the consequence that it is inappropriate to ask whether any *particular* war can be justified. They thus make life easier for their proponents than the position we are advocating; for they make it unnecessary to discriminate one war from another. But the penalty for this theoretical ease and clarity is that these views are not very useful in practice; for peoples and their governments will no doubt continue for the foreseeable future to fight wars, and other peoples and governments will continue to have to decide whether to support them or resist them. These decisions will no doubt continue to be made on the merits of the particular cases, and if ethical theory is to be listened to, it will have to be able to speak to these cases in all their particularity.

There is not nearly enough evidence to sustain the conclusion that war is built into the very structure of human biology or culture. Indeed the more cultural diversity that anthropologists discover, the less plausible is the claim that *any* cultural institution is an inevitable part of the human condition. The science of neuro-physiology is not yet far enough advanced to allow it to claim to know that any complex social interaction derives causally from the structure of the brain. More importantly, it might be the case both that the human race is prone to settle its disputes by war, and that particular men can be held morally responsible and can be blamed for particular wars. Theologians have not usually held that man's tendency to sin excuses any particular breach of the moral law. If it were true that nations are always forced into wars by irresistible pressures, it would not make sense to ask whether these pressures *should* be resisted. But if all that is being argued is that sovereign states have an inevitable tendency to fight wars, it may still be disputed whether or not this tendency *should* be resisted in any particular case.[1]

It would be possible to hold the view that although war can usually be prevented, it would usually be wrong to do so. There are probably some people, like the Kwakiutl Indians, who think that war is man's highest calling.[2] This has indeed been the reigning belief in the majority of "developed" societies throughout history. In the age of chivalry it was possible to look forward to war as the testing ground for valour; and in our century we have seen the equivalent of the classification of people as infidels, on racial, religious or political and economic grounds, and the attendant glorification of war as a holy cause. Even if war in general, or war against the infidel, is not glorified in this way, it is easy to adopt the more restricted view that any war one's *own* country chooses to fight is thereby justified. Certain kinds of unwavering nationalism encourage the view that what the government decides is inevitably what the people want, and that this is always what the rest of the world should be compelled to provide.

The view that no wars are ever justified in any circumstances is a restricted form of the more general principle that no violence is ever justified. There is a huge literature on pacifism, and we will not try to do justice to it in its entirety.[3] It is not fair to characterize the view as incoherent, either in its more general or its more restricted form.[4] The argument has been made that if absolute pacifism rules out all violence and killing, this must be because people have a right not to be made the victims of violence or killing; but if someone has this right, then we must have the correlative obligation to use whatever means are necessary to secure that he is not made a victim (of violence or killing); since sometimes the only means available will be violence or killing, it would seem that absolute pacifism sometimes requires the use of the very means it rules out. The trouble with this argument is that it restricts our attention to the third kind of right distinguished in the first chapter. It is by no means clear that ruling out a practice (such as violence or killing) always involves ascribing to people this very strong sort of right. If it did, then absolute pacifism would be incoherent in the way described.

But pacifism might be coherent without being in the least attractive. The main problem is that the adoption of the view would leave one's own country, and all those others that one could have helped, defenceless against enemy aggression. It has been argued that on the contrary there are non-violent strategies of successfully resisting armed aggression. It is certainly true that some non-violent techniques have worked in the past. Examples that are sometimes mentioned are the Civil Rights movements in India and the United States, the early history of the labour movement, and the Norwegian resistance to Hitler.[5] If it is indeed possible to rely on these sorts of techniques for national defence, the moral situation is easier. But the evidence is not strong enough that this is possible. There are serious difficulties also with understanding the difference between violence and force.[6] Moreover Gandhi's situation is not easy to generalize. He had the tradition of Hinduism behind him (though it is true that the Muslim Pathans of the "Servants of God" movement used the same techniques). He also had an opponent that was unwilling to use extreme methods (though the British soldiers did fire into the crowd).

It is not clear that the refusal to use violent means is a very strong part of our tradition. Theologians have been conspicuously divided on the issue, but have on the whole not supported the pacifist position. Thus, the Federal Council of Churches in their 1950 report, "The Christian Conscience and Weapons of Mass Destruction", backed the use of the atom bomb provided that it was a response to a nuclear attack on the United States or its allies. Paul Lehmann writes, "American Christians ... could not live out their lives in this world in disregard of fellow Christians and fellow human beings in other parts of the world", and he goes on to rule out any "categorical prohibition on the use of nuclear weapons".[7]

One form of pacifism is what has recently been called a "pacifism of scruple".[8] It is based on the argument that "killing human beings for whatever purpose is a deeply problematic proceeding; that in doing things which are deeply problematic, one should be very sure about what one is doing; that no one participating in war is capable of such assurance; and that therefore such participation is wrong". This is not an absolute pacifism. For it can countenance the use of violence to protect self or others against violence. It is primarily military violence that is found objectionable, on the grounds that the person of scruple will not want to risk obeying an order which he is not in a position to evaluate morally when what is at stake is a human life.

But there is a difficulty about this sort of pacifism, which can be illustrated by a nineteenth-century analogy. W. K. Clifford argued in 1879 that "it is wrong always, everywhere, and for anyone, to believe anything upon insufficient evidence".[9] We might call this the position of the "scrupulous believer". William James objected that "he who says 'better go without belief forever than believe a lie!' merely shows his own preponderant private horror of becoming a dupe".[10] This is not quite fair. Clifford fears making an error, not becoming a dupe, even though these may be concomitant. But James goes on to point out that we are likely to incur errors in spite of all our caution, and that it is sometimes the case that what we can achieve by accepting a belief and acting on it is of such value that it is worth overriding our initial scruples. This point is surely right even if we deny the theological application which James wants to make of it. Those in governmental positions, for instance, can have a moral obligation to decide on a policy without having "sufficient" evidence that it is the best one. This is what often makes good academics bad bureaucrats. This will be so unless we make it trivially false by saying that sufficient evidence is by definition what any decision ought to be made on.

In the case of the pacifism of scruple, it would not be fair to say that the pacifist is afraid of being untrue to his principles, rather than afraid of being responsible for a wrongful death. But it would be fair to point out that this sort of responsibility is risked fairly frequently in institutional contexts. One example would be those who work in large relief organizations. The decisions about life and death are taken at a high level, and then implemented, so to speak, "in the field". It is indeed a horrible job to distribute insufficient rice in a hungry village. But the need to have the job done overrides the scruple that the wrong people may be left without food. Famine relief raises a large number of additional questions, philosophical and practical (such as the relevance of the distinction between acts and omissions). Some of them will be discussed in Chapter 7. But it provides a good example of a case where scruples about life-and-death responsibility are overridable in the general interest. To take the obvious wartime example, it might be more important that Hitler be stopped than that the risk not be incurred of causing a wrongful death.

There is another sort of limited pacifism which needs to be considered. We might call it, pejoratively, "parasitic pacifism". It would be possible for the United Kingdom, for example, to cut its defence establishment drastically, withdraw from Northern Ireland and from NATO, and rely on America and the rest of Europe for security.[11] Such a policy might be open to all sorts of objections, moral and prudential. But it is also not a *bona fide* form of pacifism. For a pacifist would surely have scruples not only about defending his own country by violent means, but about relying on others to do this for him.

It might be that absolute pacifism would be universally acceptable in a world in which it was universally accepted. But this is paradoxical. Universal acceptance is unlikely to precede universal acceptability, and there is not sufficient reason to believe that pacifism will be accepted by enough people to make it acceptable to very many people in the foreseeable future. Moreover, the claim that the example of one nation laying down its arms unilaterally would lead other nations to do the same is not clearly supported by the evidence. Indeed, the opposite seems to be the case. In the period after the First World War, Britain adopted a policy of very heavy reductions in armed strength. Her example was not followed by even her ally France, nor did it assist her in the bargaining process during a long series of disarmament conferences. Rather, unilateral disarmament weakened her position vis-à-vis both her potential opponents and her allies and helped lead to a situation in which she was forced to re-arm under disadvantageous circumstances and, in the end, to fight for her survival. Unilateral moves toward disarmament can be used in certain circumstances to induce others to begin a process of dialogue. But unless other parties move quickly to reciprocate, unilateral action has clear limitations.[12]

It may be that it is useful for a society to have some absolute pacifists in it who can remind their fellow citizens of the horrors of war. This is useful because there is a tendency, especially in the course of a war, for consciences to get progressively blunted. But this is a role that requires, at least in wartime, an extraordinary degree of conviction, and few people would be likely to have the tenacity required, even if it were desirable that large numbers should have it. For most people, each war will be considered on its own merits, and some way to make the choices involved will be required.

One possibility needs to be mentioned in conclusion. It is what John Rawls has called "Contingent Pacifism".[13] This is the view that although a war might conceivably be justified in certain types of situations, the likelihood of such situations arising is extremely low; and it would, therefore, be reasonable to adopt a general presumption against the waging of war. The onus of proof would then be on someone who wanted to justify a war, and the forms that such a justification might take are the subject of the rest of this chapter.

THE JUST WAR TRADITION

If we make the assumption that some wars are justified and others are not, we will need some criterion for distinguishing the two. Tradition provides us with just such a set of criteria in the theory of the "just war" or, as it should more properly be translated, "the justified war". There have been two types of rules developed. One governed when the initial recourse to war was justified, and thus defined *jus ad bellum* (literally "right towards war"). The other governed what behaviour was justified during the course of a war, and thus defined *jus in bello* (literally "right in war"). To think of war in terms of this theory is to think of it as a social institution. It is not equivalent to a Hobbesian state of nature, for this would contain neither armies nor the states to raise them.[14] It may nevertheless be true that war has a tendency towards the state of nature, and the end of restraint and order. It is this tendency which makes the status of the rules of war so precarious.

If the conclusion is reached that there is no longer any *jus ad bellum* and that it is fruitless to look any more for any *jus in bello*, this will mean that war can no longer be justified as an institution. But then there will be a need for some other institution or set of institutions to take its place. For there is no sign that people have given up the objectives with which they went to war in the past. People have gone to war in order to establish or maintain political independence, to acquire or secure territory, to further or safeguard their ideologies and institutions and to acquire or protect their international position and power.[15] There is not much sign that political institutions will soon fill the role in respect to these objectives that war has played until now.

Just war theory can link *jus ad bellum* and *jus in bello* in a number of different ways. A large part of the discredit into which the theory has fallen is due to one form of such linkage. It has been held that the rules governing behaviour in war are less binding on the parties whose initial recourse to war was justified. Since both parties are likely to claim this justification, this seriously weakens any restraint on wartime conduct. It is perhaps only since Grotius that the principle has been widely accepted that the rules of conduct in war bind both belligerents alike, even where it is not the case that both belong within the same cultural or religious framework.[16] The standing of this principle has probably always been precarious and is certainly so now. A second and more promising kind of linkage would be to say that no party can be justified in starting a war in which it is planning to break the rules governing the conduct of belligerents. It was indeed the observation that "military necessity" increasingly overrode the limits on the conduct of war that eventually (though not until 1946) led to the acceptance of the renunciation of the right of the state to go to war except in the case of self-defence against armed attack.

The simplest statements of just war theory give three criteria for a justified war: it must be waged by a prince invested with legal authority, against an enemy deserving of punishment, and with the intention that good should be promoted and evil removed. But to state matters thus simply is to over-simplify. Contemporary theorists have lengthened the list and made it more plausible. Thus Richard Purtill has seven criteria which he revised from those of Joseph McKenna.[17] The first six relate to *jus ad bellum* and the last to *jus in bello*. The list goes as follows: Nation A is justified in waging war with Nation B if and only if (1) Nation A has been attacked by Nation B or is going to the aid of Nation C which has been attacked by Nation B. (2) The war has been legally declared by the properly constituted authorities of Nation A. (3) The intentions of Nation A in waging war are confined to repelling the attack by Nation B and establishing a peace, fair to all. (4) Nation A has a reasonable hope of success in repelling the attack and establishing a just peace. (5) Nation A cannot secure these ends without waging war, and it has considered or tried all other means and wages war only as a last resort. (6) The good done by Nation A waging war against Nation B can reasonably be expected to out-weigh the evil done by waging war. (7) Nation A does not use or anticipate using any means of waging war which are themselves immoral, e.g., the avoidable killing of innocent people.

The *first* criterion amounts to the claim that Nation A can only justify waging war on Nation B if Nation B is the aggressor. It is unfortunately clear that this criterion has not in the recent past put an effective limit on warfare. Julius Stone starts his book on this topic by discussing the failure of the General Assembly's Special Committee on the Definition of Aggression in 1956 to reach a consensus.[18] While the committee was deliberating, from 8 October to 9 November, Israeli forces crossed the Gaza and Sinai frontiers; the British and French governments announced in advance, and partly carried out an airborne invasion of the Suez Canal Zone; and the events occurred which led to the intervention of Soviet forces to displace the Nagy regime in Hungary. Stone ends by saying, "it is because a definition of aggression which systematically ignores demands sincerely made in the name of justice is thus not operationally viable, while an agreed definition that is precise enough to guide us and yet flexible enough to take these demands into account is beyond our reach, that the hope of basing peace enforcement on a definition of aggression has gradually faded".[19] It remains true that the principle is generally accepted that he who strikes first is in the wrong. But the participants in the conflicts of the recent past have all tended to claim that they were fighting in self-defence or in order to aid the self-defence of an ally. If the first criterion for justified war is to have a practical impact, the concept of aggression needs to be given greater exactness and clarity than has yet been found possible.

One way out of this dilemma is taken by Michael Walzer.[20] He proposes that aggression is the breach of political sovereignty or territorial integrity, that the bearers of the rights of political sovereignty are governments, and that governments can only forfeit these rights if they engage in the "enslavement or massacre" of their own citizens.[21] This seems to mean that there is an absolute ban on the use of force against a nation as long as its government does not go to these extremes. A government can thus systematically ignore the "natural rights" of its people (if we can use this phrase for the moment) without thereby providing any justification for another state to go to the aid of the people's struggle for liberation. The basis for this is a "stern doctrine of self-help", "for it is not our purpose in international society to establish liberal or democratic communities, but only independent ones".[22]

This has probably been the classic view. Hedley Bull says that there are four goals of international society that are elementary, primary or universal:[23] first, the preservation of the system and the society of states itself; second, the maintenance of the independence or external sovereignty of individual states; third, peace; and fourth, "the limitation of violence resulting in death or bodily harm, the keeping of promises and the stabilization of possessions by rules of property". But these are predominantly the goals of a policy of the status quo. And it is characteristic of such a policy that it is not able to accommodate all demands for interstate and international justice. Bull recognizes this explicitly.[24] If aggression is defined in terms of the status quo, it is likely to fall prey to Stone's objections, for if it ignores demands sincerely made in the name of justice, it is unlikely to be "operationally viable". This is because interventions in the name of justice will in all probability occur, and the concept of "aggression" will not be able to deal with them. Having said this, however, it remains true that the *quest* for a viable definition has continued in response to the renunciation of aggressive war accepted by all signatories to the United Nations charter. It may be that the most recent attempt will succeed.

The *second* criterion states that war must be declared by someone invested with legal authority. It was on the basis of this principle that President Johnson's actions were criticized when he committed American forces to a war in Vietnam without a declaration of war by

Congress. His defenders argued that the Gulf of Tonkin resolution gave authority for the commitment of troops. This principle evolved out of the long historical experience of private wars. Augustine said that "the natural order which seeks the peace of mankind ordains that the monarch should have the power of undertaking war if he thinks it advisable and that soldiers should perform their military duties on behalf of the peace and safety of the community".[25] In Protestant thought, there has been a development from Luther, who allowed Princes to use armed resistance to the Emperor, to Calvin, who allowed the minor magistrates, if they were unanimous in their opinion, to used armed resistance to the Prince. The basis is here laid for a theory of justified revolution by the will of the people.

There has been pressure in recent times to legitimate private international violence.[26] In 1949 belligerent status was given to a *levée en masse*, legally defined as "inhabitants of a non-occupied territory who on the approach of the enemy spontaneously take up arms to resist the invading force, without having had time to form themselves into regular armed units".[27] In 1968 an International Conference on Human Rights held in Tehran passed a resolution according belligerent rights to persons struggling against "racist or colonial regimes", and this was implemented in 1977 by the General Assembly of the United Nations.[28] This means that National Liberation Movements can be seen legally as having "properly constituted authority". The difficulty with this phrase is similar to the difficulty with "aggression". If the existing government of a country is by definition the only properly constituted authority, the definition enshrines a policy of the status quo. It will not, therefore, be able to handle demands "sincerely made in the name of justice" against those governments. Dissatisfaction with the status quo is what is reflected in the recent enactment by the General Assembly. But the admission of National Liberation Movements as entities which have the lawful competence to engage in "international" armed conflicts introduces a discriminatory clause into the law. Armed resistance to a government may be legitimate if that government's oppression is based on race, but not if it is based, for example, on ideology.

Is the terrorist to be regarded as a belligerent, and thus to be protected under international law? One recent treatment of this question has used Michael Walzer's analysis of the "politically divided man".[29] On this analysis it has always been a mistake to see political allegiances as undivided; but especially in the twentieth century, people are likely to have a number of competing loyalties. It can then be said that resort to terrorism or guerrilla warfare by "divided political man is neither more nor less surprising than resort to war by states". On this analysis terrorism is by definition the use of indiscriminate techniques, such as the bomb hidden in a bus station, and these are seen as no different in principle from the strategic bombing of cities practised in the Second World War; in both cases "there may be plenty of professional reasons for indiscriminate killing". A campaign of widespread assassination that aimed only at those engaged in counter-insurgency would be discriminate, and therefore not terrorism in this view. For terrorism is defined in such a way as to make it logically impossible for terrorists to observe any distinction analogous to that between combatant and noncombatant in inter-state warfare. Even the National Liberation Front in Vietnam may not have been terrorists on this definition, although 7500 village and district "officials" were assassinated by Vietcong militants between 1960 and 1965; for a concerted effort was made "to ensure that there were no unexplained killings".[30] This has an interesting consequence. One of the criteria that we are considering for *jus ad bellum* is that resort to war cannot be justified if the intention is to break the rules governing *jus in bello*. The discrimination between those who are and those who are not appropriate objects of violence is central to these rules, so that the definition of terrorism as indiscriminate precludes the justification of terrorism under this version of "just war" theory.

Some writers would say that terrorism is a kind of natural phenomenon like a hurricane or an earthquake, a kind of behaviour which is inevitable in modern societies and which cannot appropriately be subjected to moral evaluation.[31] But the terrorists themselves have not usually taken this position. They have rather claimed justification under some theory of structural violence such as that considered below. Moreover, the fact that National Liberation Movements have often refrained from indiscriminate killing suggests that terrorism in Walzer's sense is not inevitable.

The distinction between those who are and those who are not a proper object of attack is harder in the context of intra-state fighting. The National Liberation Front counted as "officials" priests and landowners who were involved in the political efforts of the enemy regime. The Baader-Meinhof gang and their followers killed a chief prosecutor, a banker and the president of the Inleyer's Federation in Cologne.[32] Some thinkers, perhaps most conspicuously Tolstoy, argue that the state itself is in effect simply a form of institutionalized violence, for all organized societies contain great inequalities of power and wealth and those inequalities are in the last resort defended by violence.[33] This view, if taken to its conclusion, would seem to imply that any citizen in any state who is enjoying comparative wealth and power is relying on the implicitly violent exploitation of those who are not. The implication (though not Tolstoy's) is that he is therefore a proper object of violent attack himself. This argument is analogous to that used by the adherents of the theory of total war who claimed that the Germans were collectively responsible for the crimes of national socialism, and could therefore legitimately be killed en masse. The mistake is the same in both cases. Even if we admit collective responsibility, and we admit the case for collective punishment, it does not follow that death is an appropriate penalty. For if the collective is responsible, it should be penalized as a collective, perhaps by dissolution. But those individuals who were not directly involved, but were implicated only as members of the collective, are punished for more than their membership if they are themselves condemned to death.

It is hard to verify or falsify the claim that all states are based on oppression or structural violence and are therefore legitimate objects of attack. Any theory of "just revolution" is likely to try to distinguish those that are and those that are not. It is not our purpose here to try to make this distinction. It is clear that ideology is likely to play a large part in any such attempt. But it is not clear that attempts like those by Amnesty or the United Nations Human Rights Commission are inevitably doomed to failure. If we allow that some measure of agreement can be reached on what constitutes "oppression", we can use Walzer's three criteria as follows: the use of armed force against a government may be justified if it is a response to violent oppression by a tyranny, if the society worked for does not itself involve oppression, and if the force used is discriminate in the sense given above. To these should probably be added that there must be a reasonable hope of success. If one looks at the recent history of Latin America, one gets the overwhelming impression that no illiberal regimes have been overthrown by the use of assassination, for example. They have simply become even more oppressive and brutal as a consequence. We can also add that a revolution is justified only after all available non-violent means of political change have been tried and only if the good achieved by the revolution is likely to outweigh the evil done in fighting it. We will then have a list of criteria very similar to that for the "just war".

The gradual widening of the scope of the phrase "properly constituted authority" shows both the strength and the weakness of the "just war" criteria. If widened any further, the criterion will become a mere tautology. Each particular use of force will be justified on other grounds and will then be said to have been declared by "properly constituted authority". But it has not yet been widened this far. It has shown surprising resilience, although its application in practice has been extraordinarily hard. In both these respects, the principle resembles the other *prima facie* principles of morality. The persistence of the principle is shown by the attempts to gear technology towards its implementation. Thus one difficulty is that in modern times increased speed of attack has worked to decentralize authority to some degree. But enormous efforts in electronic technology have been made at great expense to ensure that the decisions to use nuclear weapons remain in the hands of responsible political authorities. We are now more than three decades into the atomic age and despite the earlier fears of accidental launchings, the stability of the nuclear deterrent has been maintained. This is not to deny that some possibility (however small) exists that control may be evaded through malice or by accident or that, as the number of nuclear states and nuclear weapons grows, the probability of unauthorized war grows in some unknown proportion. But rather, it is to say that the ancient principle that war to be just must be waged by someone with legal authority retains its ancient logic as a principle of conduct for external wars.

The next four criteria can be discussed more briefly. The *third* is that the intention of a nation involved in a just war must not extend beyond repelling the invader and establishing a fair peace ("just" in the modern sense). The first of these conditions has already been discussed in relation to the first criterion. The second may seem utopian under present conditions, for the wars of this century have all released a torrent of hatred and desire for vengeance. It would seem likely that the more devastating the means of warfare used, the more difficult it would be for their victims to restrain these emotions. It would be difficult to imagine the establishment of a just peace following an all-out nuclear war. This is not in itself a reason for rejecting the third criterion. For it may be that we should retain the view that no total war could now be justified.

The *fourth* criterion raises the point that hostilities cannot justifiably be entered into unless there is reasonable hope of success. This is because the hostilities themselves cannot justifiably be chosen as an end. Modern warfare makes this particularly apparent. It was different perhaps for the Kshatriya in ancient India or the Homeric heroes. Even in the twentieth century, G. K. Chesterton could write in glowing terms of the opportunities for nobility and heroism that war afforded, and William James, though himself against war, could write of "the moral equivalent of war" as though the cessation of war would leave a gap which some other glorious and demanding enterprise would have to fill. But the weapons of contemporary war are at once duller and more devastating. They are duller because, though sometimes technologically fascinating, they involve less and less personal contact with the enemy. If war can no longer be chosen as an end, it can only be justified by the reasonably high probability that it may be a means to something that can be chosen as an end. This criterion is thus entirely congenial to a consequentialist.

The *fifth* criterion states that war can only be justified as a last resort. Presumably first resorts would be such alternatives as economic, social, or political boycott, and negotiations, either through unilateral or multilateral means, or through such an agency as the United Nations.[34] Donald Wells has argued against this criterion. He says, "the sheer presence of the doctrine of 'last resort' makes the compromise contingent on negotiations inadmissible". But it is hard to see what he means. For the mere fact that some dire alternative is available if all else fails does not *logically* interfere with the choice of some less drastic alternative. And the claim that such a choice is *psychologically* impossible is hard to square with the fact that both Russia and the United States have threatened war without actually resorting to it. Perhaps what Wells means is that the availability of the last resort makes it *easier* to ignore the possibility of compromise. But this would only be true if the last resort could reasonably be used. If the last resort is total nuclear war, its "availability" makes compromise more likely rather than less. The normal practice of states is to engage in diplomatic discussion before hostilities are begun. This is the reason why diplomacy evolved and why it is likely to continue as long as the state system exists. If war is considered as one alternative among others, the costs and risks of war will be weighed against those of the peaceful alternatives. If the war being considered is an all-out nuclear war, it is hard to see what greater costs and risks any alternative policy could present.

The *sixth* criterion is a straightforwardly consequentialist one. Richard Brandt has formulated the principle in more technical terms as follows: "a military action is permissible only if the utility (broadly conceived so that the maintenance of treaty obligations of international law could count as a utility) of victory to all concerned, multiplied by the increase in its probability if the action is executed, on the evidence (where the evidence is reasonably solid, considering the stakes), is greater than the possible disutility of the action to both sides multiplied by its probability".[35] Thus stated the principle applies to *jus in bello*. But it can be widened to apply to *jus ad bellum* if we include reference to the declaration of war as well as to military action. In this form, the principle is simply an application of the consequentialist principle itself to the ethics of warfare.[36] It can be argued that this criterion alone is sufficient to rule out the justifiability of a total nuclear war. For it does not seem that any resultant good could justify the destruction of whole societies. "To say that one should choose the death of millions rather than accept survival at the price of subjection to tyranny is neither a powerful nor an appealing argument. For against the certainty of massive infliction of suffering and death, one would have to weigh the possibility, however far distant and faint, of an escape from bondage into freedom."[37] But to say that this criterion rules out the use of total war does not imply that it rules out the *threat* of such war. This needs to be independently argued. Moreover it does not imply that the criterion rules out the use of limited nuclear war.

The *seventh* criterion gives the heart of the traditional theory of *jus in bello*, which is the distinction between combatants and non-combatants. In the language of the United Nations "grave breaches" legislation, it is a "grave breach" to make "the civilian population or individual civilians the object of attack".[38] This is a distinction which could not be honoured in all-out nuclear war. If we accept the criterion, the question is whether there is any kind of limited war which would allow it to be honoured. The distinction itself is probably best seen as one of degree rather than kind. There are obvious problems about categorizing munitions workers, for example, or recruits in training. But there seem to be clear cases at either end of the spectrum. Small children clearly are not engaged in the hostilities and volunteer troops clearly are. John Ford provided a list in 1944 of well over one hundred typical civilian professions, none of which is directly engaged in fighting, though they may all aid the war effort indirectly to a greater or lesser degree.[39] The point needs to be made that it was always the case that some members of the population were directly involved and others indirectly to a greater or lesser degree. This is not something new in modern warfare and it is therefore difficult to see why it should provide a reason for dropping the distinction between combatants and non-combatants.

This criterion, however, like the others with the exception of the sixth, should not be taken as giving an absolute prohibition. It may be, for example, that the bombing of Hiroshima was justified and not that of Nagasaki. This would be because the harm was in one case proportionate to the good achieved but not in the other case. In *Shimoda–v.–Japan*, a Japanese civil court denied damages to survivors of Hiroshima and Nagasaki but characterized the bombings as "contrary to the fundamental principles of the laws of war", because international law forbids indiscriminate or blind attack on undefended cities.[40] But it also allowed for the possibility that there might be, although there was not in this case, military necessity of sufficient magnitude to justify such action.

It is instructive to look a little more closely at the case of strategic bombing. Sir Solly Zuckerman has provided us with the conclusions of a quantitative study of the total effects of the air raids on Hull and Birmingham, which he prepared for the Ministry of Home Security in April 1942. He stated that "there is no evidence of breakdown of morale for the intensities of the raids experienced by Hull or Birmingham (maximum intensity of bombing forty tons per square mile)" and that "loss of production was caused almost entirely by direct damage to factories".[41] He also details the dispute with Sir Arthur Harris and others about the effectiveness of bombing cities as opposed to railways. It seems, to use the principle stated by Richard Brandt, that the evidence was not reasonably solid, considering the stakes, that the bombing of German cities would be effective. Moreover, it seems likely that the motivation for the raids was at least partly retributive. Thus Churchill said in a radio broadcast of 1941 that the British Air Force would make "the German people taste and gulp each month a sharper dose of the miseries they have showered upon mankind".[42] The raid on Dresden may have shortened the war by a few days, or it may not have. But this by itself is not sufficient justification. It may even be that the bombers were diverted from other tasks which would have ended the war even sooner, with far less loss of life and property. Churchill, in fact, issued a minute six weeks after the attack which "bluntly said that any further attacks on German cities would hinder the Allies more than they would hurt the Germans".[43]

But if bombing Dresden was wrong, this does not show that strategic bombing could not have been justified under any circumstances whatever. If bombing the cities had indeed been the only way to win the war, and if winning the war was indeed vital to the interests of humanity, then a justification for the bombing could perhaps be mounted that would be consistent with the consequentialist principle. But in the Second World War, the Allies carried out a strategy which was not, at least in its later stages, justifiable in this way. Why might this have been? There are at least three reasons which can be given and doubtless there are many more. The first is that it was not widely understood in 1944 how greatly the accuracy of bombing techniques had improved since 1941. The second is that the attacks on English cities had given rise to a desire to retaliate in kind. The third is that there was a widening gulf in the high command of the air force which made communications and, therefore, a change in strategy more difficult. It is very possible that these three reasons are interconnected.

What needs to be pointed out is that these three factors were not inevitable. It does not seem plausible to argue that either these or equivalent factors would always interfere with the observance of the rule of war in question in any modern war. The case is one in which it would have been not only morally but prudentially reasonable to abide by the rule and in which a firmer intuitive distaste for breaking it would have worked to everyone's advantage. What we should probably conclude is that this seventh criterion for a "just" war is a useful one, if it is seen as giving a *prima facie* rule. There is a strong presumption that a war is not justified if it involves, for example, the strategic bombing of cities. But this presumption is rebuttable in certain circumstances, and what these circumstances are will be discussed in more detail in Chapter 4, in relation to the attack on Hiroshima.

DO THE RULES DO ANY GOOD?

It is true that the rules of just war have been honoured more in the breach than the observance. Sir Hersch Lauterpacht said that "if international law is in some ways the vanishing point of law, the law of war is, perhaps, even more conspicuously at the vanishing point of international law".[44] Even by the end of the fifteenth century, "the normal state among Christians was assumed to be peace, tempered by a readiness to repel the infidel", but "in practice nothing was more likely than war among Christians and, in order to leave them free to pursue it, overtures of peace to the Turk".[45] It is not clear that the breakdown of mediaeval Christendom and the rise of sovereign states decreased either the frequency or the brutality of wars, and certainly the Thirty Years' War of religion matched in ferocity the struggles of any era.

There have been three major attempts in modern history to outlaw the use of war as an instrument of national policy. The first was the Covenant of the League of Nations. Without going into a full consideration of the complex legal details, it may be said in brief that the Covenant restricted but did not eliminate the right of states to go to war. All disputes were to be submitted to arbitration, judicial settlement or inquiry by the League Council. While numerous procedural difficulties existed in the system, these were by no means fatal. The real difficulty lay in the simple but deadly fact that the League did not have the power to arrive at a final decision binding upon the parties. The League system could only recommend terms of settlement and each member could decide for itself whether or not to apply sanctions to violators of the Covenant.

The Pact of Paris (1928) was completely devoid of enforcement provisions, although it bound all parties to renounce war as an instrument of national policy. All disputes were to be settled by peaceful means but no specific obligation existed to submit such disputes to binding settlements. Although war no longer constituted a legal remedy,[46] nothing was put in its place, with the inevitable result that states anxious to revise the *status quo* resorted to war in violation of their pledges. There can be no doubt that Japan violated the League Covenant and the Pact of Paris in Manchuria in 1931 or that Italy violated her obligations to the League when she attacked Ethiopia. But other signatories took no effective opposing action. It is, therefore, impossible to resist the conclusion that under the existing political, economic and social conditions, the mere sense of moral obligation, which had been too weak to overcome the legal deficiencies of the Covenant and the Paris Peace Pact, was too feeble to support a world-wide response to aggression.

In our own time we have witnessed a large-scale effort to control war. Indeed, the United Nations Charter has abolished all private wars. Force is no longer a legal instrument of self-help except in the case of self-defence against armed attack, although the effect of this provision is weakened by the simple fact that great power unanimity is required in all cases involving threats to and breaches of the peace. The great powers have reserved the right of veto over any use of force or war mandated by the United Nations, and this has significantly weakened the enforcement provisions attached to the renunciation of aggressive war. Since this veto can be used to protect their vital interests, and since these interests have expanded to the point where they are virtually global in scope, the effect is to prevent action under the Charter to enforce the prohibition against aggressive war.

It is thus hard not to be sceptical about the extent of the legal changes brought about by the United Nations Charter and the charges of aggressive war brought by the victors at the International Military Tribunal at Nuremberg War Crime Trials. States now do not admit they have gone to war when they decide to use force. Self-defence is pleaded or some other rationale, as when Russia invaded Czechoslovakia or when the United States waged war in Vietnam. The most optimistic conclusion available is that there has been a gradual change in the norms to which states express their commitment, even though these norms are fairly consistently violated in practice. It has been said that "of man-made law it must always be remembered that, if it could not be bent or broken, it would not be law. The law lays down the rules, it does not ensure that they will be obeyed. What has come about with the abandonment of the right to war — with the admission that war is not a legal or sanctified form of force — is a change of norms, and this is a change that cannot but be symptomatic of a still wider shift in international attitudes."[47] We can see these principles as providing a useful *prima facie* proscription of the use of war as an instrument of national policy.

The rules defining *jus in bello* have not fared any better. It seems as though modern war has a kind of logic of its own. A survey of the American Civil War, the two World Wars, and the war in Vietnam would show that the course of each of them was marked by a gradual erosion of the moral principles with which each of them began. The law of warfare in the air provides the most eloquent example.[48] The first attempt to obtain international agreement about the dropping of explosives from the air occurred at the first Hague conference in 1899. The second Hague conference in 1907 put down in Article 28 a centuries' old rule to the effect that attacks upon or bombardment of undefended towns, villages, dwellings or buildings was forbidden. Yet in the war of 1914–1918, the raids over London and southeast England were followed by those over the Saarland and towards Mannheim and Stuttgart. After the war, the Washington Conference of 1922 set up a commission of jurists whose General Report specifically forbade attack from the air for the purpose of terrorizing the civilian population or of injuring non-combatants. Article 23 stated that where bombing targets were so situated that they could not be bombarded without the indiscriminate bombing of the civilian population, then there was to be no bombing at all. In 1933, only Britain stood out against the total abolition of aerial bombardment, apparently because she thought it might be useful in policing the remoter parts of the Empire. But again, in the period from 1940–1945, the bombing of open cities like Rotterdam and the onslaughts on London and other British cities were followed by the bombing of almost all the great German cities. Tokyo and other Japanese cities were set on fire by the use of napalm bombs, and in the end, the two atomic bombs exploded over Hiroshima and Nagasaki. The experience of mankind since the first Hague conference of 1899 suggests that legal restraints on war based upon one kind of military technology will not survive as weapons technology changes. It is a long road from attempts to prohibit the use of dum-dum (expanding) bullets to the mushroom-shaped clouds over Japanese cities and every mile of it is marked by the wreckage of the traditions of *jus in bello*.

But what follows from the observation that many of the rules of war did not in fact succeed in limiting the scope or methods of this century's wars? It does not follow that these rules were inappropriate or that the time spent in formulating them was wasted. For first, they provided a basis for retrospective censure and punishment. Second, they articulated a change in norms, even if not a change in practice. Third, it remains true and important that most of them would have worked to everyone's advantage if they had been observed.

Once the shooting stopped in 1918, nations tried to justify their actions by charging one another with responsibility for the war. The Germans were forced to accept civil liability for "all damage done to the civilian population of the Allies and their property by the aggression of Germany by land, by sea, and from the air".[49] The former Emperor of Germany was to be arraigned for "a supreme offence against international morality", although the Dutch government refused to surrender the royal refugee and thereby prevented formal action being taken.[50] Twelve persons were tried by a German court in Leipzig in 1921 for violations of the laws of war and six were convicted. In 1945 the consciences of men over a large section of the globe had revolted in horror and indignation before the spectacle presented by the acts of Hitler and Nazi Germany.

International lawyers have argued about the legality of the Nuremberg trials, [51] but most of the world agreed that the calculated murder and torture of literally millions of innocent people was a massive and indefensible violation of all human standards and deserved a swift, sure punishment.

Secondly, there is a change in norms represented by the Hague conferences, the disarmament conferences between the World Wars, and the international legislation since 1945. Each war was followed by a genuine revulsion against the methods used by both sides. This revulsion has, at least in some cases, been reflected in an attempt to limit practice in the actual course of a war. It is true that no nation is likely to abide by such limitations in a supreme emergency. Machiavelli said, "When the entire safety of our country is at stake, no considerations of what is just or unjust, merciful or cruel, praiseworthy or blameworthy must intervene." We might not agree with the imperative "must (not) intervene", but we would agree with a qualified indicative "are (not) likely to intervene". But nations are not always in a state of supreme emergency in wartime, even though they may tend to think they are.

The conduct of the American navy in Vietnam is instructive in this respect.[52] Two separate naval operations were involved, "Operation Market Time" and "Operation Sea Dragon". The former was concerned with policing the three-mile territorial sea limit of South Vietnam and an additional nine-mile contiguous zone. The Seventh fleet, which carried out the operation, was given legal standing by legislation in South Vietnam, paraphrasing the Geneva Convention, which gave it the authority to prevent infringements of customs and immigration laws, especially those relating to the infiltration of arms, supplies and personnel. "Operation Sea Dragon", however, was designed to cut off in the North the logistic support for Communist "armed attack" in the South. It was based on the recognition of the territorial waters of North Vietnam and was compelled to observe the right of innocent passage. Fishing boats and any other shipping which did not meet the "indices of logistic support for the war" were immune from attack. There were points common to both operations, "merchant shipping as such could not be taken in prize. Attack on civilians had to be avoided in order to comply with the laws of war and the Red Cross conventions. The distinctions between military and civilian targets and between attack and harassment and interdiction, put a premium upon positive identification which was unusually strict." Undoubtedly the rules were frequently broken, but it seems clear also that they did put some limitation on the practice of one of the belligerents. Indeed, some would claim that it is the one-sidedness of this limitation which raises serious questions about the ability of the western nations to fight protracted counter-evasive wars.

Thirdly, a number of the rules which were broken would in fact have worked to the long-term benefit of both sides if they had been observed. This claim needs to be understood in the light of the theoretical discussion of rules in the first chapter. It is true in general of moral rules, and the rules of war are an instance, that we should adopt the rules with the greatest acceptance utility. Good prudential rules are those whose acceptance maximizes benefits for the individual. Good moral rules are those whose acceptance does so for all those affected. It was argued in the first chapter that prudence provides the securest basis for morality. But a good moral rule is not *justified* by being shown to be in someone's interest. That is merely what is likely to make him accept it. It is always possible that a particular rule is not in someone's interest, and that if he realizes this, he may refuse to adopt if for his own use. The justification for the rules of war, then, is that they are in the general interest. But it is also in the general interest that they be as effective as possible, and this means that they must be as attractive as possible to the belligerents. There is, thus, a difficult balance between making a rule stringent enough for people in general to be significantly benefited by its observance and flexible enough for it to be possible for each belligerent to observe it without sacrificing long-term national interests. Those who are sceptical about such rules deny that such a balance is possible.

Let us take as an example the rule against ill-treating prisoners of war, a rule which has been only partially observed in this century.[53] A rule such as this, if accepted by both sides in a war (especially if they are both well provided with supplies), is likely to work for the benefit of both sides. For the military benefits of mistreating the prisoners are not likely to be substantial, and it is an advantage that they should return after the war to their own countries with as little bitterness as possible. Moreover, the news that one's own troops, when captured, were being mistreated or even killed would be likely to strengthen the resolve not to surrender or to retaliate against the enemy prisoners in one's own hands.

But what if there are military gains to be won by mistreating or killing prisoners? The Department of the U.S. Army Field Manual states explicitly, "A commander may not put his prisoners to death because their presence retards his movements or diminishes his power of resistance by necessitating a large guard, or by reason of their consuming supplies, or because it appears certain that they will regain their liberty through the impending success of their forces."[54] The manual states that this rule, along with the others it gives, may not be disregarded on grounds of "military necessity" since considerations of military necessity were fully taken into account in framing the rules.

This seems to reflect one of the two standard views of the rules of war, that they cannot be overridden by considerations of military necessity because these have been given their full weight in the decision to promulgate the rule.[55] The other standard view is that the rules all carry with them an implicit clause of exception, "unless military necessity dictates otherwise". For a consequentialist of the sort described in the first chapter of this book, both of these views are misleading. For a consequentialist, the status accorded to considerations of military necessity depends on the value of the military goal in question. Suppose it is necessary to break one of the rules for the success of a comparatively unimportant mission. In this case, the rules should not be broken. Or suppose the breaking of the rules is necessary for the winning of a war that should never have been started in the first place, or at least should now be stopped. In both these cases, the appeal to military necessity should not have much force. But it will always be possible for the consequentialist to think of hypothetical circumstances in which the appeal to military necessity can override a rule; although strictly it will never be military necessity itself which overrides the rule, but the *moral* necessity of trying to ensure the success of some particular military action.

We have already referred to a principle, stated in consequentialist terms by Richard Brandt, which gives the conditions under which a military action is morally legitimate. There are many problems with the implementation of a principle of this sort. It allows for a large measure of discretion on the part of the military authorities. It is also likely that each side will be convinced of the overwhelming importance of its own victory to humanity at large. But even so, Brandt's principle does not license the conclusion that "it is permissible and lawful to kill and maim and destroy, provided only that it will help to win the war".[56]

A consequentialist commander-in-chief, convinced of the benefits to humanity that would arise from the victory of his forces, might be able to justify in some situations breaking the rules against the mistreatment or even the murder of prisoners of war. It is this sort of point that makes consequentialism seem so disreputable. For once this possibility has been allowed, it may seem that the only effective barrier to barbarism has been removed. If it is no longer perceived that there is an absolute ban on certain methods of warfare, will not any combatant be able to rationalize the conclusion that his present situation is one to which the ban does not apply?

One might take as an example the following situation: "Small detachments on a special mission who are accidentally cut off from their main force, may take prisoners under such circumstances that men cannot be spared to guard them or take them to the rear, and that to take them along would greatly endanger the success of the mission or the safety of the unit."[57] These two considerations, danger to the mission and to the safety of the unit, need to be distinguished. International lawyers seem to agree that the first is a less good justification for breaking the rule than the second.[58] There is one consideration of long-term interest that might deter a military commander even if he believed that the victory of his own side would be beneficial for all and that the killing of prisoners was necessary to win the war. This is that in the long run the example of someone keeping the rule even at considerable cost might have the effect of making future warfare more humane. Unfortunately, it might also have the effect of confirming the impression that altruism in warfare leads only to defeat. In general, no nation is likely to agree, even in the absence of a present threat, to a rule that substantially reduces its chances of victory. This is the limitation on all the rules of war. Their acceptance is likely to be contingent upon their not interfering unduly with the very process they are supposed to control.

But there is a reply to the argument that to remove the absolute status of the rules of war is to remove the only effective barrier to barbarism, which is the individual conscience. For a consequentialist will respond that if the rule is a good one, the situations in which it can be justifiably overridden will be extremely rare. He will refer to the two-level analysis of moral thinking outlined in the first chapter. A good rule, such as that against murdering prisoners of war, will be one whose observance usually maximizes the general welfare. This fact justifies its inclusion in army manuals and its use in the training of soldiers. The more deeply ingrained it is, the more useful it will be. For it will come to have an intuitive appeal to those making the relevant military decisions and those who decide to break it will accordingly feel the sting of conscience. But the justification of the rule is not that it feels intuitively right, but that its general acceptance maximizes the general welfare. It is, therefore, always possible that a commander may be justified, despite his feeling bad about the decision, in deciding to break it. But if it is a good rule, the situations which justify breaking it are likely to be enormously less frequent than those in which fallible moral agents want to break it. It is, therefore, an advantage if those who do decide to break it do so with reluctance and feel accordingly guilty about what they have done. For they are then less likely to break it when it is not justifiable to do so.

Michael Walzer objects to this account on two related grounds: first, that it is psychologically incoherent and second, that it imposes unnecessary suffering.[59] The point he makes is that the more a person is persuaded on consequentialist grounds of the merit of breaking a good general rule in a particular situation, the less guilt he will feel. How then can there be an internal conflict between the feeling of guilt and the belief that he is justified? But this objection supposes that the amount of guilt we feel is under our control, which is probably not the case.[60] If the disposition to feel that a certain kind of action is wrong is deeply enough entrenched, the mere recognition that the feeling is inappropriate in a certain situation will not be enough to remove it. Moreover, if a person believes that a rule is a good one, he will, if he accepts the above analysis, believe that it should be broken only on very rare occasions, and there will very seldom be sufficient evidence to make it certain that one of these occasions has arisen. The agent who is prepared to judge that it has will, therefore, always have to allow that it is quite likely that he is mistaken and therefore that he is doing something horribly wrong.

Walzer's second point is that it imposes needless suffering to suggest that people should feel remorse for what they were, on the consequentialist principle, justified in doing. It is true that someone who makes his decision by balancing what he thinks are the probable consequences will not be likely to have the complete ease of conscience than an absolute ethics can provide. This is because of the inevitable limitations on his knowledge and his impartiality. It is possible that he will have decided rightly in some difficult situation, even though the decision does not "feel" right because of the intuitions which he is overriding. Walzer mentions the case of the members of a firing squad who are prevented from knowing which of them fired the fatal shot by the distribution of some rifles loaded with blanks. The purpose is to relieve them from the remorse which they might still feel for killing another human being, even if they believed that he deserved to die. Should we not rejoice, he asks, every time the stratagem works, since "it subtracts one from the number of innocent men who suffer"? But consider an analogous case. Should we rejoice if a bombardier is relieved by not knowing whether it was his bomb that killed the civilians in the village, which he believes is hiding guerrillas, and which he has been ordered to destroy? It seems that in this case our doubt about whether or not the bombing could be justified would lead us to hope that he would continue to feel guilt, even though he had agreed of his own free will to carry out the raid. But this is just the point. We should always be doubtful about whether a rule of war, if it is a good one, can justifiably be broken in a particular situation. We should, therefore, usually hope that those who do break it will feel guilty about it even though they have justified it to themselves. For the pain involved is hardly commensurate with the utility of such feelings being general.

An interesting sidelight on this is provided by the fact that after the Second World War, Sir Arthur Harris, who directed the strategic bombing of Germany, was not rewarded with a peerage unlike other well-known commanders. Moreover, the bomber pilots were not honoured by a plaque in Westminster Abbey, although they had suffered far higher casualties than those pilots of Fighter Command who were so honoured.[61] It would be consistent both to think that the attacks on German cities were militarily necessary (though there are reasons to doubt this) and to refuse to praise those who carried them out. This is rather like the policy of Basil the Great (Bishop Caesarea in the fourth century), "killing in war was differentiated by our fathers from murder ... nevertheless, perhaps it would be well that those whose hands are unclean abstain from communion for three years".[62]

Richard Wasserstrom makes two major attacks on the validity of the rules governing *jus in bello*, which he calls "the laws of war".[63] He claims to be attacking only their primacy over the principles governing *jus ad bellum*. But his arguments, if they were good, would work in favour of the stronger claim that the laws of war do not have moral force at all, or at least that we should not "embrace such a code and insist upon its value". The first argument is that the laws are morally "incoherent" and the second is that they produce more harm than good. He gives as an example of a code which would be incoherent in his sense, a criminal code that made criminal only various thefts but allowed all acts of violence against persons. It would be incoherent in that it could not be "rendered intelligible in terms of the moral principles that justified making theft illegal"; for if theft is morally wrong, then violence against persons should be wrong too. In the same sort of way, if killing prisoners is morally wrong, so should killing non-combatants be. But, Wasserstrom claims, the laws of war do not distinguish "meaningfully" between combatants and non-combatants. It can be objected to this that incoherence, in this sense, is a feature of the domestic criminal code as we now have it, and perhaps a desirable feature.[64] Destructive gossip, for example, is morally wrong and so is the falsification of customs declarations, but the former is not a criminal offence for good reasons. Even if there is not a good reason for some particular incoherence in a code, it is not clear that this shows that the whole code should be abolished.

But more importantly, Wasserstrom's reason for saying that the laws of war do not "meaningfully" distinguish between combatants and non-combatants is that any distinction that might be made can be nullified by considerations of military necessity, or as he rephrases it "military utility". He is discussing these laws as though they all had an implicit clause of exception, "unless military necessity dictates otherwise". But, as we mentioned earlier, it is not *any* military utility that justifies suspending the rules, for a consequentialist, but only military objectives of overriding moral significance. It is not unique to the laws of war that they are overridable in this way, but common to all general moral rules, as discussed in Chapter 1.

Wasserstrom's second claim is that the consequences of the general acceptance of the laws of war are in fact harmful. He suggests that soldiers who have been trained to accept them will end up with less respect for the value of life, for they will have learned that anything whatever can be justified by appeal to military advantage. He argues, finally, that the tendency is always for the laws to change to fit the techniques of modern war, rather than *vice versa*, so that the effect of our respect for these laws is in practice to license ever increasing brutality. But what is needed here is an extraordinarily difficult balancing judgement. We have to judge how likely it is that a substantially more stringent set of laws would gain acceptance, one which gave no place to military necessity as a legitimate exception. The suggestion given earlier in this section was that no rule is likely to be accepted by belligerents which substantially reduces the chances of victory. If this is true then we have to balance all the lives that have been saved by the admittedly partial observance of the present rules (for example, those against killing prisoners and bombing hospitals), against the number of lives saved by the general observance of the more stringent laws multiplied by the low probability of this general observance. In the judgement of the present writers, the consequences are probably better of having the rules more or less as they are.

PREVENTIVE WAR

The chance is always present, however remote it might be, that one of the great powers might achieve another weapons breakthrough of the dazzling proportions of 1945. Would the state possessing such a weapon and believing war to be inevitable be justified in striking the first blow? This is the ancient doctrine of preventive war advocated by Alcibiades, practised by Caesar and all the greatest masters of aggressive statecraft. The technique has been used to preserve the balance of power, to forestall a military attack, or to take full advantage of a transient superiority in power.[65] A restricted principle of preventive war has recently stated as follows: "States may use military force in the face of threats of war whenever the failure to do so would seriously risk their territorial integrity or political independence."[66]

But in the first place it is clear that the technique has proved in many cases to be a foolish and dangerous method of conducting state policy. Austria's pitiful attempt to check Pan-Slavism in her empire by means of war actually resulted in the complete destruction of her position as a great power in Europe. Hitler's preventive war against Russia proved to be a singularly mistaken venture, and it played a great part in his final downfall and death. Japan's attack on Pearl Harbor did not have the desired results, nor did Israel's invasions of Sinai in 1956 and 1967.

A second point worthy of note is that many of the examples of supposedly successful preventive war in history are really examples of a tactical as distinguished from a strategic attack. Most of these purely tactical operations occurred either during the war or in the period just before a struggle broke out. Thus the British attack on the French fleet at Oran occurred while a desperate war was already being waged.

With respect to the justification of preventive war, Winston Churchill posed an interesting thesis when he considered whether the Western powers would have been justified in going to war with Hitler during the Munich crisis. He writes:

The first duty of Ministers is so to deal with other nations as to avoid strife and war and to eschew aggression in all its forms, whether for nationalistic or ideological objects. But the safety of the State and the lives and freedom of their own fellow countrymen, to whom they owe their position, make it right and imperative in the last resort, or when a final end of definite conviction has been reached, ·that the use of force should not be excluded. If the circumstances are such as to warrant it, force may be used. And if this be so, it should be used under the conditions which are most favourable. There is no merit in putting off a war for a year, if, when it comes, it is a far worse war or one much harder to win. These are the tormenting dilemmas upon which mankind has throughout its history been so frequently impaled.[67]

One can agree with Churchill that no state has an obligation to commit suicide. If State A has conclusive evidence that State B plans an all-out attack upon it, then State A may feel justified in taking some kind of preventive action. Yet such arguments always leave one uneasy, as when one finds German military leaders arguing that France should be attacked in the 1904 to 1907 period rather than waiting until the nation grew in strength, or Churchill arguing during the same period that the German menace had to be faced and fought out some time or other.[68] The foundation for our uneasiness is that such arguments rest at bottom on the assumption that war is inevitable. But this assumption is usually precarious. In the case of Churchill's argument for war against Germany, Britain and Germany had in fact come close to settling many of their outstanding grievances in the weeks before the July crisis of 1914 and it is by no means certain that the two countries would ever have come to blows had not the foolish and impetuous diplomacy of Imperial Austria set in motion the great alliance systems of the day.[69] On the other hand, Hitler's activities were so blatantly aggressive, so indicative in their whole context of highly hostile intent toward Britain and France, that they come very close to providing an example of inevitable war. But even in this instance, it would not have been necessary to engage in a preventive war in the sense of a sudden, unannounced attack upon Germany. Rather, Hitler could have been told quite bluntly that the Western powers were determined to defend Czech independence. In this fashion the onus for the decision as to the inevitability of war would have been placed upon the shoulders of Hitler, where it properly belonged.

Another source of uneasiness concerning the theory of preventive war is the ease with which it can be corrupted and distorted. It is so easy to pass imperceptibly from the idea of preventing a brutal, premeditated attack, to the idea that a state is justified in suppressing the growth of a rival by violent means. But no state can claim a moral right to greatness and a corresponding right to crush its rivals by military force.

Writers of great repute such as Gentile and Francis Bacon have, however, argued that preventive war was legitimate in order to preserve the balance of power.[70] Grotius's answer to this argument was that, "One never finds oneself in perfect security. It is not to the ways of force but to the protection of providence and innocent precautions that one ought to look for response against an uncertain fear."[71] Other responses might be made. In the first place attempts to estimate with any degree of accuracy the existing power situation at any given moment are notoriously inaccurate. Examples are legion but one of the best is the belief on the part of most military experts before the Second World War that the Soviet army was weak and that Poland was a stronger ally.

But the fundamental argument against the doctrine of preventive war is that conditions have undergone a radical change since the time of Bacon and Gentile. Given the dangers of a holocaust capable of destroying entire nations, preventive war becomes itself an exercise in potential suicide. Stripped to its essentials, the doctrine of preventive war simply carries to their logical conclusion the ancient ideas of *raison d'état*. By that doctrine, national values and interests are no longer merely regarded as worthy of defence if attacked, but are exalted to the point of justifying outright conquest or suppression of an emerging rival. Such a doctrine was dangerous enough in the age of muskets and the cavalry charge, but in terms of present-day weapons it is an anachronism which contains the seeds of potential ruin for all states alike.

4 Three Hard Choices

THE RETURN OF THE RUSSIAN PRISONERS

Since this chapter is going to evaluate a number of historical political decisions, it is worth making a few preliminary remarks about what may and what may not be expected from such an evaluation. This historian, according to Hugh Trevor-Roper,[1] can only present, not solve moral dilemmas. It would certainly be presumptuous to flaunt an "obvious" moral answer to these dilemmas, with the benefit of hindsight, as though the people involved at the time had no perception of the moral as well as the prudential issues, and the complexity of the interaction between them. But it would be equally wrong to claim that we should make no moral judgement at all about the political decisions of the past. We have argued in this book that moral concerns are germane to current decisions in international relations. The relevant differences between the present and the past in this context are that we can judge with more accuracy what the consequences of past decisions were, and at the same time we are less sure of what the climate was in which these decisions were made. We are, therefore, in one way in a better position to make a judgement, and in another way in a worse one. Trevor-Roper says at the close of his introduction to a book which discusses the return of the Russian prisoners after the Second World War, "This is not a book which calls for judgement: it calls, as good books do, for reflection." We would prefer to say that it calls for reflective judgement.

The present moral character of a people is displayed most conspicuously in the shared perception of its past. The policies of statesmen are either influenced by, or dictate, moral interpretations of the policies of their predecessors. To take an example of a modern realist, George Kennan said in 1951, after an analysis of the war with Spain, "Perhaps the ruling of distant peoples is not our dish", and

"Republics cannot properly have subjects."[2] A people and its leaders would be seriously impoverished if they could not use the categories of "good" and "bad" or "right" and "wrong" to describe their past. There will often not have been an "obvious" moral answer. Sometimes, if the dilemma was too cruel or the options too equally weighted, there may have been no moral answer other than choosing lots. It may be that even here an ideal observer could have discerned which line of action would have produced the lesser evil; but for the rest of us there may be no way of doing this.[3] But there is no reason to suppose that this is always the case, and in the absence of such a reason, it is legitimate and even important to make the attempt to form a reflective moral judgement about the past conduct of international policy.

The first case we will consider is that of the return of the Russian prisoners in 1944–47. On 28 May, 1944, Clark Kerr, British ambassador to Moscow, informed Molotov, Stalin's Foreign Affairs Commissar, that there was "a large Russian element" that had been "forced to serve with the German armies in the West".[4] He wanted the Russian government to issue an assurance that these people would be treated leniently on their return to Russia, so that they could be induced more easily to desert the German army. Molotov's reply was that "the number is very insignificant", and that a special appeal to them "would not be of political interest". It can be surmised that the reason for this reply was partly that it was politically embarrassing for Stalin to have to admit that there were large numbers of Russians who were not loyal enough to the communist regime to prevent them joining the Germans. But it was the British experience that roughly ten per cent of the prisoners they captured were in fact Russians.

Certainly many of them had not fought willingly. The conditions inside German prisoner of war camps had been appalling. Some Russians were forced to enlist at gunpoint, others by the prospect of enough food to live on. Still others were deceived into thinking that they would be joining only the supply services. There was thus a distinction in theory between those who were traitors who had volunteered to join the Germans in order to fight against the communists, and those who had not. It has been argued by Rebecca West that it is not possible to owe loyalty to a state that does not afford one the protection of its laws. A case may be made that even the volunteers were not traitors in the full sense if they had suffered beyond endurance inside Russia before the war. But in any case, the distinction between willing and unwilling was extremely hard to maintain in practice. It would have necessitated an elaborate hearing for each prisoner to determine the degree of constraint, and in many cases there would not have been sufficient information to reach a satisfactory answer.

This was one of the reasons offered to the British cabinet for adopting the policy that all prisoners, without distinction, should be returned. This is certainly what the Russian government came to demand. Moreover, on 17 October Molotov raised the question whether the consent of the individual prisoners would be required. The reply of the British Foreign Secretary, Anthony Eden, was that the British government "merely wanted these men, within the limitations of British law, to be placed under Soviet administration and discipline until they could be repatriated".[5] The policy of forcible repatriation was adopted before the Conference at Yalta in February 1945. What is chiefly interesting for the purposes of this book is the process by which this policy was arrived at.

On 17 July, the cabinet resolved to return all the prisoners without considering either which of them were traitors or how they would be treated on their return. But it was objected on these two points that the treatment accorded to them by the Germans had often been appalling and that they were being sent to an almost certain death. Eden's reply on 2 August summed up the main arguments that won the day. First, the behaviour of the prisoners in France had "often been revolting". It was not appropriate to be sentimental about them. Second, Britain did not want to be "permanently saddled" with a number of them. Third, Britain had no right whatever to refuse to return them. In the version on 3 September, he said "no legal or moral right". It was not a proper concern what measures any allied government, including the Soviet government, took as regards their own nationals. Fourth, the failure to return them would arouse the gravest suspicions on the part of the Soviet government. Fifth, there were many British and American soldiers who would fall into Russian hands when German-occupied territory was liberated by the Red Army. It was necessary to ensure that these men be returned and, therefore, that goodwill in the matter of prisoners be maintained.

These arguments are of different kinds. Some of them appeal exclusively to the national interest and some do not. The appeal to the need to get British soldiers back was of the former kind, but not the appeal to the revolting behaviour of the Russians and to the right of allied governments to do as they pleased with their own nationals. These two latter points were addressed to two moral arguments raised by Lord Selbourne, then Minister of Economic Welfare. Lord Selbourne did not think these men deserved to have their wishes in this matter ignored just because they had fought, however unwillingly, for the enemy, and he did not wish to be responsible for sending them to their deaths.

Eden's two counter-arguments were not strong ones. Some of the Russians had behaved badly. Some of the Cossacks, especially after June 1944, had "robbed like bandits ... raped women and set fire to settlements".[6] In England, some of the Russian prisoners were refusing to obey British authorities in the camps and were staging a sort of strike. There was no doubt that the decision to discriminate between prisoners would make a substantial demand on British time and energy. But when used to show that the Russians as a whole did not deserve sympathy, these considerations were insufficient. To label such sympathy "sentimentality" as Eden did is to beg the question. Secondly, the claim was dubious that there was no right to refuse to return its nationals to an allied government. Britain had traditionally offered asylum to anyone fleeing persecution. It was true that propaganda during the war had emphasized praise of the heroic fighting on the Eastern Front rather than criticism of internal Russian policy. But Eden knew what fate was likely to befall those who were tainted with disloyalty and what many of those who chose to fight for the Germans had suffered in Russia before they left. The argument was later made that asylum was traditionally offered only to those who reached British soil, not to those who fell into the hands of the British army. But at least for those who did reach British soil, there was a traditional right to stay if they wanted to, and this right was violated by the cabinet's decision. A conflict between *prima facie* rights may be understood in terms of a conflict of obligations such as the obligation to provide asylum and the obligation to honour the political integrity of allied governments. It is at least clear that this dilemma is partly a moral one and that any solution to it is properly open to moral debate.

P. J. Grigg, the Secretary of State for War, responded to Eden by allowing that "in war we cannot, as you say, afford to be sentimental". But he confessed that he found the prospect of forcible repatriation "rather revolting", and he expected public opinion to reflect the same feeling. He raised two other points: "There is also the danger that if we hand them back there may be reprisals on our men in German hands, but I think that that risk is probably growing appreciably less, and that the Germans have problems enough to think about without keeping an eye on what happens to Russians whom they forced into the German armies." He recognized the danger that the Russians might not cooperate in sending back British and other Allied prisoners. But he "was not convinced that, whatever we do, the Russians will go out of their way to send our prisoners westwards at once or to deal with them in any special manner". He concluded by saying, "If we hand the Russian prisoners back to their death, it will be the military authorities who will do so on my instructions, and I am entitled to have behind me on this very unpleasant business the considered view of the Government." Eden accordingly prepared a cabinet paper for 3 September, repeating most of the same arguments, and on 4 September, the cabinet approved his proposals.

A similar debate was held in the United States, but the action already taken by the British made any dissenting decision more difficult. Initially only those who claimed Russian citizenship were returned. This left the option to those who wanted to stay to claim to be Germans. But, as George Kennan reported from Moscow, demands were growing in the Soviet press and among officials "for immediate and total repatriation", and "the prestige of the Soviet Union will suffer if it becomes generally known that some Soviet citizens are not accepting with enthusiasm offers of repatriation". Plans for the Yalta conference were already at this stage under way, and Eden was told by the Foreign Office that if the American policy were adopted, "all chances of early agreement would disappear". At the Yalta conference itself, a secret agreement was made to return all Russians, by force if necessary, into Soviet hands.

But there was still the question of who was a Russian. Britain and the United States did not recognize as Russian possessions the Western Ukraine, Western Byelorussia and the Baltic states of Estonia, Latvia, and Lithuania. An English officer, Brigadier Firebrace, was thus given the task of sorting out by linguistic tests who were Russians according to the borders in existence at the beginning of the war. A Soviet officer was present at these sessions, and thus heard many of the prisoners beg to be shot on the spot rather than be returned to Russia. Firebrace believed that their fate was thereby sealed, but he only once intervened to prevent the return of someone who was in his judgement a Russian.[7] Britain was not prepared at this point to break unilaterally an agreement she had made with her allies.

In the space of two months in 1945, 1,393,902 Russians were returned from Europe. The conditions were so chaotic that it was difficult to give individual attention to those who claimed not to be

Russian citizens. No doubt there were many such who were sent back. This is certainly true of the Cossacks. Most of the senior Cossack officers had left Russia by 1920, and so did not come under the Yalta agreement which covered only those who were Russian citizens at the outbreak of the war. But it was argued that if the Soviet government was accommodated in this matter, it might be more likely to cooperate in the treatment of Poland and to try to moderate Tito's activities in Yugoslavia. In order to get the Cossacks back to Russia, deception and violence were used on a large scale. Perhaps as many as 27 people died on 1 June in the process of transferring 6500 into Russian hands, most of them by suicide.[8] A mother leapt from a bridge with her children and a father shot his wife, his three children and himself. About 50,000 were handed over in the five weeks from 28 May.

It is hard in retrospect to recapture the atmosphere in which these decisions were made. But there are three factors which should be mentioned. First, there was an overwhelming desire to end the fighting. After the German surrender, it would have been politically hazardous for any British or American government to suggest that large numbers of troops should stay in Europe to secure Western interests against the Russians. Second, Stalin had been portrayed throughout the war as a great war leader and a defender of democracy. There was, therefore, a great initial reluctance to think about the fact that the war in Europe had resulted in raising yet another totalitarian regime to a position of overwhelming power. The third factor is the hostility with which all captured prisoners were regarded. Those who were guarding them had in many cases seen friends and fellow-soldiers killed before their eyes. It was extremely hard to feel any sympathy or to make any fine distinctions between them.

At any rate by the middle of 1945 resistance to the policy of forcible repatriation was hardening. Field Marshal Alexander wrote to the War Office on 23 August about the use of force, "Such treatment, coupled with the knowledge that these individuals are being sent to an almost certain death, is quite out of keeping with the principles of democracy and justice as we know them." His resistance led to a note of protest from the Russian ambassador and embarrassment in London. But at the beginning of October, General Eisenhower suspended the policy and only those were returned who had actually been in the Red Army or who had collaborated actively with the Nazis. The Foreign Office objected that this was a breach of the agreement with the Russians, which it was, and that it would, as the new Secretary of State Ernest Bevin said, "aggravate existing difficulties". It would also, he pointed out, be extremely hard to distinguish without being arbitrary those who were traitors from those who were not. These were both familiar arguments used throughout the controversy. Bevin added a point which played the same role as Eden's claim that the behaviour of the prisoners "had often been revolting". Bevin said, "Among the civilians there may be many whose conduct has been no less reprehensible" (than that of acknowledged traitors). He might have continued, "we cannot afford to be sentimental about this". The British position was that "we are therefore in favour of avoiding discrimination".

General Richard McCreery, the General Officer Commanding British Forces in Austria, responded by sending a telegram to the War Office on 16 December. "A high percentage of Soviet displaced persons consists of women and children against whom the use of force by British soldiers would be contrary to normal British practice ... Troops are also not available for the rounding up of the 1500 (or 1800) Soviet citizens believed to be at large. The Commander-in-Chief believes that the practice of forced repatriation of Soviet citizens will inspire such displaced persons to become deserters who would almost certainly become bandits in preference to dying of starvation. There is also a danger that such a policy might likewise lead to desertions of other displaced persons such as Poles, Yugoslavs and Hungarians."[9] This response is in some ways like that of P. J. Griggs to Eden a year earlier. In both cases, there is a mixture of moral and prudential concern and an appeal to traditional British standards of morality.

But the difference between August 1944 and December 1945 lay in the changing perceptions of Russian intentions. In 1944 and the first half of 1945 there had been a consensus, not shared by Griggs, that it was important to mollify Stalin. But the forcible return of the prisoners continued until 1947. Churchill's Iron Curtain speech was delivered on 5 March 1946. Operation "Eastwind", the return of the last 255 prisoners, was carried out after the orchestrated "elections" in Poland and other violations of the Yalta agreement by the Russians. It seems that the mollification continued after its usefulness could no longer reasonably be relied upon. There is in any case a great uncertainty about the degree to which Churchill and Eden believed that post-war cooperation would be possible with the Soviet Union. Churchill at least may have thought that the chances were very small.

One interesting feature of the whole episode is that those who intervened most consistently in favour of the prisoners were the high levels of military command, for example, Griggs, Eisenhower, Alexander and McCreery. These were the people who had to superintend the dirty work, and it is interesting that it was often for at least partly moral reasons that they objected to it. The assimilation of respect for morality to respect for law in this case breaks down. For the diplomats appealed to the law both before and after Yalta as a justification for forcible repatriation. It was those who wanted to let the prisoners stay who were moved by the considerations that many of them had collaborated with the Germans unwillingly, that many of them had not collaborated at all and that many of them would probably die on their return. It is easy to see why the diplomats were reluctant to let the prisoners be an obstacle to the attainment or the maintenance of peace. But in the end thousands of Russian citizens escaped forcible repatriation because individual officers turned a blind eye, or because the policy was resisted and finally changed at a high level. We cannot tell whether the return of the prisoners did make the Russian government more favourably disposed to British and American interests after the war. But it is hard to believe that the hope that it would was sufficient to justify the return of those, like the Cossack officers, who were not covered by the agreement. And it is equally hard to see how the hope itself could have been justified after 1945.

THE USE OF THE BOMB

The second series of events we shall consider is much better known and has inspired a much larger literature. The bibliography on the use of the atomic bomb against Japan extends to approximately 400 titles.[10] It is almost impossible to state the facts without interpreting them in a way favourable to one's final evaluation of Truman's decision. In order, therefore, to warn against any potential distortion, we will state our conclusion in advance, that the dropping of the bomb on Hiroshima can probably be justified but that the bomb on Nagasaki cannot. The important part of the analysis for the purposes of this book is not so much the final verdict but the demonstration that moral concerns were relevant to the decision, that they were invoked and that they exercised an important moderating influence.

In the first place, although the Japanese were suffering defeat at every turn in the Pacific theatre, they were resisting American advances with tenacity. In April 1945, 107,000 of their garrison of 120,000 men on Okinawa had to be killed before the island was captured. The United States suffered 80,000 casualties in the same battle. Some 300,000 Japanese were killed in the recapture of the Philippines. The Japanese navy was no longer a major fighting force but kamikaze suicide raids were inflicting heavy losses on the United States fleet. These raids had sunk 34 American ships including three aircraft carriers and damaged 285, and it was known that the Japanese were assembling several thousand aircraft to attack an invasion fleet.[11]

The Japanese had over two million men trained and ready on the home islands. The Joint Chiefs of Staff advised the President, despite Navy disagreement, that an invasion would be necessary. Their reasoning was based on past experience – no great power had ever surrendered and agreed to enemy occupation in the absence of an invading army. Their plans, therefore, called for a sea blockade and intensified bombing, invasion of Kyushu by November and the main island of Honshu by March 1946. The forecast called for a one-year battle with the likelihood of several hundred thousand U.S. casualties and many times that in Japanese lives. The B-29 bombing of Tokyo on 9 March had burned out over 15 square miles, killing 100,000 people. Nagoya, Osaka and Kobe had suffered severe damage. Millions of people had become refugees.

Even if an invasion were not attempted and the Japanese were induced to surrender by blockade and 'conventional' bombardment, casualties would still have been enormous. The Russian invasion of Manchuria, the steady advance of Chinese forces towards the coast, and the starvation conditions and bombing inside Japan would have led in all probability to a far higher loss of Japanese life than the two atomic bombs.[12] In any case the Army Chiefs of Staff had persuaded the President that an invasion was necessary, so that even if they were in fact wrong, Kyushu would most likely have been invaded if the Japanese had not surrendered by 1 November.

It has been argued that if the demand had not been made for *unconditional* surrender, the Japanese would have surrendered earlier. This amounts to the claim that it was a political failure that led to the use of the atomic bomb. It is often pointed out in this connection that the Japanese did not in fact surrender unconditionally, but insisted on the single condition that the imperial system should be continued. Is it the case that they would have surrendered earlier if they had been assured that this condition would be met? It is true that there was an active peace party in Japan and that cables were intercepted, starting on 12 July, which showed that the Foreign Minister Togo had instructed the Japanese Ambassador in Moscow to "endeavour to obtain the good offices of the Soviet Union in ending the war short of unconditional surrender". But it is not clear that this party was strong enough to win the day against those who wanted to fight to the bitter end, or at least to give a convincing demonstration of Japan's will to resist on its home beaches. The War Minister and two Service Chiefs were in favour of pressing for three additional conditions even after Hiroshima. They wanted to prevent occupation, and to permit Japanese control over demobilization and any trial of war criminals. It is difficult to believe that the American recognition of the right of the Emperor to stay would have been enough to change their minds about fighting on. One historian has concluded that the atomic bombing of Hiroshima and Nagasaki created "that unusual atmosphere in which the theretofore static factor of the Emperor could be made active in such an extraordinary way as to work what was virtually a political miracle".[13]

Recognition of the Emperor in the Potsdam declaration of 26 July would probably not have ended the war itself or made the use of the atomic bomb unnecessary. But it might have been desirable none the less. The reason in favour of it was that the authority of the Emperor was the only thing that could make an orderly transition from war to peaceful occupation possible. The reason against it was that propaganda during the war had made of Hirohito a figure like Hitler and Mussolini, and it was difficult to undo the effect of this on public opinion. In this case, as in the return of the Russians, the Allies were to some extent the prisoners of their own propaganda. It should also be mentioned that it was the view of some that the Imperial system was the root cause of Japan's militarism and that it therefore had to be eliminated in the interests of lasting peace.

The other notable exclusion from the Potsdam declaration was any mention of the atomic bomb itself. Would an explicit threat have made any difference? It was the opinion of Truman's advisers that there was a substantial difference between the conditions under which the bomb had been successfully tested at Alamogardo and the conditions of actual combat. If something were to go wrong and there was a 'fizzle', it might do serious damage to America's credibility with the Japanese. It was therefore better not to mention the bomb before its effectiveness had been demonstrated in Japan. It is important to ask whether it was necessary to carry out this demonstration on a Japanese *city*. But we will consider this question later in relation to alternative uses of the bomb that might have been less costly in terms of human life.

Those who say that the bomb should not have been used point out legitimately that the decision to use it was flawed in many respects. We will look at a number of the less good reasons for the decision. But the existence of these does not affect the claim that the decision was in the end justified. It merely shows how difficult it was and is to separate the good reasons from the bad in matters of this complexity.

First of all, the figures available to Truman were misleading. Robert J. Oppenheimer had estimated 20,000 persons killed by each bomb, and Truman reported that he "had no qualms if in the long run millions of lives could be saved".[14] In fact, about 110,000 were killed and the number saved was not in the millions, though it is impossible to say how large it was with any precision. The main reason for Oppenheimer's figures was that he had assumed that the population of the attacked cities would have taken shelter. But in fact the 509th Composite Group, consisting of about 1800 Air Force officers and men under the command of Colonel Park W. Tibbets, had been flying small groups of three planes since 20 July and dropping 'pumpkins', single large bombs loaded with TNT. Since these had done no appreciable damage, the Japanese had got used to them and therefore ignored the flight on 6 August. In this way, the overall political objective was defeated by the independent initiative of the local military commander.

Secondly, the development of the bomb had cost in excess of two billion dollars. Any decision not to use it would have had to face serious attack in Congress and would thus have been politically hazardous. Stimson, the Secretary of War, said, "The entire purpose was the production of a military weapon; on no other ground could the wartime expenditure of so much time and money have been justified."[15] It has been suggested that the decision to use the bomb was motivated partly by a desire to justify the expense of developing it.

Thirdly, the bomb was seen as simply another weapon, "as legitimate as any other of the deadly explosive weapons of modern war".[16] This had not been the case at the beginning of the war. The émigré scientists who had initially pressed for the bomb's development had done so in the fear that Germany would get there first. But in the period from 1942–5, it seems to have become accepted by almost everyone in a position of authority that the bomb would actually be used by the Allies if it were developed in time. Thus the work went on at full speed at Los Alamos even after the discovery that the Germans had not in fact been nearly as close as had been assumed. Einstein, however, whose intervention in 1939 had been crucial in persuading Roosevelt to back the necessary research, said after the war, "If I had known that the Germans would not succeed in constructing the atom bomb, I would never have lifted a finger."[17]

Part of the explanation for this change may lie in the fact that the development of the bomb was put under military control in 1942. But many of the scientists involved also came to think that it should be given a military use. It is perhaps more accurate to say that the progress of the war itself had blunted the sensibilities of the decision-makers. For there is a steady progression from Franco's bombing of Guernica in 1937 to the bombing of Hiroshima in 1945. Hitler's bombings of Warsaw and Rotterdam were undertaken to support troops about to enter those cities, and this was denounced by Churchill in 1940 as "a new and odious form of attack". But in 1940/1 it became apparent to the British that daylight raids were too dangerous and that night-time raids could not pinpoint targets with any precision. Under Air Marshal Harris Hamburg, and in the end all the major German cities, were exposed to "obliteration" bombing. Lord Cherwell's minute in 1942 showed that the purpose included the destruction of civilian morale. He thought it would be possible to render a third of the German population homeless by 1943.[18] The British decision was based partly on desperation. It was not clear what else there was to do to stop Hitler. It was also based partly on the desire for retribution. But it is fairly clear that the strategy was continued after its usefulness was put in serious doubt by the development of more sophisticated equipment.[19] After the bombing of Dresden, Churchill withdrew his support from the strategy. But the fire-bombing of Tokyo led to more destruction than the bombing of Dresden. It seems likely that there was a gradual hardening of attitude during the war and a general readiness to use weapons as they were made available, so that the bombing of Hiroshima fits into a previously established pattern.

One result of this can be seen in the fact that Hiroshima and Nagasaki were described as military targets. Truman said to the nation on 9 August that the first atomic bomb was dropped on Hiroshima, "a military base", in order to "avoid, in so far as possible, the killing of civilians".[20] But it is difficult to see how any target could have involved the taking of many more civilian lives than those that were actually chosen. The two cities were, it is true, "devoted to war production", but that by no means justifies describing them simply as "military bases".

Another factor which made the decision harder to avoid was the change in administration. Roosevelt had not told anybody before his death on 12 April 1945, what, if anything, he had decided about the use of the bomb. He had agreed with Churchill that "when a bomb is finally available, it might perhaps, after mature consideration, be used against the Japanese who should be warned that this bombardment would be repeated until they surrender". Truman said that he "regarded the bomb as a military weapon and never had any doubt that it should be used". His ease of conscience is understandable if the decision was to a large extent inherited. General Groves said, "Truman did not so much say 'yes' as not say 'no'. It would indeed have taken a lot of nerve to say 'no' at that time."[21] There is no evidence that during the period from 25 April, when he was briefed by Stimson, to 3 August, when the die was cast, Truman ever seriously considered not using the bomb.

Finally, it seems that the decision was motivated at least partly by the desire for retribution. In this respect it was like the British decision to bomb the German cities. Truman said, "We have used (the bomb) against those who attacked us without warning at Pearl Harbor, against those who have starved and beaten and executed American prisoners of war, against those who have abandoned all pretence of obeying international laws of warfare."[22] He seems to be saying that the Japanese, including the inhabitants of Hiroshima and Nagasaki, have lost their right to non-combatant immunity because of their collective responsibility for the crimes he mentions. But the assumption here is highly suspect. Even if the inhabitants of the two cities had been one and all directly involved in war crimes, it would not have followed that it was justifiable to obliterate the cities like a modern Sodom and Gomorrah.

We have looked at a number of bad reasons for the decision. But it remains to insist that there were a number of good ones. This is particularly clear from the diaries of Stimson, who was himself a lawyer and tremendously conscious of the demands of morality and international law. The most important point is that he made an effort in good faith to see whether the bomb could be used in a less devastating way and still be effective in ending the war. He instructed the scientific panel of the Interim Committee to try to come up with an alternative. But if the Japanese were, for example, warned which cities would be hit, they might put prisoners of war in those cities or make the delivery of the bomb militarily difficult. A demonstration over empty country would not have been impressive, since the main visible effect of an attack was in terms of the destruction of buildings. "Only the reality of what the bomb actually could do to a city would be certain to shock Japan out of the war."[23] Moreover, there was a real danger that the military authorities would try to hide the effects, for they apparently tried to do this even after Hiroshima. The same two arguments apply to the bombing of a purely military installation. And there was in this case the additional point that the purely military targets had already been severely bombed, so that again the effects would not be so apparent. The details here are not as important as the fact that the scientific panel included a number of highly intelligent people who wanted very much to find an alternative to using the bomb on a city. They were unable to find any "acceptable alternatives to direct military use".

The bombing of Hiroshima was in a sense a last resort. It is also true that without Stimson's moral concern, the first choice of target would probably have been Kyoto, the ancient capital of Japan and the centre of her civilization for more than a thousand years. The target committee observed that "Kyoto has the advantage of the people being more highly intelligent and hence better able to appreciate the significance of the weapon."[24] Kyoto was moreover surrounded on three sides by hills, and thus made an excellent target on purely military grounds. Stimson was under pressure from his advisers to accept Kyoto as a target but he stood firm.

His agreement to cities as legitimate targets came only after he had extracted a promise from his Assistant Secretary for Air that the bombers would conduct "only precision bombing" against purely military objectives. He then called in General H. H. Arnold, Commanding General of the Army Air Forces, who told him that the destruction of war output could not be achieved without the destruction of civilians. Stimson saw clearly that "in the conflagration bombings by massed B-29's he was permitting a kind of total war he had always hated". His reaction was to come close to a total despair about the possibility of fighting modern war justly. He said that he was "implicitly confessing that there could be no significant limits to the horror of modern war".[25] But while this pessimism is understandable, it is seriously misleading. It gives expression to a sense of despair which Stimson may well have felt. But in fact his actions did put a significant limit. It should be remembered that the policy he approved was not the policy carried out. He was anticipating that the second bomb would not be dropped until after sufficient pause for the Japanese War Cabinet to think through the implications of the first one, and he was anticipating that the first bomb would cause 20,000 deaths and not 70,000. The cry that "War is Hell" was for Stimson, though not necessarily for Byrnes or Truman, an expression of moral turmoil. In terms of the investigation of this book, what is important is that Stimson was engaged in thinking morally about the war and that this did impose some limitation on what he was prepared to allow.

There is a set of long-term consequences that we have not yet considered. It is the opinion of some commentators that the bomb was aimed not so much at Japan as at Russia.[26] It is certainly true that many people were thinking before 6 August 1945 of the implications of the new weapon for international relations after the defeat of Japan. Niels Bohr, for example, whose work in atomic physics had contributed largely to the early theoretical discoveries, tried in vain to persuade Roosevelt and Churchill in 1944 that it was essential to inform the Russians about the development of the new weapon. Bohr thought that this was an essential preliminary to the achievement of international control of atomic energy and the avoidance of a catastrophic arms race after the war. It appears to have been Churchill's view that control of the bomb should stay in American and British hands. Roosevelt appears to have agreed, for he signed an aide-memoire at Hyde Park on 19 September 1944, stating that "Full collaboration between the United States and the British government in developing tube alloys (the code name for the atomic bomb) for military and commercial purposes should continue after the defeat of Japan unless and until terminated by joint agreement." One motive for dropping the bomb may have been to demonstrate its power to Russia and perhaps to bring the war with Japan to an end before Russia could make too much progress in Manchuria. But the opinions of Truman, Roosevelt and Churchill in the first half of 1945 about post-war cooperation with Stalin are difficult to diagnose with any certainty. There is not enough evidence to contradict the plain impression given by Stimson's diaries that the main motives behind the use of the bomb had to do with the saving of American and Japanese lives.

Some of the scientists used the argument in favour of the use of the weapon that it would have such a profound psychological impact on the world that the bomb would never be used again.[27] President Conant of Harvard, who had been involved in the top administration of the development of the bomb since 1941, wrote to Stimson that "one of the principal reasons he had for advising (him) that the bomb must be used was that that was the only way to awaken the world to the necessity of abolishing war altogether". It is not clear to what extent Stimson considered this argument. He did say later that the atomic bomb "made it wholly clear that we must never have another war", but that is rather different. Again this was probably not central to his decision-making process or to that of Truman's other main advisers. It is very difficult to evaluate now whether the bomb did have the effect that Conant predicted. Certainly no atomic bomb has been given combat use since 9 August 1945. But the *threat* of its use has dominated international relations for thirty years. All we can safely say is that these long-term effects of Hiroshima and Nagasaki are too uncertain to enter into an ethical analysis as brief as this one.

So far we have mentioned Nagasaki only in passing. The bombing of this city is a second case where the independent initiative of the local military commander interfered with the political goals of the President and his advisers. The original schedule called for the second bomb to be dropped on 11 August, but the schedule was advanced two days by Colonel Tibbets because of the prospect of at least five days of bad weather after 9 August. It is fairly clear that this advance left too little time for the Japanese War Cabinet to reach a decision after Hiroshima and after the Russian invasion of Manchuria on 9 August, which was a response to Hiroshima. In fact, the Japanese surrender came on 10 August. There is not sufficient evidence to show that the deaths of 40,000 people and the injury of an equal number in Nagasaki played any substantial role in persuading Japan's leaders. The original rationale for dropping two bombs was that it was important to show that America had more than one and could carry out its threat of "complete and utter destruction". With the benefit of hindsight, we can say that this was not in fact necessary.

The utilitarian argument that the dropping of the bomb on Hiroshima was justified relies largely on the claim that it saved thousands of lives, American and Japanese. Stimson was also under a special responsibility to look after the welfare of the men in the armies "he had helped to raise". He says that no one in his position "could have failed to use (the bomb) and afterwards looked his countrymen in the face". He was aware of the war-weariness of the Americans fighting in the Pacific theatre and the need to spare them further sacrifice. The opposition to these arguments comes largely from either the absolutist view that nothing whatever could justify ignoring non-combatant immunity or the weaker view that even if something could justify this, it would not be the goal of securing unconditional surrender. The first of these views is made more palatable by the application of the principle of double effect. But even so, it would seem that an adherent of this view would be able to justify the killing of 317,000 Japanese in the Philippines, 107,000 in Okinawa, to forbid the killing of 110,000 civilians by the two atomic bombs, and to condone the killing of ten times that number of Japanese and Allied soldiers in Manchuria, China and the Japanese home islands.[28] For he would be able to allow the "side effects" of the invasion, including the deaths of thousands of civilians from freezing and starvation and the general breakdown of the fabric of society, as long as these were not "directly intended".

There is in traditional Roman Catholic moral theology a proportionality clause which requires a proper proportion between the evil effect permitted and the good effect intended. Here "the calculation of consequences or the weighing of anticipated greater goods, or lesser evils, plays its proper role."[29] This principle might be used by a just war theorist to deny that he would reach the paradoxical position outlined in the last paragraph. It will certainly be used by those who make the weaker of the two objections given above; for they will ask how important proportionately was the political goal of reducing the Japanese to unconditional surrender, or at least to surrender on the sole condition that the Emperor could stay? Walzer states the objection forcibly, "In any case, if killing millions (or many thousands) of men and women was militarily necessary for their conquest and overthrow, then it was morally necessary – in order not to kill those people – to settle for something less."[30]

The moral implications of the policy of unconditional surrender cannot be surveyed and evaluated unless the background of the policy is understood.[31] It did not originate with Roosevelt in a sudden impetuous and ill-considered gesture at Casablanca. In fact, it had been considered by the Joint Chiefs of Staff, presented to the British government and approved after debate by the British War Cabinet. In short, it was an agreed-upon Allied policy. Its roots went deep into the experience of the First World War when the German surrender had been conditional upon acceptance of Wilson's Fourteen Points. It was believed – and there is good evidence for the belief – that postwar German governments and the military had used the terms to create a stab-in-the-back legend and a myth that the German Army had never suffered defeat. After all, battles were not fought on German soil and German armies had marched back into Germany with their bands playing. Allied leaders were determined that, on this occasion, neither opponent should be able to claim that a complete defeat had not been inflicted on their armed forces and in the future to raise in the public mind the possibility of a victorious future war. In addition, the question of what particular terms should be offered to the enemy was potentially divisive to the alliance, and might have led to a bidding game and a separate peace. This latter fear was present in the minds of all the parties, and the damage it could cause to Allied unity is apparent when one considers the suspicions that Stalin felt and the recriminations which he heaped on Roosevelt over the secret negotiations for the surrender of German forces in Italy.[32]

Finally, the policy rested in the last analysis upon a firmly held conviction that German and Japanese aggression had their roots in the social and institutional structures of their respective nations and that it was necessary to make fundamental changes in these societies if future aggression was to be avoided. In fact, these changes were implemented in the occupations of Germany and Japan and it would be hard to deny that they accomplished a good many of the goals envisaged. Militarism and an expansionist spirit are conspicuous by their absence in both countries. In short, with hindsight the policy can be justified by its success.

A more sophisticated criticism might be that ultimately peace would depend upon the creation of a new and stable balance of power in which the defeated states would come to play a part and that the total destruction of German and Japanese military power would lead to dangerous instability and a conflict among the victors.[33] Such thinking was probably alien to Roosevelt's outlook, which was based on Wilsonian ideas of a new League of Nations and on the idea of the cooperation of the surviving great powers.

It might still be argued that, even if the above analysis is accepted, a more flexible attitude to negotiations could have ended the war earlier and saved countless lives. This is a matter of judgement and involves matters of considerable political and diplomatic complexity. All the evidence at the time clearly indicated that the Hitler regime would have fought to the end. The military in Japan were a determined lot and believed that they could utilize Soviet mediation in order to avoid complete defeat and occupation. This belief meant that the Japanese leaders were minded to continue the war even if the position of the Emperor were assured. Our judgement is that only the dropping of the bomb, combined with Soviet entry into the war, ended their hopes of lenient terms.[34]

APPEASEMENT

The decisions' about the return of the Russian prisoners and about the use of the bomb illustrate two different ways in which the different levels of moral thinking can be used by political leaders. In the first case, it can be argued that Eden moved too quickly from the level of intuitive moral conviction in order to override it by appeal to consequences. In the second case, Stimson allowed his intuitions more weight and although he overrode them in the end, they played a sufficiently large part in his decision to force him to sanction the use of the bomb as a 'last resort' and to prevent the bombing of Kyoto.

There are examples of political decision-makers who stayed at the intuitive level too long. One case that comes to mind is Chamberlain's attempt to "appease" Hitler before the outbreak of the Second World War. Again there is a large literature on this, and we will not discuss it in detail.[35] It is not possible to be dogmatic about Chamberlain's thought processes because he has not revealed them in much detail. It is possible that he never had any hope that he would succeed in appeasing Hitler, but that he did hope to unite the country behind him when Hitler inevitably marched into Prague. It was apparently Hitler's view at the end of his life that he lost the war when he signed the Munich agreement and that he should have forced war on France and Britain over Czechoslovakia in 1938. Perhaps, then, Chamberlain saw Munich as the only way to win the eventual and inevitable war with Germany. This is possible, but it does not fit at all well with the evidence we do have. There are, for example, Chamberlain's comments on his return about "peace in our time", but these might be put down to propaganda. There is, more significantly, considerable evidence of his single-minded and consistent hatred of war. Thus Robert Boothby, studying Chamberlain in the House of Commons, noted that his "hatred of war burns him up. One felt that there were almost no limits to which he would not go in order to prevent the horrors of war which he so vividly described, and the thought of which, I am convinced, never for a moment leaves him ... One would not, at first sight, suspect the Prime Minister of being an emotional man; but when the question of peace or war arises, his passion knows no bounds. This is at once impressive, formidable and dangerous."[36]

Chamberlain's overwhelming desire to make peace made it difficult for him to believe that Hitler would "take responsibility for starting a world war which may end civilization for the sake of a few days' delay" in settling the Czechoslovakian problem. After Munich he said to a cabinet colleague, "You see, my dear fellow, this time it's different; this time he has made the promises to me." He continued to advise the Germans to ignore the pronouncements of the Foreign Office, he promised trade concessions, loans and perhaps a return of Germany's African colonies. It was Hitler's view that "This fellow, Chamberlain, shook with fear when I uttered the word 'war'. Don't tell me he is dangerous." In thinking of Chamberlain as a coward, Hitler misjudged. But he did not err in sensing Chamberlain's hatred of war. It is possible to make the historical judgement that Chamberlain, by allowing this hatred to dominate his political action, encouraged Hitler's misjudgement, and thus contributed to the outbreak of the very war he so desperately hoped to avoid.[37]

This judgement is not by any means certain. It might, for instance, be argued that Chamberlain was simply a realist and knew that Czechoslovakia was not defensible after the Anschluss into Austria. But if we do interpret the policy of appeasement as a genuine attempt to make a secure peace, it is a good example of a series of decisions that stayed too long at the intuitive level, where the intuition in question is that war should be avoided at any cost. Eden, on the other hand, dismissed as "sentimentality" the intuition that the Russian prisoners deserved compassion. The desire to accommodate the Russian government led to a policy of returning even those prisoners *not* covered by the Yalta agreement (such as the Cossack officers), whom Stalin particularly wanted back. Both Eden and Chamberlain operated a policy of appeasement, but (though again this is a matter of judgement) it does not seem in Eden's case that there was a bedrock of principle from which the policy was derived. Stimson's case is different. He eventually decided to overcome his resistance to a form of "total" warfare which he had always hated. But the repugnance he felt was not brushed aside as "moralism" or "legalism". He went almost to the other extreme; rather than declare morality off limits, he was tempted to despair morally of the acceptability of any wartime decision, given the conditions of modern warfare. The practical effects of these two positions may be the same, as we discussed in Chapter 2. But Stimson's tendency towards pessimism did not in fact result in his ceasing to work for the least bad option available.

In general, the necessity to decide when to override a moral intuition may well be the single most difficult aspect of political life. Any attempt to lay down simple guidelines is likely to be unsuccessful. The examples given in this chapter are designed to illustrate how such intuitions can be overridden too soon or too late, and what a decision might be like that got the solution approximately right.

5 Deterrence

THREATS AND INTENTIONS

After the end of the Second World War, and the use of the atomic bomb on Japanese cities, America came to adopt a defensive justification for the retention of nuclear weapons. This change was never entirely credible to her international opponents. But to judge from the strategic literature, especially after 1949 when the Soviet Union demonstrated its nuclear capacity, strategic thinking in the United States became defensive, the focus being on 'massive retaliation' and deterrence. It is true that some argued even after 1949 that it was better to risk death than to risk communist take-over. This would imply that in the face of Soviet expansionism, America should first threaten and then, if necessary, use its nuclear weapons, even at the risk of Russian retaliation. This was at least one implication of the jingle "better dead than red" and of the demand for "roll-back" in Eastern Europe. But most people would not choose death for a large portion of mankind rather than accept survival at the price of subjecting themselves to a tyranny. It is one thing to risk one's own life for the sake of freedom. It is another thing to risk the physical destruction of civilization.

But is not a defensive nuclear policy, which relies on the threat of massive retaliation, risking just this sort of catastrophe? The central moral difficulty in the carrying out of a strategy of nuclear deterrence is that such a strategy depends upon the threat to do what does not seem to have a moral justification. Communist lives are no less valuable than capitalist ones. It is not clear why it should make any moral difference that the Russian lives would be taken in response to the bombing of, let us say, American cities. From a consequentialist point of view, the fact that millions of people, even civilian people, have been killed by an attack on one's cities does not justify the reciprocal killing of millions of enemy civilians. George Kennan has put it this way, "Let us suppose there were to be a nuclear attack of some sort on this country and millions of people were killed and injured. Let us further suppose that we had the ability to retaliate against the urban centres of the country that had attacked us. Would you want to do that? I wouldn't ... I have no sympathy with the man who demands an eye for an eye in a nuclear attack."[1] It is perhaps worth pointing out that an intuitionist who just knows that vengeance is wrong is in a more ambiguous position than the consequentialist when it comes to arguing with someone who just knows that vengeance is right.

But what follows from the failure to find a moral justification for massive retaliation? In particular, does it follow that there cannot be a moral justification for the *threat* of massive retaliation? Our answer would be that this does not follow. It would only follow if a threat were the expression of a conditional intention. A conditional intention is an intention to do something if some condition, such as a Russian attack on West Berlin, is fulfilled. But the connection between threats and intentions is a tricky one. The dictionary defines a "threat" as a "declaration of an intention or determination to inflict punishment, injury, death, or loss on someone in retaliation for, or conditionally upon, some action or course".[2] But there is an ambiguity in this definition.

The intention which is "declared" may or may not be present. We can take an example that has nothing to do with nuclear deterrence in order to illustrate the ambiguity. A mother may tell her child that he will get a spanking if he knocks over his mug one more time. She may indeed have formed the intention to spank him if he does it again. But she may also *not* have decided whether to do so or not, and she may be waiting to make up her mind until after she sees what happens next. The person making the threat may have formed the intention not to do what he is threatening, or he may not have decided whether to do it or not. There are intermediate possibilities. He may have decided to do it if his opponent increases his provocation, but not if he stays at the same level. There are in principle an infinite number of degrees of commitment to a threat. Some writers seem to assume that a threat is either in earnest, or a "mere bluff", but the truth is not so simple. In any case, a threat may be a bluff and still be a threat. If a threat of massive retaliation is the expression of what is in fact a commitment, its moral status is quite different from that of a purported expression of a commitment.

That the deterrent threat is *not* the second of these is argued in two recent treatments of the ethics of deterrence, that of Michael Walzer and that of Barrie Paskins and Michael Dockrill.³ Michael Walzer starts by allowing that the deterrent threat essentially involves the commitment to murder millions of non-combatants in enemy cities. He then concludes that although this is wrong, there may well be no other way "in a world of sovereign and suspicious states" to avoid the intolerable situation in which "advances in technology should put our nation, or any nation, at the mercy of a great power willing to menace the world or to press its authority outwards in the shadow of an implicit threat". The word "commitment" presents an immediate difficulty. For threats are not in themselves commitments. Walzer's argument that deterrence involves the commitment to mass murder runs as follows, "No doubt, killing millions of innocent people is worse than threatening to kill them. It is also true that no one wants to kill them, and it may well be true that no one expects to do so. Nevertheless, we intend the killings under certain circumstances. That is the stated policy of our government, and thousands of men, trained in the techniques of mass destruction and drilled in instant obedience, stand ready to carry it out. And from the perspective of morality, the readiness is all. We can translate it into degrees of danger, high and low, and worry about the risks we are imposing on innocent people, but the risks depend on the readiness. What we condemn in our government ... is the commitment to murder."⁴

Now there is an interpretation of this argument which is straightforward, and telling. But it does not fit the text at all well. This interpretation is that Walzer is arguing that making deterrence an institution increases the risk that the threat will have to be carried out. But if this were his point, he would surely make reference not to the training and discipline of those manning the deterrent, but to the possibility of human and mechanical error. His argument seems to be, rather, that because the stated policy of the government is to kill under certain circumstances, this must be the government's intention. But what follows is not this, but that killing is the *stated* intention of the government under certain circumstances. There may be a great difference between a stated intention and a real one. There is also a distinction between readiness and intentions, though it is not easy to state clearly. Taken in its most straightforward sense, it is false to say, "From the perspective of morality, the readiness is all." I am, for example, when buying a book, ready to try to return it if it turns out to be missing some important pages. But do I therefore have the intention of trying to return it in those circumstances? In any case, the possibility of the pages being missing is rather remote, and my readiness in this respect explains very little about my action. What makes readiness important morally is the combination of the moral importance of what I am ready to do and the *likelihood* of my actually doing it. This is where the training and the discipline of the armed forces become relevant, though they point to the opposite conclusion from Walzer's. The training and the discipline is important mostly because it makes the use of the nuclear weapons less likely. Both the Soviet Union and the United States have set up elaborate mechanisms for guarding against the use of the power which they have admittedly equally elaborate mechanisms for unleashing upon each other. The deterrent has not been used except as a threat for thirty years and this is because of the care taken by all the great powers that it should not be.

We can go further than this. The threat of retaliation has preserved its deterrent effect, without having to be implemented, despite astounding technical changes: medium-range bombers, long-range bombers, liquid-fuelled missiles, solid-fuelled missiles, Polaris submarines, MIRV'd missiles, etc. It has survived astonishing developments in the accuracy of targeting and detection. In addition, it has survived periods when one side alone had nuclear weapons, when one side alone had effective means of delivery and when one side had a substantial lead in both weapons and delivery systems. It has continued to function even though none of the major technical advances associated with it were developed simultaneously by the two superpowers. It has survived despite numerous crises which occurred throughout this long experience of asymmetrical development. In fact, then, deterrence in the nuclear age has a peculiar stability – a stability which has survived enormous changes in weapons, in ratios of striking power and periods of political turmoil.

It contrasts with previous systems of deterrence in many ways. Their disadvantages were numerous: military force could be translated, often effectively, into political gains; imbalances of power could be exploited and often led to war; the decision to go to war and use maximum force could be defended as potentially successful; the build-up of military capabilities added useful increments to one's position compared to an opponent's; the overall results of war could be presented as a viable option. The total result was a system which prevented war in some instances but which proved ineffective in cases involving serious great power rivalries. These disadvantages led many people to suppose that nuclear deterrence would not work any better. But nuclear deterrence operates within a different set of constraints: military force, even preponderance, cannot easily be translated into political gains; imbalances of power, even if considerable, have not produced decisions for war; decision-makers cannot believe in the utility of maximum force;[5] increments of nuclear power do not translate automatically into clear military advantages; the overall results of general war have ceased to be a viable option.

Paskins and Dockrill, like Walzer, argue that a strategy of nuclear deterrence involves the conditional intention to bomb the enemy's cities. Their conclusion is that since such an intention violates the principles of proportionality and non-combatant immunity, and since in addition it makes "trusting to luck the foundation of security", it cannot be morally justified. Unfortunately their argument is both complex and unclear and it needs to be sorted out and responded to in some detail.

First, Paskins and Dockrill try to rule out the justification of deterrence that it involves bluff rather than conditional intention. They secure this result by stipulating that it is only appropriate to call a threat a "bluff" if it involves the intention not to carry out the threatened response if the threat fails. But it is not at all clear that this stipulation reflects ordinary usage. For it seems more natural to allow that a bluff might involve the pretence of intention to carry out a threat, where the intention was not yet present. Paskins and Dockrill insist that in a bluff the intention must be not to respond in the way threatened. But it is more natural to allow that a bluff may simulate an intention to respond in a certain way, whether or not the intention has in fact been formed to back down if the bluff is called.[6] The use of the word "bluff" can, indeed, be restricted just as that of any word can be; but it will remain true that there is a significant difference between conditionally intending to bomb a city if provoked and threatening to do so without yet having formed an intention one way or the other.

A refinement would be to distinguish, as Maxwell does, between a strategy of bluff and a strategy of simple deceit.[7] Maxwell makes the distinction in the context of a discussion of the rationality of an irrevocable commitment. He suggests that the pretence that there is an irrevocable commitment to retaliate, or that one has lost all control over the final outcome, is a strategy of simple deceit. A strategy of bluff would be one that attempted to produce the appearance that one would *choose* to retaliate, if provoked. It would thus give the appearance of a conditional intention, though not the appearance of an irrevocable commitment. In any case, a bluff will not need to involve an actual conditional intention.

Paskins and Dockrill claim that "that which holds the deterrent together is the concept of conditional intention". But there is an ambiguity here. It is true that a threat purports to express a conditional intention. This is certainly true as long as deterrence is supposed to depend on political will and not merely on military capability. What is supposed to deter is not the mere fact that one could retaliate, but the fact that one might decide to do so. To this extent it is true to say that the concept of conditional intention "holds the deterrent together". But we are not given any argument to rule out the possibility that the conditional intention which the threat "expresses" may not yet have been formed. A decision-maker may prefer to make a bluff while still keeping open all his options as to actual response. It is not legitimate to conclude that because threats must at least masquerade as the expression of conditional intentions, that those intentions must themselves be in place before a threat can be made.

Paskins and Dockrill go on to argue that the conditional intentions which they think are necessarily involved in a strategy of deterrence are morally vicious. They give three reasons. Such intentions break the principles of proportionality and non-combatant immunity, and they rely to an intolerable extent upon good luck. The principle of proportionality, on their analysis, requires "that people think what they are trying to do, remember what they are trying to do, avoid being side-tracked into doing something else". It is tempting to remark that this principle might be adhered to by the most ruthless political realist. But the authors' intention is to insist not only on the deliberate proportioning of means to ends, but on the restriction of what ends can properly be pursued in war. In particular, they are concerned with the Kantian formula, "Always treat humanity, whether in your own person or in the person of another, as an end, and never merely as a means." It may be that on their view of the principle of proportionality, it entails the principle of non-combatant immunity, which they also defend on the basis of the Kantian formula. If so, they do not have two independent arguments against a strategy of nuclear deterrence. At any rate we can agree that the intention to bomb a city would be impossible to justify unless some proportionate good could be achieved, and that in the context of the struggle between the superpowers this is exceedingly unlikely. The satisfaction of the desire for revenge would not, for a consequentialist, be a proportionate good. But if a strategy of deterrence does not necessarily involve a conditional intention to retaliate, the consideration of the principle of non-combatant immunity is not conclusive. The important point is that it is not always true that whatever is wrong to do is wrong to threaten. This is only true if "threaten" means "intend (conditionally) to do", which it often does not.[8] It is vital in assessing the moral status of a threat to assess the probability of its being carried out.

This brings us to the authors' third objection. They claim that deterrence "introduces an unacceptable quality of giving hostages to fate". Their discussion of luck is difficult to follow. They give a story as an analogy. Bandits invade one's house and snatch one's child, and one is faced with the options of either threatening to destroy the house, the family and the bandits (by exploding the gas), or letting the bandits take the child to a horrible death. If nuclear deterrence were like threatening to explode the gas in this situation, it might (they think) be justifiable, for our situation might be said to fall into "the class of situations in which there is strong moral reason for doing something with consequences of a hideous sort which are possible but extremely unlikely".[9] But the authors claim that nuclear deterrence is not like this, but more like the same story as above with the added feature that the bandits place honour above life; in this case, one would be making the threat "in the firm knowledge that this will very likely result in the death of all".

Now the apparent difference between these two cases is one of probabilities. The threat is much more likely to have to be carried out in the second case than in the first. But Paskins and Dockrill explicitly discount this difference. Their assumption is that a threat implies a conditional intention, and therefore that a deterrent threat by a state implies the conditional intention to make use of the ordered structures of society to carry it out. The authors conclude, "deterrence makes trusting to luck the foundation of security – if only in the sense that if there is a major nuclear war then we will all have been very unlucky".[10] This may be intended as a sort of pun. In English, as in the equivalent Greek, it is possible to use "lucky" as a term of congratulation and "unlucky" as a term of condolence, without any implication that the unexpected has occurred. But "trusting to luck" is different. We use the phrase when someone is taking an unreasonable risk. To trust that I will not be run over when I perform my kerb drill properly and then cross the street, is not to trust to luck but to trust in the low probability of an accident. Those who trust deterrence are trusting in the low probability of any of the great powers using their nuclear weapons against each other. This cannot be called "trusting to luck" independently of an assessment of what the probabilities in fact are.

It is possible that a great power might have formed a conditional intention of the sort Paskins and Dockrill describe. It is possible even that it might have made an "irrevocable commitment". Would it be rational for a country to adopt such an intention, or such a commitment? The word "rational" is notoriously slippery. Sometimes it is used by one person to describe those actions or decisions of another person which the first person finds intelligible in terms of his own value structure. Sometimes it is used to describe actions or decisions that can be made intelligible in terms of the agent's values. On this second view to say that an action is rational is to say at least that it is consistent with the agent's values, whatever those may be. This is closer to the decision-theoretic account of rationality as involving the intention to maximize expected utility. Game theorists have developed more rigorous versions of what constitutes utility maximization; but we will not need to make use of them in our present context. It is hard to deny that it might be rational in the second sense to make an irrevocable commitment. It might be the case that a state considered that some interest was at stake that was not worth fighting a nuclear war for, and which the enemy did not think was worth such a fight for either. In such a case, the first state might decide to make an irrevocable commitment to the use of nuclear weapons in order to "raise the ante". Such a decision might be rational in the above sense. A doomsday machine, which would guarantee retaliation without any political decision being involved, would be an embodiment of such an irrevocable commitment.

But such a policy might be rational in the second sense without being rational according to the values of most of us, or without being moral. It has sometimes been thought that the use of a doomsday machine or something like it would be moral because it would remove the responsibility for the retaliation from the retaliator. For might it not be said that it is the opponent who should bear the responsibility – he after all had been told that an irrevocable commitment had been made, and he, therefore, brought the destruction upon himself? General Sherman apparently held similar views about the responsibility of the South for the devastation wrought in the final stages of the Civil War. But the proper reply to this is Aristotle's reply to the defence from drunkenness.[11] The drunkard argues that his victim could see that he was drunk and should not have tried to stop him. Aristotle replies that the drunkard was responsible for getting drunk, and therefore responsible for the consequences.

The same sort of response is appropriate to a strategy of threatening to lose control. A nation may make its limits plain. It may say that it is prepared to respond rationally within these limits, but if pushed beyond them, it will not be able to control itself; and it will not answer for the consequences. In the face of such a threat, it might be argued, any opponent who pushed that nation beyond its stated limits would bear the responsibility for the retaliation which followed. But again this defence will not do. It is an attempt to produce an excuse in advance for a military action.[12] It is analogous to the excuse that a husband might offer in a court of law, after shooting his wife's lover when finding them in bed. He was overcome, he might say, by a kind of temporary insanity. But temporary insanity cannot be used as an excuse if it has been deliberately planned for. The excuse is not, therefore, available for a *policy* of deterrence that relies upon the threat of loss of control.

There are, however, other reasons for moral discomfort with this sort of policy. It will not be easy to secure credibility for such strategies. For the purpose of making an irrevocable commitment, or deliberately planning to lose control, is to enhance in the eyes of one's opponent the value one attributes to some object. It will not be worth trying to do this for stakes such as national survival which it might be rational to *decide* to defend with maximum force. For the value, for example, of national survival to a nation does not need to be enhanced in the eyes of its opponents. But if, as we shall argue, the credibility of a threat depends on the enemy's perception of the relative size of the stakes at issue, together with their perception of the relative military capabilities, then any expression of an irrevocable commitment to defend an object which one would not have *chosen* to defend is not likely to be believed. One's opponent will be more likely to suppose that one has adopted a strategy of "simple deceit", in Maxwell's terms, and that one has retained control of the final decision while pretending to abandon it. The more the level of a threat corresponds to the actual value of a stake to the nation making the threat, the more stable the deterrent is likely to be.

In fact, neither the United States nor the Soviet Union has adopted the policies of irrevocable commitment or threatened loss of control. There is no doomsday machine, and neither party has, for example, delegated decisions about the use of nuclear weapons to junior officers so as to introduce a greater element of "luck".[13] They have preferred to threaten retaliation, but to keep the actual decisions firmly in the hands of their political leaders. What has deterred, at the strategic level, is the *possibility*, however remote, that the leaders of the other side might decide to use their second-strike capability. As a matter of history, the reliance upon irrationality or luck has been avoided, most probably because of its attendant risks; if one side knows that this is what the other side is doing, this can all too easily give rise to a series of regressive expectations, in which each side argues from initially incomplete evidence that the other has set the whole deadly process in motion. Keeping the decision in the hands of political leaders has the virtues of comparative predictability and intelligibility.

What we are suggesting, then, is that the maintenance of the nuclear deterrent is morally justifiable as long as it does not involve the conditional intention to use the weapons beyond their deterrent function. There is one objection to this view which we have not yet mentioned, though it may be implicit in Walzer's comment, "the readiness is all". We will call it "the objection from the rank and file". Even if the president and his advisers have not formed a conditional intention to bomb Russian cities, and they may very well not have done so, what about the armed forces? A strategy of bluff, in the sense discussed above, requires for its implementation "thousands of men trained in the techniques of mass destruction and drilled in instant obedience". Do not those "manning" the deterrent have to have formed a conditional intention to fire the missiles, for example, if so ordered? If so, then we may be justifying the maintenance of the deterrent by absolving the top military commanders from immoral intentions while all the while requiring immoral intentions of the rank and file. For if it is immoral to intend massive retaliation, it is surely immoral to intend to carry it out if so ordered. The objection runs, then, that a strategy of bluff puts thousands of people in a morally indefensible position.[14]

There are various possible responses to this objection. One is to deny that those manning the deterrent have to have formed the conditional intention to carry out the order, for example, to fire the missiles. Perhaps they too have not yet made up their minds what to do, although they have had to act in all the drills required of them *as though* they had decided. Another response is to deny that the intention to obey the order is immoral. For someone carrying out such an order would be very unlikely to be in a position to know or to evaluate the reasons behind the order. Our argument is as follows. Most of those "manning" the deterrent will not be in a position to know whether in obeying orders, through all the various stages of alert, they are implementing a strategy of threat or of actual use. But if there are some who will be in a position to know this, they should not, if they want to avoid immoral intentions, form the antecedent intention to obey the orders before these are given. If it is argued that they do have to form these antecedent intentions, then the response must be that this is still the lesser of two evils. For against the wrong required of them, if it really is required of them, has to be weighed a greater wrong – their country would not be able to resist the demands of any opponent who is both armed with nuclear weapons and less scrupulous about the intentions it requires of its armed forces.

It is true that the American army, like the West German, but unlike the British, has a manual which includes an explicit instruction that each soldier is required to evaluate morally the command which he carries out. Suppose a soldier has reached the position advocated in this chapter, that massive retaliation cannot be justified although the threat of it can be. If so, then the fact that he is following an order will not make much moral difference to him, since the manual puts him under the requirement *even as a soldier* to evaluate the order morally.

However, the suggested picture of a single soldier making the single fatal decision is unrealistic. In fact, there are thousands of people making thousands of decisions all of which are necessary, but not sufficient, for the final use of the weapons. The position is thus extraordinarily complex. For each person following an order has to allow the possibility that the chain of operations will stop before the final button is pushed. It would be morally preferable if the final action, which in the popular imagination is the pushing of a button but may in fact be something quite different, were taken by the originator of the policy – the president or his immediate subordinates. The developments in communications technology have made this increasingly possible by allowing the centralization of control mechanisms. If this is possible, then a satisfactory response to the objection about the rank and file is available. For each of the innumerable antecedent decisions necessary for the use of the weapon can be taken in good faith by a member of the armed forces who agrees with the position of this book; he may, after all, be implementing, through all the various stages of preparation, a policy of threat rather than use.[15]

But perhaps there do have to be people who both know that they are taking the last and irreversible step, and who are not in a position to know the policy reasons behind it. It is admittedly unsatisfactory to say, in response to this, that the members of the armed forces do not need to have made a conditional intention to obey orders. For even if in theory they are required to evaluate orders morally, in practice most of them probably will not; and the system of military training and discipline is designed to encourage them not to do so. It is probably unrealistic to suggest that there could be widespread independence of mind in the matter of obedience in an efficient military force. However what is in question is not a general independence of mind but the absence of a very specific conditional intention, or the suspension of judgement by those involved about what they would do if they *both* knew that the step they were ordered to take was the last and irreversible one *and* they were not in a position to know the reasons for the order. The only people who have been in such a position so far are those who dropped the bombs on Hiroshima and Nagasaki. There is evidence from their subsequent lives that their state of mind was in fact extremely unstable. It is plausible to suggest that none of us could in fact know how we would respond in such a situation. Those men had undoubtedly formed the conditional intention, when they entered the aircraft, to drop the bombs. Their mental health was in a sense sacrificed to the general welfare. But the present point is that they played a highly specific role. A consequentialist is forced to weigh the wrong done to them against the benefits of a deterrence policy in general.[16] The large majority of those in the armed forces will *not* have to form these intentions, and will not be in any position to do so. This argument is not supposed to be a justification for a massive retaliation but for allowing some members of the rank and file to form the conditional intention to obey the orders to fire the weapons *if* there is no way that this can be done by those responsible for the policy of deterrence itself. If on the other hand this centralization of control *is* possible, then nobody is required to form the conditional intention in ignorance of the reasons. In either case, there is a response available to the objection from the rank and file.

THE SPECTRUM OF DETERRENCE

Strategic thinking has not in fact maintained the emphasis on massive retaliation which it adopted after 1949. If we look at the field of strategic studies, we can trace a clear line of development. The first reaction to the atomic bomb was to believe that war between atomic powers had been made impossible. The second reaction was to try and avoid this sensible conclusion by providing alternatives to all-out nuclear war – war with tactical nuclear weapons, strategies of limited strategic strikes or flexible retaliation, theories of escalation and crisis managment. They were all designed to make it possible to think of *winning* a nuclear war. But the position is now more ambiguous. One analysis of the change is as follows, "Read these elaborations today and you bring away from then one unmistakeable impression. They possess all the cogency, all the intellectual rigour, and all the irrelevance of the scholastic writings of the Middle Ages. And why do they do so? The answer is that during the 1960s the response of the strategists was steadily displaced by another – this was a return to the first massive reaction to the atomic bomb."[17]

The value of this quotation is that it draws attention to an important feature of the current situation. No theory of limited war can uncouple strategy from the final deterrent as long as this is maintained by the great powers. But an emphasis on the threat of unlimited nuclear war distorts the strategic picture, for there is in fact a whole spectrum of deterrence: Choices in the real world are not confined to waging all-out attacks on cities or doing nothing; they include conventional war, the possible use of a variety of tactical nuclear weapons and limited nuclear strikes on military targets, to name but a few. In short, a range of options exist which create the possibility but not the necessity of escalation to ever greater levels of violence. It might be argued that although this range of options exists physically, it is not available psychologically because of the *fear* of inevitable escalation. We do not want to deny that the fear of escalation is one of the foundations of peace. But allowance must also be made for the secondary fear of what would happen if this initial fear were overcome, that is to say if deterrence were breached. It is this second fear that should produce the range of options mentioned above. For it it does not, this makes the intitial fear into a self-fulfilling prophecy. Escalation to general or total war will be inevitable if there are no intermediate levels of conflict available.

We would like to stress three principles in considering these various levels. First the principle that the strategy of a state should be consistent with its declaratory posture, second the principle of non-escalation, and third the principle of parity. By "declaratory posture" we mean the stance taken by a country in its declarations of intent towards other countries. As stated, the first principle is inconsistent with a strategy of bluff. For a bluff is a form of deceit. It declares an intention that may not in fact have been formed, or which may be the opposite of the intention that has been formed. Thus a bluff involves a dissonance between strategy and posture. If we want to allow that bluff is justifiable as a strategy, we will have to rephrase the principle. We might say that the strategy of a state should not be more aggressive.than its declaratory posture implies, although it may on occasion be less so. The fundamental justification for such a principle is a moral one. For it is a specialized statement in the international context of the obligation of truthfulness. We do not agree with Kant that there is an absolute moral proscription on lying. But there is a *prima facie* rule against it. A recent full-length treatment of this subject has analysed four basic sorts of morally relevant reasons that can be given for lying.[18] A lie may be permitted in self-defence in a crisis; or if the person to whom one is lying has "no claim to normally honest answers" because of his behaviour; or if there is no likelihood that the practice of lying will spread because of the present lie; or if, finally, the likely harm to a liar from his lie, including the harm to his character, is less than the harm from telling the truth. There are numerous difficulties in applying these excuses to the international context: the identification of enemies is liable to paranoiac exaggeration (though it is likely to be easier in a nuclear context); the dismissal of peoples as outside the moral community has alarming historical precedents; international trust is peculiarly fragile, and the example of a country telling the truth even at a cost might have a significant impact (though this needs discussion); and a lie to an enemy can very easily backfire, as in the U-2 incident, which damaged seriously the U.S. government's credibility with its own people. The trust of a people in its government is a matter of such importance that it should not lightly be put in jeopardy. Often the likely harm to a nation from planning a more aggressive policy than it is stating in public is greater than it thinks. It is not in the interest of a democratic country for its citizens to be disillusioned with the statements of its political leaders.

If NATO, for example, is not planning for a first-strike capability, it would be desirable for some explicit declaration of this to be made. There is a cost involved in this, namely the possible loss of some deterrent effectiveness that might arise from leaving the first-strike option open. But, first, the Russians will no doubt continue to be uncertain whether or not the NATO forces will strike first if it is in their interest to do so. Second, any loss in deterrent effectiveness will be outweighed by the gain in moral consistency. Since the Second World War, the U.S. has normally taken the posture of a defender of the *status quo*. A no-first-strike declaration would be consistent with this posture and would tend to consolidate it, although there are undoubtedly scenarios that could be constructed in which a first strike could be justified on the basis of self-defence or the defence of an ally. Consistency between strategy and declaratory posture is important for the morale of the Western nations.

This principle has implications for targeting policy. If it is the declaratory posture of a nation that it does not intend to launch a first strike against enemy cities, it is consistent with this, though not strictly required by it, that no missiles and no bombers should be targeted on those cities. One possible alternative policy would be to target fifty per cent of all missiles and all bombers on purely military targets and to leave the other fifty per cent not targeted at all. The targeting could be changed very quickly if there were an attack so that very little deterrent effectiveness would be lost.

The second principle mentioned above was the principle of non-escalation. This principle states that the level of force used against an enemy should not exceed that used by the enemy.[19] A conventional attack should be met by a conventional defence; tactical nuclear attack by tactical nuclear defence, and so on. A consequentialist will be able to think of scenarios in which this principle needs to be overridden.[20] But it can be maintained as a useful general principle for one main reason; it decreases the risk of general or total war, once the initial breach of deterrence has been made.

This is clearest in the case of a no-first-strike policy for the use of strategic nuclear weapons.[21] As the great powers reach approximate parity in arms (in accordance with the third principle mentioned above), a first strike against an opponent will be less likely to be a tolerable risk. This is at once a prudential and a moral argument. It is in the interest of all the great powers and also of the rest of the world that a general or total war be avoided. But the argument can be extended to each level of escalation. Each move to a higher level of conflict brings closer the possibility that the great powers may be led to use their full arsenals. But there is a second reason behind the principle of non-escalation. Certainly in the case of the strategic nuclear weapons, a no-first-strike policy is consistent with the values represented by international law and by the declaratory posture of most nations of the world. We can use an extension of the argument used in favour of the first principle. There it was suggested that it is in the interest of a democracy for strategy to be consistent with declaratory posture. Here the argument is that the declaratory posture of most nations in this century has been to condemn aggression. This is not to say that their strategy has been consistent with this or that the definition of 'aggression' is at all straightforward. But a first strike would be under most definitions a form of aggression, and the morale of a nation may be seriously undermined if its military strategy is inconsistent with the values for which the nation claims to stand. Last, but not least, each escalation of levels of force increases the range of potential victims. Any taking of life requires to be justified, and the burden of proof gets progressively heavier as the number of lives that will be taken increases.

But the principle of non-escalation is a *prima facie* one; it will sometimes be right to override it. The sentence quoted in the third chapter from Richard Brandt gives a summary statement of when it will be right to override it on consequentialist grounds: an action which escalates the level of conflict "is permissible only if the utility (broadly conceived so that the maintenance of treaty obligations of international law could count as a utility) of victory to all concerned, multiplied by the increase in its probability if the action is executed, on the evidence (where the evidence is reasonably solid considering the stakes) is greater than the possible disutility of the action to both sides multiplied by its probability".[22] It may even be that an escalation across the nuclear "firebreak" can be justified on these grounds. This is a question which involves a whole set of considerations: the targets that are hit, the number of weapons used and the radiation yields. In fact, a large-scale conventional battle extending over several months could easily result in both civilian and military casualties far in excess of those produced by the use of a few tactical weapons confined to the battlefield. For similar reasons a demonstration strategic nuclear strike on a military target might produce very few casualties and bring a conventional conflict to an abrupt halt. It is conceivable, then, that it might be right to take the initiative in escalation. But it is still important to say that this would need to be demonstrated and that there is a principle here which would be overridden.

The threatening of a nuclear first strike against a non-nuclear power is not so liable to the objection from the danger of escalation to unlimited war. The threats against Japan in 1945 came into this category, though they were not explicitly nuclear threats, as do the threats against China over Korea and the offshore islands. Putting one's forces on alert, as the U.S. did in 1973, is a revealing intermediate strategy. The intention was to deter the Russians from intervening in the Middle East. Putting the forces on alert was not itself a threat to use nuclear force. But it conveyed to the Soviet Union the seriousness with which the U.S. viewed their actions. It can perhaps be seen as the threat of a threat, and there might be a number of similar intermediate possibilities.

The third principle mentioned at the beginning of this section was the principle of parity. This principle states that a country should have available to it, or available to its allies, the whole range of weapons available to its enemies. This principle is necessary in order to allow the flexibility of response called for by the second principle. If a country or an alliance does not have available to it, for example, conventional forces of sufficient size and scope to counter the conventional forces of its enemies, it will be forced either to escalate or to surrender in the face of a full-scale conventional attack. The debate centres most often around the forces in Europe. At the level of conventional arms, it is a controversial question whether at the moment the NATO forces in Europe do have parity. It seems to be the conclusion of the specialists that in Europe "the overall balance still appears to make military aggression seem unattractive".[23] This means in effect that a responsible ethical choice has been made in the broad sense that excessive reliance has *not* been placed on the threat of nuclear weapons. The principle was contravened by the policy of "extended deterrence", which minimized conventional forces in Europe during a time of Western strategic superiority. This policy relied on the threat of immediate escalation without response at the conventional level. It seems to be the case now that the balance is such that only a major attack would require a move to the next level of force. Moreover, NATO forces have been designed primarily for defence whereas their opponents have forces suited to offensive operations.[24] This suggests a consistency between Western strategy and posture. The question of parity in tactical nuclear weapons is again hotly disputed. If it is the case that NATO is presently in a position of weakness, parity should be restored. For otherwise the threat to respond at that level without escalation loses credibility. In general it is true that a declared policy of defensive strategy will only be credible if it is backed by sufficient forces at each level so that deterrence can be sustained without escalation.

The principle also implies that there should be no more than a parity of force available. For superiority will not convey defensive intentions to an opponent. The implementation of this in practice is notoriously difficult. For as both of the superpowers have independent research establishments, different histories of weapons build-up, and different strategic strengths and vulnerabilities, parity is not going to be a matter of numerically equal forces, but of equal power. Since the situation in this respect is never static, there is need for constant re-evaluation, and the constant danger of each side erring too far on the side of caution in its assessment of the other side's capabilities as against its own. We will deal with these difficulties again in the chapter on disarmament and arms control. Doubt might reasonably be expressed about the plan for new mobile MX missiles, for this might seriously disturb the balance.[25] A proponent of parity may find himself at one moment recommending the deployment of more forces in Europe, and at the next recommending against the development of new missile technologies in the United States.

The arguments for parity, then, are first that it keeps open a range of options and second that it improves credibility. Exceptions to the principle, dealing with the need to allow for a margin of error and the difficulties of assessing relative strengths, will be mentioned in the chapter on arms control and disarmament. The connection between parity and credibility is an important one. We can take the credibility of a threat as dependent upon two factors – the relative military capabilities of the parties and the relative size of the stakes at issue between them.[26] If one country is to find the threat of another country credible, it must believe first that the second country has available the force it is threatening to use, and second that this force is proportionate to the value attached by the second country to the object at stake. The crisis over Hungary and the Cuban missile crisis provide interesting examples. In the case of Hungary, the U.S.S.R. faced the possible collapse of its inner ring of defences just as the U.S.A. did in Cuba. Russia was as far in advance of the U.S.A. in local conventional capacity in Hungary as the U.S.A. was in advance of Russia in Cuba. The difference between the two is that the U.S.A. did not threaten to use nuclear weapons against Russian cities in the Hungarian crisis, though the administration was under pressure to do so, but it felt free to do so in the Cuban crisis. The difference is explicable in terms of the above analysis of credibility. A U.S. threat over Cuba was credible, whereas a threat over Hungary would not have been. This gives us a connection with the principle of parity. If the forces available to both sides are approximately equal, then what will make the threat to use this force either credible or not will be solely the estimate of the values attached by each side to the objects at stake. This may be one reason for the stability of the deterrent. Each side has recognized a distinction between marginal stakes, survival stakes and a range between these.[27] Hungary and Cuba represented stakes in the intermediate range. Their importance was such that a defeat for Russia in the first case or for the U.S. in the second could have seriously disrupted the balance of power. If the superpowers' approximate parity in armaments continues, we can expect the deterrent to remain stable as long as the values attached in practice to the stakes at issue remain compatible.

We might plot a graph with levels of force on the vertical axis and the size of stakes at issue on the horizontal. On the vertical axis the range would be from conventional force at the bottom, through tactical and strategic nuclear weapons, to the entire arsenal of the superpowers at the top. On the horizontal axis, the range would be from marginal stakes through 'landslide' stakes (where the issue may affect the relative positions of powers in the international hierarchy), to survival stakes. A threat by the U.S. to use a certain level of force will be maximally credible relative to a certain size of stake. We can then plot a threat-credibility curve (strictly, a cumulative probability distribution curve), which would probably take an S-shape; it would show a gradual rise as force was threatened in response to attacks on Angola or Afghanistan, then a steep rise through those made on members of NATO, especially if U.S. troops were involved, and it would flatten out at the top over attacks on minutemen or on U.S. cities. The curve would not start at zero or end at one hundred. For the mere existence of the military technology poses a threat even if no force is explicitly threatened and the stake is extremely small. The threat to use the entire arsenal is not likely to be maximally credible even for the highest stakes, because of the possibility of loss of nerve or of a decision that massive retaliation is immoral.

What makes the deterrent work is the residual uncertainty created by the mere existence of the nuclear weapons. The only way to remove this would be to abolish the weapons and the technical knowledge of how to build them. This is now no longer possible. Having said this, however, it should also be said that the uncertainty could be substantially reduced by a successful multilateral disarmament. There are a number of reasons for thinking that this would be, if possible, a better solution to the world's problems.[28] *First*, there is the constant possibility that the deterrent may become unstable. It is true that it has already survived surprisingly well, as we discussed earlier. But it is always possible, for example, that a nuclear power might make a huge advance in weapons technology and might decide to seize the advantage. *Second*, a policy of deterrence assumes the rationality of the nuclear powers; and this assumption, though so far substantiated, is not inevitably so. There has been so far what we might call a "Genghis Khan complex"; no political leader has wanted to be known as the first to unleash the forces of destruction. But, as Churchill said about Hitler in his bunker, there may come a leader about whose mental processes we can only "draw a blank". *Third*, there is the point that the longer we rely on the deterrent, the more used we become to the idea of the destruction we are threatening against others and in the end against ourselves; we become dangerously less ready to move decisively towards disarmament and arms control. For all these reasons (and there are others that could be given), a policy of deterrence is not one that can be pursued with much enthusiasm, either from a moral or a prudential point of view. What is needed is a full-scale commitment to work for an alternative way to keep the peace, while at the same time realizing that the deterrent is necessary to maintain some sort of balance in international relations while this work is done.

It may seem paradoxical to advocate that we *both* maintain the deterrent *and* work for disarmament and arms control. But the paradox is only apparent. The situation is illuminated by a reference back to the two-level theory of moral thinking presented in the first chapter. The relations between the great powers will no doubt continue to fluctuate between cold war and détente, with direct armed conflict as an option beyond cold war and cooperative disarmament as an option beyond détente. The goal of moving these relations towards cooperation and away from conflict cannot be achieved in the absence of an interim balance. The hope is that balance will lead to restraint and restraint to concert or cooperation. Balance is seen, on this view, as a necessary but not a sufficient condition for progress in this direction. We do not think that there is enough evidence to say either that this progress is inevitable, as Kant thought, or as some modern pessimists have said, that it is impossible.[29] An ideal observer, or archangel, would know how much progress was possible at each stage; to push for more than this would lead in the long run to disillusion and therefore to regression. In using the critical level of moral thinking we are trying to approximate as closely as possible to this sort of knowledge and to prescribe how much effort and how much hope is justified in the movement towards international cooperation. This is the subject of the following chapters. But the apparent paradox will be resolved, though not the practical difficulty, if we take account of the different levels. At the critical level we can decide that it is of fundamental importance to foster the intuition that a policy based on mutual terror is morally repugnant; only by fostering this will there be any hope of reaching a less dangerous system of world order. But we can also decide at the critical level that the intuition has for the time being to be overridden in the interests of present peace. The overriding of a sound intuition will leave, and should leave, an uneasy conscience and the intention to do everything possible to remove the cause of the difficulty. In this case it will leave the intention to use restraint and to encourage communication even in the face of rejection and hostility, as long as this is compatible with protecting the genuine interests of one's country.

NUCLEAR PROLIFERATION

No discussion of the ethics of deterrence can be complete without considering, however briefly, the issues posed by nuclear proliferation. The problems involved are extremely complex, combining issues of developing technology, pressures for energy growth and the familiar dilemmas of security and prestige. Together they form the potential nightmare, for coming generations, of a serious erosion (if not a complete breakdown) of deterrence. What follows is a summary of leading opinion with particular emphases selected by the present writers.[30]

Perhaps the first thing to be said is that early efforts to deal with the problem of proliferation foundered on a combination of power politics and insufficient knowledge of some of the technical processes involved. This was true, for example, of the Acheson–Lilienthal Report and the Baruch plan of 1946; the former relied on a mistaken belief that plutonium left in a reactor long enough would be spoiled for weapons use, and the latter, acting on this assumption, proposed an international authority to own and supply this "safe" material. For reasons of strategic interest, the Soviet Union turned down the Baruch plan. Meanwhile, acting on the belief that plutonium could be made safe for civilian use and that the supply of uranium was limited, the United States through the Atoms for Peace Plan spread civilian nuclear technology quite widely by subsidizing research reactors and power reactors.[31] There seems also to have been a certain confusion of thought involved in this process; it seems to have been believed that the promotion of peaceful uses of atomic energy would discourage military uses. Certainly the accounting and inspection procedures of the International Atomic Energy Authority were inadequate for the task of controlling the spread of weapons technology. These initial difficulties were compounded enormously by the intensity of the Cold War which, among other things, prevented the achievement of a comprehensive test-ban treaty forbidding all nuclear testing. Some idea of the extent of the weapons developed as a result of thirty years of testing by the United States is indicated by the following figures: there were seventy-four different types of weapons tested, fifty of these were produced, and twenty-six of these fifty are currently in operation using thirty-three different weapons systems.[32] About one thousand nuclear tests have been carried out by the Soviet Union and the United States over the past thirty years.

The Cold War was the main but not the only reason for the failure to take reasonable steps to halt proliferation. Early beliefs that proliferation would proceed rapidly, and that the issue involved great urgency, turned out to be unfounded. This seems to have reduced efforts to face the issues squarely. At any rate, it was not until 1970 that the two superpowers agreed on a Nuclear Non-Proliferation Treaty. This treaty provides that nuclear states will not give non-nuclear states nuclear weapons or help in their acquisition; and reciprocal promises are made by the non-nuclear signatories, who agree to accept international inspection. The nuclear powers for their part agree to assist in the development of civil nuclear energy, to negotiate a comprehensive test ban, to cease manufacture of nuclear weapons and to reduce stockpiles.[33] Two great powers have not signed (e.g. France and China), two near-nuclear powers (India and Israel) also refused, as did three with nuclear ambitions (Argentina, Brazil and South Africa). Several others displayed great reluctance to ratify the treaty.

It is important to recognize that the NPT by itself will not be sufficient to prevent the spread of nuclear weapons. A recent conference of sixty-six nations – the International Fuel Cycle Evaluation Conference – convened by President Carter to determine whether existing nuclear plants could be replaced by facilities that would not produce bomb-grade materials, concluded that there were no technical means of doing so.[34] Their report is particularly sobering since their calculation is that as many as two thousand nuclear plants may be built around the world by the year 2000.

Meanwhile the Carter Administration's efforts to halt or slow down proliferation have produced mixed results. The Nuclear Non-Proliferation Act of 1978 set tighter standards for export licensing but apparently unduly restricts the Executive's bargaining leverage. Pressures on France and Germany to block multi-billion dollar deals with Korea, Brazil and Pakistan have embittered our allies and produced only partial results in two of the cases. Carter's decision to hold back on the development of a billion-dollar breeder reactor has been viewed with scepticism by the major industrial nations since these can be fuelled with uranium waste from enrichment plants and would provide a major energy resource. For example, it is estimated that 300,000 tons of uranium waste contains more energy than all U.S. coal reserves and more than all the oil in the world.[35] Probably breeder reactors, because of their enormous size, cost and complexity are beyond the capabilities of all but a few countries.

It may well be too late to stop proliferation by an embargo on reprocessing plants and uranium-enrichment plants.[36] This is because of the widespread knowledge of nuclear technology and the incentives which exist for states to obtain civilian nuclear energy. There is however a variety of approaches that might reduce the drive toward the acquisition of a weapons capability:[37] increasing the supply of natural uranium and enrichment services, purchasing plutonium in spent fuel-rods, offering inexpensive reprocessing services and bringing spent fuel and plutonium under international control. These methods probably would not eliminate nuclear proliferation. They would, however, slow the rate at which it occurred and avoid a rush to nuclear weapons technology. A sudden, sharp increase in the number of states with nuclear weapons would be inherently destabilizing for many reasons; as the number rises so does the probability of miscalculation, accident or unauthorized use, and so do the possibilities of escalation and the creation of regional instability.

Beyond this the actual incentives and disincentives for the acquisition of nuclear weapons have to be tackled on a broad front. Incentives include the aspiration for great power or regional status, the desire for prestige and the fear of territorial insecurity. Disincentives include fear the weapons might be used, fear of sanctions, costs in resources, etc. Since many states are involved in serious quarrels with their neighbours and many have great ambitions for status and prestige, and since several are rich beyond the dreams of avarice, the outlook is not bright. What appears to be possible is a combination of measures: the creation of nuclear-free zones, the offering of security guarantees, the settlement of regional disputes and a non-use declaration with respect to non-nuclear states. What does not seem to be feasible is either severe economic sanctions or some kind of imposed Soviet–American condominium. The superpowers can and should face frankly the fact that they have it in their power to reduce the pressures for nuclear weapons acquisition by signing a comprehensive test-ban treaty and by negotiating significant reductions in their nuclear stockpiles. Unless a firm intention to proceed in this direction is made clear, the likelihood of local nuclear wars will almost certainly rise and the current stability of deterrence may well be seriously eroded.

6 Arms Control and Disarmament

It is tempting to view with cynicism attempts by the nations to render themselves less dangerous through disarmament. We will look in this chapter at some of the reasons for pessimism about the chances that these attempts will be successful. Our conclusion will not be that failure is inevitable, but that success will only come if proposals for arms control are accompanied by more general attempts to relax political tensions. Disarmament cannot stand as an independent goal, and the difficulties which have faced diplomats both before and after 1945 bear witness to this. There has indeed been a striking continuity in the sorts of difficulties they have found, and we will be discussing to what extent the situation has changed since the development of atomic weapons.

In the first place, the object of any disarmament agreement is to contribute to the achievement of peace and security between states. By "peace" the diplomats do not mean merely the absence of war but an equilibrium of power such that the existing situation is not changed by the use of armed force.[1] The concept of security means that the vital interests of states are to be protected against changes by force or subversion.[2] On these definitions, the connection between peace and security is clearly an intimate one. The main problem of disarmament is how to achieve a diplomatic situation satisfactory to all the powers concerned without recourse to violence. The key word here is "satisfactory", for the chief lesson of all disarmament negotiations in the past century or more is that "arms could not be limited without perpetuating a settlement intolerable to several states".[3] Professor Tate who examined the record from the end of the Napoleonic Wars to 1907, showed in detail that no plan which would freeze the status quo was acceptable to the powers during this entire period.[4] At the turn of the century the great powers all had ambitions which they refused to give up. France had ambitions in Alsace-Lorraine after the Franco – Prussian War, the Eastern question was still unsettled, and the great powers were all involved in varying degrees in attempts to partition China into spheres of influence.[5] Today we have unsettled territorial problems in the Far East, Eastern Europe and the Middle East. The modern phase of the struggle for Africa is just beginning.

In these encounters no great power has ever been willing to face its opponents without arms sufficient to protect what it considers to be its vital interests. This was true of the nations throughout the last century; and it is true, apparently, of the powers today and for much the same reasons. In the nineteenth century the possession of armaments was looked upon as evidence of the total power of the state.[6] Competition in arms took the place of war with the result that the superiority of the British Navy and of the German army (after 1871) was accepted by all statesmen.[7] Much the same situation exists today. Great Britain thought it necessary to develop first the atomic bomb and then the hydrogen bomb in order to maintain her place in the front rank of the great powers.[8] France and China followed suit. The constant testing of atomic and hydrogen weapons since 1945 has not been merely for the purpose of gaining information but to remind the world in the first instance that the United States was the world's only atomic power and, after 1949, that the Soviet Union had attained the select circle. Unquestionably, the announcement by the Soviets on 26 August 1957 that they had successfully tested the prototype of an intercontinental ballistic missile was intended as a demonstration of their (temporary) superiority in this field of endeavour.[9]

The striking similarities which exist between the past and present efforts of the powers to achieve peace and security through disarmament suggest that there are certain more or less endemic problems which tend to frustrate such efforts. One of the most glaring and obvious of these is that the security needs of the powers tend to vary widely owing to differences stemming from geographical location, the size and skill of their populations, the natural resources of each and the amount of space available for defensive manoeuvre and dispersal of people and cities. In the pre-1914 period, for example, British defence needs were largely met by the maintenance of a navy equal in power to the navies of the two largest powers in Europe.[10] That is to say, Britain felt that her geographical position required her to maintain a position of predominance at sea particularly in the

European theatre. It was only the difficult economic situation presented by the years immediately following the First World War and strong public pressures in favour of peace which led the British government to try and maintain their position by international conventions at Washington in 1921/22 and at London in 1930 and 1935.[11] The coming of air-power radically transformed the defence needs of all states. This was apparent to acute observers long before 1939[12] and was borne out by the grim experiences of bombing in the Second World War.

United States security needs are quite different in nature from either those of Great Britain or the Soviet Union. This was true during the 1920s when Britain and America tried to arrive at a naval agreement relative to cruisers. Britain wanted a large number of small cruisers because she had a great many bases from which to operate them while the United States desired a small number of large cruisers for precisely opposite reasons.[13] In the first SALT negotiations, the Soviet Union claimed the need for a larger number of nuclear submarines than the United States since the transit time required was much larger. This meant, of course, that Soviet subs could spend less time on station than their U.S. counterparts. Again, it would seem that the United States is relatively *less* vulnerable to attack by atomic and hydrogen bombs than, say, Great Britain; but, owing to the concentration of her cities in the northern and eastern sections of the country and upon her coasts, she appears to be relatively *more* vulnerable than the Soviet Union. Whether this relative difference would prove really important or not if war came cannot, by the nature of things, be known for certain; but it is probable that these differing security needs among the powers do make agreement more difficult. It was this fact that all the great powers have different defence needs which rendered futile efforts to differentiate between "offensive" and "defensive" weapons in the inter-war period. Madariaga's parable of the disarmament conference of the animals describes this dilemma beautifully. According to this story the lion wanted to eliminate all weapons but claws and jaws, the eagle all but talons and beaks, and the bear all but an embracing hug![14]

A second major impediment to successful disarmament is the uneven development of weapons systems in various states. There is rarely, if ever, a point in an armaments race where all the powers are more or less equal to one another. This is one of the primary reasons for the failure of *quantitative* disarmament proposals; for no one has ever found out a method of measuring the relative effectiveness of navies versus armies or the relative war-making capacities of states. This problem of ratios, as it is called, bedevilled the discussions at the Geneva Disarmament Conference of 1932 under the guise of German claims to "equality" with France,[15] and was partly responsible for the failure of the Soviet Union's proposal, made in 1948, for a one-third cut in the land, naval, and air-forces of the great powers to be accompanied by an unconditional ban on atomic weapons. Acceptance of such a proposal would have resulted in overwhelming Soviet superiority; for although they did not then possess atomic bombs, they did maintain vastly larger armed forces of a conventional type. The discrepancy in weapons systems also tended to dictate American proposals between 1946 and 1950 to the effect that, before the atomic bomb was renounced as a weapon, "an adequate system for control of atomic energy [should be] agreed upon and put into effective operation ...".[16]

Indeed, past evidence suggests that the discovery and development of a new weapon tends to precipitate an arms race in that particular weapon. This was true for example after the British completed the Dreadnought in 1906, for the Dreadnought was so powerful that all other ships became relatively impotent. Until other nations built a fleet of these ships British naval supremacy was assured.[17] A similar race for the atomic bomb was precipitated by its development and use in 1945. It was achieved by the Soviet Union in 1949, and by Great Britain in 1952. The race for the hydrogen bomb was completed by the United States in 1952, the Soviet Union in 1953 and Great Britain in 1957. Another race went on in the field of missiles and here the Soviet Union was the first to test successfully a weapon of intercontinental range.[18] Naturally, the United States refused to talk seriously of limitations until its own tests were completed. It is almost impossible to achieve any kind of arms limitation in such a situation (at least until the other powers have developed the new weapons for themselves) for the leading power is tempted to use the new weapon for national political advantage while the powers who are behind will resist agreement until they have caught up.[19] This suggests the possibility that the nation-states may have become increasingly the prisoners of their own technology and that as long as ever-newer and ever-deadlier weapons loom over the scientific horizon the cause of any form of disarmament may be hopeless. Certainly the technological developments since 1945 have occurred with such rapidity that they would not have provided a stable foundation for a political agreement even if no other obstacles had intervened. Success in arms limitation may turn out to be dependent in large measure upon the failures of science to penetrate certain technical barriers in the weapons field.[19a] A third and closely related obstacle to disarmament is the uncertainty attendant on scientific discovery. It is tempting for governments to wait quietly for a major technological breakthrough which would give them a powerful edge in either their defensive or offensive capabilities or both. The Western powers have been particularly exposed to this temptation, for their scientists developed the atomic and hydrogen bombs first and, in general, they have had a larger number of scientists of the front rank than the Soviets. But this reasoning is open to serious objection for, to begin with, no one can predict the rise of a scientific genius. Such a person might accomplish major discoveries in a critical area of knowledge which would lead in turn to a major shift in military and world power. Again, the Soviet Union has demonstrated that, owing to their virtually unlimited governmental powers, it is possible to concentrate a high proportion of a nation's scientists in military endeavours and attain results out of all proportion to the total available scientific manpower.

The most potent stumbling-block in the path to an effective disarmament agreement, however, is the existence of international political tensions. When tensions are extreme states draw back from any proposal which threatens their position of power. At such a point an armaments race is the *result* of tension but, as the race becomes progressively more competitive and as the arms of one state produce first fear and then countermeasures in the opponent, the struggle then becomes a *cause* of political tension in its own right. Certainly it is very difficult to see how any extensive agreement can be achieved with a struggle for power raging over large areas of the globe.

The role of tensions in preventing disarmament becomes doubly significant if one looks at political tensions in the *internal* affairs of states. Observers going back to Aristotle[20] have agreed that tyrants require outside enemies in order to justify their harsh and arbitrary measures within the state. Moreover where there are no legitimate means of transferring power the resulting instability can prove deleterious to international negotiations. This is apparently what occurred in the summer of 1957 when the struggle between Mr. Khrushchev and other members of the Praesidium had come to a head. It was perfectly apparent to observers on the scene that the Soviet delegation was waiting to see the outcome before proceeding with the negotiations.[21] Above all, it is far from clear whether any state, totalitarian or democratic, would tolerate the levels of intrusion demanded by really rigorous inspection procedures. Certainly all Soviet proposals on this point have been very carefully hedged about with detailed qualifications.[22]

An appraisal of the armaments problem is made more difficult by the fact that the word "disarmament" can mean several different things. It can mean *unilateral* disarmament. It can mean international *limited* disarmament or it can mean *abolition* of armaments. The unilateral type was practiced by Great Britain from 1919 to 1931 with the result that the influence of British diplomacy declined and her ability to maintain peace was weakened.[23] "Foreign governments took advantage of the popular pressure behind the British government to extract support of some favourite policy in exchange for agreement on disarmament."[24] There is presently no indication that the great powers are remotely interested in the risky experiment of unilateral disarmament, nor that they are ever likely to undertake such a course of action.[25]

States have traditionally endeavoured to arrive at a limited international agreement on arms. This pattern was typical of conferences held between 1921 and 1935 and is still the pattern even following the advent of atomic-hydrogen weapons. Yet it is apparent that in the era of hydrogen war certain doubts haunt the minds and hearts of the negotiators. The reason for these doubts is, we believe, that a disarmament agreement covering only part of the existing weapon systems would be perceived as relatively unimportant, except insofar as it constituted a temporary break in existing tensions. For there is the almost universal fear of escalation to unlimited war. The logic of the situation therefore tends to drive on the negotiators from limited disarmament to *abolition* of armaments — a very different thing. *Abolition* of arms in contrast to arms *limitation* implies a fundamental change in the structure of the nation-state system; for it requires the abandonment of the use of force as an instrument for the resolution of disputes and for changes in the existing world power structure. In short, abolition of arms means that for the first time men everywhere would be forced to face up to the whole problem of peaceful change until now very largely the preserve of scholars and dreamers.[26]

PRESENT DILEMMAS

So far we have emphasized the fact that present disarmament difficulties are not by any means new to statesmen and those charged with the responsibility of resolving such tangles of power and purpose. But there is one vital respect in which our present situation is very different from past human experience, and that is the *scale* of destruction now possible.[27] Authorities are agreed that there is no upper limit to the size of the bombs that can be made. Bombs of the range of those already tested would produce "terrible fire damage within a circle of twenty miles' radius" with the result that it would require fewer than one hundred such bombs to devastate a country the size of France.[28] The scale of destruction can be better grasped perhaps if we note that "a single hydrogen bomb of 20 megatons, equivalent, that is, to 20 million tons of TNT, possesses fifteen times the destructive power of the total high explosive thrown into Germany in the whole of the last war, and about one hundred times the total high explosive delivered on England in the same period".[29] In addition, there is no doubt that the genetic damage caused by extensive use of atomic and hydrogen weapons in an all-out war would be extremely serious.[30]

The deadly situation brought about by the advent of nuclear weapons has become even clearer since 1955. Since that date both the Soviet Union and the United States have admitted that there is no method now known by which stockpiles of nuclear weapons can be detected.[31] It was this fact which lay behind President Eisenhower's aerial inspection scheme of July 1955. Soviet refusal to accept this proposal led to the notorious U-2 flights, followed by an increasingly sophisticated network of reconnaissance satellites. These last have eased somewhat the phobia for secrecy which held back previous arms control proposals. They do not of course eliminate the problem, since at a certain level of disarmament even small numbers of missiles secretly held back from inclusion would pose a mortal danger to an opponent. Hence the inspection problem emerges at a later stage in any plan and probably demands a reserve stock held by an international authority. Such an authority would be in fact an embryo world government.

At the present state of political development, such an authority is not acceptable to the great powers. What they have evolved is a partial condominium in the shape of the Nuclear Non-Proliferation Treaty which came into force in 1970. By this treaty the nuclear 'haves' agreed not to transfer nuclear weapons to any state and the non-nuclear powers agreed not to receive or manufacture such weapons. The main organ of control is the International Atomic Energy Agency. The agreement has grave weaknesses – it lacks effective sanctions, the inspection system seems inadequate and the necessary political provisions for universal cooperation are lacking. Some states like Brazil have resisted signing since they wish to develop nuclear energy for peaceful purposes. Still others such as Israel feel that a nuclear option (or unadmitted stocks of bombs) would provide a last-ditch type of security. Permanent technical or military inferiority is not a good basis for a lasting agreement.[32] In other words, until the superpowers are prepared to safeguard their security by means other than nuclear arms, they are unlikely to persuade others to renounce for ever the acquisition of nuclear weapons.[33] Treaties to demilitarize Antarctica (1957) and the moon, as well as other celestial bodies (1956), will really prove of very little help unless the great powers come to grips with the substance of the problem confronting them. Regional prohibitions, such as the one applying to Latin America (1967) are a start. Better safeguards, fuel assurances, development of fuel cycles which cannot be used for weapons – all these will help but not resolve the problem.[34] Expressions of goodwill, unaccompanied by far-reaching attempts to deal with the arms race and the security issue, will not be enough.

The arms race now consumes an estimated $350 billion worth of resources each year. It is too simple to say that disarmament can only follow political settlements and that the arms race is a mere result of the political tension. The truth surely is that the two go hand in hand. The arms race is in fact itself a variable of incredible power in the struggle for the world. For a severe and prolonged arms race produces fear and tension in its own right and makes any political settlement extremely difficult. As long as there exists a prospect of one side gaining an advantage in the balance of arms, no political agreement is likely since the new balance could then be used to secure a more favourable arrangement.

If, therefore, any diplomatic settlement is going to be accepted, it is not likely to be one which completely satisfies either side. A demand for complete satisfaction is tantamount to a refusal to negotiate. For the growth of weapons is so complex and various that the lead in arms will inevitably sway back and forth in the course of decades, with the result that the opponent who is temporarily losing the race in a particular weapon will, if he wants complete satisfaction, refuse agreement until he attains equality. A series of ever-increasing cycles of arms expenditure results. It is a race without an end, with first one side then the other getting the lead. At any point along this vicious spiral war may well occur, either because the tensions become too great to bear, or because of a diplomatic miscalculation based on a false estimate of one's own ability to outbluff an opponent who is temporarily behind in the contest. Unless the arms race is resolved, the competition for influence among the great powers will continue to be characterized by fear, hatred and perhaps violence – violence on a scale beyond the imagination's ability to comprehend it.

The Strategic Arms Limitation talks so far give little reason to hope that significant progress is just around the corner.[35] It is true that quantitative limits were set on anti-ballistic missiles in the first SALT agreement. However, qualitative improvements were not covered in that agreement and intensive research continues in this area. On ballistic missiles the 1972 agreement amounted to a five-year freeze on launchers. This meant that the Soviet Union could have 2424 of which 950 could be submarine-launched. The United States was permitted 1710, including a limit of 710 submarine-launched missiles. The agreement took no account of bombers, nor did it deal with warhead numbers. In the 1974 agreement at Vladivostock, both sides agreed to permit multiple warheads on a total of 1320 missiles. This latter figure apparently represented the number planned by the United States, including those to be fitted aboard its new Trident submarine. This means, in effect, that neither side was interested in reducing its on-going programmes.[36] In the case of the United States, this meant that the Pentagon was prepared to have the Soviet Union achieve these extremely high levels rather than accept a reduction in America's own forces. In sum, the strategic arms race has continued with SALT merely formalizing the planned efforts of the parties.[37]

Meanwhile, the combination of multiple warheads and increasing accuracies has raised fears of a first-strike against land-based missiles. This has been particularly true in the United States, since the Soviet Union, while catching up in accuracy, has a distinct advantage in the size of its missiles. Fears are expressed that in the 1980s the Soviets will achieve a 25–1 advantage in the ability to destroy land-based missiles.[38] Pressures are mounting, therefore, to undertake sophisticated programmes of mobile missiles and/or to increase the number of undersea launchers. Efforts to deal with new weapons, such as the cruise missile or the new Soviet bomber, will be tackled in the SALT III negotiations.

The agreements concluded in SALT II do mark a step forward in that a limit of 2250 delivery vehicles has been set. However, this limitation does not deal with the hard fact that the Soviet Union has a distinct lead in deliverable megatons and in throw-weight. The best guess seems to be that the Soviets will have a 7–1 lead in megatons and a 5–1 advantage in throw-weight by 1985.[39] The United States will continue to maintain a substantial advantage in total warheads until 1982, after which this lead will decline. It does seem likely that even after this latter date the United States will continue to lead in bomber- and submarine-launched warheads.

It is important to grasp the fact that the first SALT agreements did nothing to prevent the production of new weapons systems. Indeed, the Russians developed four *new* ICBM's, two *new* submarine-launched types and a new bomber in the interim period. The U.S. deployed one *new* submarine-type missile and is testing another. Fortunately the new SALT agreements only permit one new type of ICBM (inter-continental ballistic missile) to be deployed until 1985 so that some slowdown in the competition has occurred. But unless future negotiations can limit new systems already developed, a new round in the missile race could occur fairly rapidly. Meanwhile, the United States has to face the fact that certain asymmetries have come about which indicate that the momentum of the missile race may have shifted in favour of the Soviet Union. The key question then becomes "Can these asymmetries be translated into strategic gains in the event of war *or* into political gains if war is avoided?". Certainly it is difficult to deny an overall shift in the strategic balance in favour of the Russians, or that the increasing vulnerability of land-based missiles will be a feature of the strategic landscape in the 1980s. Whether this shift will affect the fundamental stability of the strategic balance in the sense that it will make a massive (or limited) strike on land-based missiles a live option is very doubtful. Such a strike would encounter several grave risks – the problem of fratricide (one's own missiles exploding incoming "brother" missiles), the launch-on-warning option, and, above all, the terrible gamble that massive retaliation would not be ordered in the desperate atmosphere resulting from a "successful" attack. It is difficult to believe that any political objectives would justify such a hideous risk.

Soviet strategic advantages could, however, produce plausible potential gains in the political field. These could be, for example, increasing strains in NATO as doubts grew regarding U.S. vulnerabilities and, perhaps, a Soviet "victory" in some brink-of-war crisis. This last could be very dangerous indeed, since, having invested billions to achieve a lead and remembering their backdown in Cuba, the Soviets might feel compelled to demonstrate that these costly efforts were "worth their weight in political leverage".[40] There certainly would be tremendous pressures on the Soviets not to back down. The United States, on the other hand, knowing that the strategic momentum has passed to Moscow, might be reluctant to accept a crisis decision which confirmed that the strategic advantage lay with the Russians. The dangers inherent in this sort of situation are in fact increased by the differing military doctrines of the parties.[41] The United States has emphasized secure second-strike forces, limited war forces to extend deterrence and the avoidance of threats to Soviet second-strike forces. The Soviets, on the other hand, have stressed preemptive strikes against an impending attack, degrading of the second-strike by massive civil defences and deterrence as a function of aggregate military capabilities. This divergence of views does *not* mean that the Soviets could actually make a preemptive strike work but rather that such an attitude might lead them in such a direction in a crisis.

At any rate, one can conclude that we could be entering a less stable period of nuclear deterrence with increased possibilities for miscalculation. What is the correct course to pursue? Details aside, we suggest that insistence on the logic of American attitudes to deterrence (no threats to second-strike forces, etc.) is not enough. Moscow must be convinced rather, by Western programmes and by their attitudes, that they are not prepared to accept significant inferiorities in the area of strategic threats to land-based missiles; that, while they prefer reductions to increases as a way of achieving parity, they are determined to attain it. If they do not do so, Soviet political influence will grow, Western confidence will decline and overall stability will be eroded. The most likely result will be a sharp rise in spending on missiles, after a new panic, and a huge increase in missile numbers. In such an atmosphere political agreements and increased cooperation would be the victims.

Finally, some progress needs to be achieved in the burgeoning field of arms sales. In 1977 U.S. sales were about $11.3 billion and for 1978 sales totalled $13.2 billion. The Soviet Union's efforts in this field of endeavour are relatively modest by U.S. standards, a mere $4 billion. Very little effort has gone into seeking agreements with other major NATO suppliers — Britain, France, Sweden, Belgium to name a few — let alone the Soviet Union. This trade now includes not just "obsolescent" weapons but very advanced weapons systems, weapons so advanced that they require the employment in host countries of large numbers of U.S. trained personnel.[42] In 1965 fourteen developing countries had supersonic jets and eight had ground-to-air missiles. In 1976 forty-four had jets and twenty-six had missiles. Many countries now have begun defence industries and some states – Iran and Saudi Arabia for example – now finance part of the development of certain weapons.[43] The international arms trade is a buyer's market. One result is that weapons are transferred from one country to another. Again, stockpiles grow to the point where war can be waged without great power agreement. Terrorists may be able in the not-too-distant future to buy new weapons such as missiles and advanced electronic systems.

The great powers engage in this enormous trade for a variety of reasons; for example, to enlarge the production "run" of a weapon and thus lower its cost, to obtain foreign exchange, to test weapon effectiveness in actual war, and to promote political stability or instability. It is difficult not to agree with the judgement that "the likelihood that the major suppliers can agree ... on guidelines for the limitations of arms exports ... remains low."[44]

In conclusion, we must face squarely the fact that present efforts at arms control, while they have introduced some restraints into the competition, have not prevented a huge increase in Soviet military power. Nor have they done very much to inhibit technical developments which threaten to create new and dangerous instabilities in deterrence. Moreover, continuing political tensions are clearly threatening to vitiate the effects of those agreements which exist, at least judging by the angry Senate debates over whether to ratify the SALT II accords.

Several paths of possible action remain open at this juncture. The Western powers must make it clear that, while they are not prepared to accept permanent military inferiority, they are ready to try by negotiation to achieve significant reductions in arms and to expand the political détente with the Soviet Union.[45] This last point is of vital importance for it is difficult to believe that new military agreements could be achieved in the face of rising tensions and increasing Russian pressures whether in the NATO area or in the Middle East.

If such negotiations proved fruitful, it might then be possible to embark upon measures which led to significant disarmament. The alternatives are not pleasant to contemplate. Vast new programmes of military research will produce new weapons systems and these will tend to outrun efforts to control them. Technology will be in the saddle and will ride mankind.[46] But this is not our inevitable future. It may be that all we are capable of at the present is partial agreements. This is not satisfactory as a final goal, and will not remove the dangers of an increasing arms burden, new unknown weapons, the gradual spread of nuclear weapons to new states and increasing tension and fear which could end in a disastrous conflict. But we need to let the goal of general and complete disarmament, which alone can remove these dangers, inform our diplomacy as an ideal. As always with ideals in politics, there is a precarious middle path. Utopianism can lead to selective blindness or disillusion. Cynicism can lead to apathy and indecision and can become a self-fulfilling prophecy. It is true that the nuclear age has not produced significant changes in the attitudes of the superpowers to the basic problems of arms control and disarmament. Agreements are reached but they tend to be on matters which effect the competition in arms only marginally. Quantitative curbs lead to qualitative improvements. Limits tend to be set at levels which embody existing force-planning. Negotiations lag behind new weapons developments. The task of calculating the balance of overall military strength has proved as insuperable as it did in the inter-war period. Differences in geographical situations, military doctrines and political objectives have prevented significant reductions in the overall level of arms. Indeed, this level goes on increasing at an ominous rate. But what is the proper response to this situation? We can put the matter in the terms of the first chapter of this book. Those involved in the arms control process need *both* to hold on to their intuition that nothing short of general disarmament will lead to a peaceful world *and* allow the movement towards this goal to be continually hampered by the need to compromise in favour of the moral claims of national security or the balance of power or a vulnerable ally. To complain that this is logically inconsistent is to fail to understand the nature of moral thinking.

But this is not to say that it is not in practice enormously difficult. The long-term goals of general disarmament and the evolution of a peaceful world community need to be kept in view as objectives for the future. They will not be achieved, however, if short-term efforts continue to be swallowed up or bypassed in the continuing struggle for power. Hence, it is vital for the superpowers to agree on political restraints which will begin to reduce tensions and permit a reduction in the pace of the competition in arms whether conventional or nuclear. Beyond this basic principle there is no one clear path to enhanced security. It is easy to suggest possible alternatives: a determination on the part of the Western powers to demonstrate their will to match growing Soviet military power as a necessary condition for any progress; an agreement to curb or eliminate new nuclear weapons systems by a comprehensive agreement to ban all nuclear tests; nuclear-free zones and limits on the sale of conventional arms as well as restraints on military activities in regions, such as the Middle East, where potential conflicts could lead to serious confrontation and escalation; the strengthening of safeguards against nuclear proliferation and, eventually, drastic reductions in nuclear weapons to an agreed-upon level of minimum deterrence.[47] Clearly the possibilities of these short-term alternatives are dependent upon available political opportunities and changing circumstances. It requires a quite sophisticated judgement to determine on each occasion how likely they are to succeed and how much they reduce the dangers of nuclear war and conventional conflicts which could get out of hand. No easy moral generalizations concerning these short-term objectives are possible. But, because such measures could lead to reduced tensions and progress in either arms control or some degree of disarmament, they, and other measures like them, should be pursued with resolution and imagination. To achieve more is almost certainly impossible given the present strained international climate. But not to press ahead would be a failure of moral nerve and might well lead to a series of major conflicts, an accelerating arms race and a potential disaster of the very first magnitude.[48]

7 The Problems of World Order

When we face honestly the perils and problems which make up the world scene, it is easy to abandon hope completely. It *is* possible that events have grown so complex and the pressures so relentless that we will not be able to escape the disaster created by our own ambitions and fears, and above all by the power placed in our hands by modern science wedded to the nation state. To accept this vision of the future is to adopt a counsel of despair. For if we cannot avoid this disaster, then we do not have the obligation to try to avoid it. The alternative is to seek by every possible means the long-term goal of world order – the evolution of a peaceful and just world community in which inter-state conflict is minimized if not abolished and in which procedures are established for the peaceful settlement of disputes. This is the goal of reasonable men in most governments as it has been the vision of scholars and dreamers for centuries past. To work for this goal is to accept that progress towards it is not impossible. Moreover now that mankind has the potential ability, in the shape of nuclear weapons, to destroy his own civilization, the avoidance of nuclear war has become for all nations an ethical and political imperative. This is a challenge which they cannot escape and which is harder than any they have ever had to face.

At this point, however, agreement ends for the simple reason that arguments proceed on different premises. We will try to set out clearly and succinctly the basic assumptions which underlie the arguments that follow. *First*, no sudden transformation of the existing state system by a grand design can be achieved, all schemes to the contrary notwithstanding. Such schemes simply assume what they need to prove and thus beg all the major questions at issue. There is not a master plan for world order in the sense of an effective, on-going scheme of action, agreed to and deliberately pursued by the powers. The fundamental reasons which prevent such a solution are the determination of states to maintain the elements of sovereignty, including the use of armed force, and equally vital, a lack of consensus on basic political values.

Second, the rivalry between the Soviet Union and the United States will persist into the foreseeable future. This competition can be reduced or expanded but it cannot be eliminated under present conditions.

Third, no effective international institutions exist capable of dealing with the major problems of war and peaceful change.

Fourth, demands for economic development will continue at an accelerated rate under the pressure of growing populations and increasing poverty in the Third World, despite the threat of global pollution.

Given the above premises, is it possible to suggest a set of *prima facie* ethical principles which would serve as guidelines in the evolution of state policies? The essential idea behind such a set of principles is that there should not be an outright competition without thought of limits and with no rules for avoiding collision. It is true that the conflicts which would likely emerge from an uncontrolled competition need not be nuclear or even, in many instances, large in scope; yet the danger of such struggles becoming both large and nuclear would exist. Further, even if such dangers could be avoided on one or more occasions, their continued occurrence would inevitably raise the stakes and the risks for the parties as the process went on. For in such encounters someone would lose and someone would win, and there could come about, perhaps by imperceptible degrees, a perceived shift in the world balance of power. Such a moment would be a time of maximum danger and might produce decisions which could lead to the breakdown of deterrence.

In short, it would appear as if the great powers are embarked upon a time of intense competition — by intervention through proxies, by arms aid on a very large scale, by playing upon the internal weaknesses and instabilities of the other states and, to some extent, by the active use of the blacker arts of power politics. In view of the potential dangers of this process, the perfectly rational course of action would be complete abstention by the great powers. For many reasons this will not happen; and unilateral abstention would mean the defeat of the virtuous abstainer. Some competition, even fairly intense competition, is likely. But such a contest should be entered into with a full recognition of the hazards involved and a clear admission that it is a lesser evil, a stage on the road to a more civilized and productive relationship. For it does make a world of difference, both practical and moral, that such a choice be made with an appreciation of its limitations. It is *not* a game to be played for its own sake, as if it were the final goal of policy.

We would suggest that there are five *prima facie* principles which might be useful in the present situation. There is an obligation *first*, to maintain an overall balance of power such that no state is in a position to engage in large-scale expansion; to maintain the central balance of nuclear power and regional balances (in particular the European balance); and to avoid any attempt to achieve an overall superiority such as would result, for example, from the large-scale rearmament of China or Japan; *second*, to exercise restraint through limitation upon coercive intervention; *third*, to reduce the dangers of direct confrontation; *fourth*, to work for a more equal distribution of the world's resources; *fifth*, to strengthen existing international institutions and to build, wherever possible, new international regimes which would help resolve emerging issues of energy, the use of ocean resources and the like.

These five principles taken together could, if acted upon, maintain the elements of order present in existing world politics and, at the same time, gradually expand upon these to decrease tensions and build more lasting forms of cooperation among states. The fourth would, if acted upon, assist in making the existing order more just. We recognize, however, that progress in these matters will not be linear, that setbacks are bound to occur and that the whole effort could easily revert to unrestrained competition and war. Moreover, the *prima facie* rules may have to be modified or overridden if sufficient mutual reciprocity does not develop.

FUTURE MILITARY TECHNOLOGY AND THE BALANCE OF POWER

The first of these principles is difficult to apply for many reasons. It is notoriously difficult to know what power is and what counts as an equal amount of it. We mentioned this difficulty in the previous chapter. Morgenthau divides the elements of national power under eight headings: geography, natural resources, industrial capacity, military preparedness, population, national character, national morale, and the quality of diplomacy.[1] But his list is constructed for the purposes of his own analysis, and different lists could be made. In any case, the principle that the balance should be maintained requires constant assessment of a large number of variables, most of which are extremely hard to measure. Martin Wight said that to assess the balance, and know the threshold between agitating it and overthrowing it, was "the highest art of the statesman".[2] The most conspicuous of these variables is military preparedness, though it is not much more easily measurable than most of the others. We would like to discuss some of the new military technologies and how they affect the balance between the powers. For some of the new weapons, if they are built, may put enormous pressures on the other side and may make the balance much more difficult to maintain in the future.

There have been opportunities like this in the past, which have not been taken, to control problems before they become unmanageable. Thus it would have been comparatively easy, following the Second World War, to control atomic weapons through the control of fissionable materials. But as stockpiles grew it became necessary to try to control delivery systems in the shape of aircraft, a much more difficult problem. Inspection and control was delayed in fact until the age of the ballistic missile and the difficulties of control have been multiplied enormously. Similarly, the great powers today have an obligation to do what they can to prevent the growth of the number of nuclear powers and the dissemination of stocks of atomic-hydrogen weapons. For it should be clear that such a growth in nuclear capability and such a dispersal of weapons would gravely complicate the problems of control and increase the probability of wars occurring through accident or design. In short, the powers cannot justifiably permit themselves to be overwhelmed by events when, in point of fact, the dilemmas can be foreseen and forestalled. The problems do not have to be solved if they can be *avoided*.

Some of the most pressing examples of this kind of ethical dilemma occur in the area of developing military technology, and there are here some additional difficulties.[3] Development is a constant process with no precise lines which mark off new from old weapons. Historically, military men have had very great difficulty in perceiving the implications of new technology and hence tend to prefer to insure against uncertainty by keeping as many options open as possible and stressing the need for flexibility. Many (but not all) technologies cannot be tested in actual combat, and so judgements must rest on data which are bound to be inconclusive.[4] Rarely have technological assessments of weapons arrived at in peace been supported by the test of war.[5] This fact alone precludes any form of dogmatic assertion whether it be military, political or ethical in nature. Yet choices are being made which have serious implications in all these areas and therefore some assessment of the problems they pose is demanded.

It is undeniable that some link exists between technological change and arms control but the relationship is not a simple one. Early theories which held that the arms race was a straightforward action–reaction phenomenon[6] are not supported by the evidence.[7] The sad truth is that no really adequate explanation exists at this point in time; hence no clear-cut conclusions can be drawn concerning ways to check, much less to eliminate, arms competition. This is the beginning of wisdom in these matters. But can we say more? Yes, we can, but answers will depend upon judgements concerning the actual experience of states and this experience is subject to sharply differing interpretations.[8]

The orthodox arms control view is that a series of agreements beginning in the 1950s and continuing in the present SALT negotiations have limited, and have prospects of continuing to limit, arms competition. This view grew up in the period 1958–61 and became accepted doctrine for the Arms Control and Disarmament Agency established by the U.S. Department of State in 1961. Briefly, these views rested on the felt need to stabilize nuclear deterrence through technical control of arms. The idea was to include measures of arms control which would keep an unstable balance stable and prevent escalation.[9] The main developments proceeded from a criticism of the policy of massive retaliation enunciated by John Foster Dulles. It questioned the credibility of this policy when applied to the defence of areas not of vital interest to the United States, advocated the use of tactical nuclear weapons in certain circumstances (Kissinger), argued the feasibility of limited war strategies (Osgood, Halperin), warned against the dangers of escalation (Knorr and Read) and urged the need for superpower communication and active cooperation (Schelling). Arms control measures were seen as necessary to reassure the two giants that no surprise attacks were in the offing. Hence the Surprise Attack Conference of 1958 which attempted to provide technical solutions to specific problems of strategic stability. The drive for a comprehensive ban on nuclear testing followed. It resulted in a three-year moratorium which was broken by the Soviet Union following failure to agree on technical means of verifying such a ban. This failure led to the signing of the

Partial Test Ban Treaty (1962) banning nuclear tests in the air, outer space and under water. Even the arms control advocates were forced to admit that the latter treaty "placed no significant restraint on the development of new nuclear weapons".[10]

The lesson of this period of arms control effort was that significant arms control cannot be achieved through purely technical means but only if the effort extends also to the political relations of the superpowers. This lesson, alas, was *not* in fact learned. Technical means were employed again in the effort to halt nuclear proliferation by means of the Non-Proliferation Treaty, the halt on anti-ballistic missile deployment, a restraint on MIRVs (multiple independently targetable re-entry vehicles) and the freeze on strategic forces at the Strategic Arms Limitation talks. Except for the ABM treaty, which did prevent deployment but not continued research, it is highly doubtful whether the other agreements had any significant impact on either the proliferation of nuclear weapons or the expansion of the missile forces of the superpowers. India, for example, developed a nuclear weapon, Israel is believed to have done so, and several other states seem to be in the process of building and/or purchasing nuclear reactors. As for SALT, the follow-on temporary agreement at Vladivostock provided for an enormous expansion in warheads, a number which almost certainly reflected the upper limit of superpower plans and desires.[11] The latter development is particularly revealing. In fact, the United States began deployment of MIRV warheads in 1972, three years before the first Soviet test and by the time of SALT II had 800 deployed, whereas the Soviet Union had none. The Vladivostock agreements then went on to permit *each* side 1320 MIRVs, which meant in effect that the United States preferred to have the Soviet Union build up to that level from zero rather than to drop any of its own deployed MIRVs.[12] Nor did the United States propose to trade any follow-on systems such as the Trident submarine or the B-1 bomber.

This suggests not only that great powers are reluctant to surrender a technical lead if they have it but that they may not even be prepared to use it to bargain for significant restrictions on an opponent. At first sight this seems odd, perhaps even irrational. But there are a number of reasons for this behaviour. There is, first of all, the momentum of programmes planned and carried out by powerful military and civilian bureaucracies. Perhaps more significantly, there are the advantages of even a temporary lead in other political bargaining, the unattractiveness of the extensive and perhaps unachievable controls necessary for effective monitoring, and the prospects of continuing asymmetries in technical development with their consequent effects on political attitudes to deterrence. To condemn these reactions as irrational is to fail to see how little can in fact be achieved by purely technical arms control measures. For arms control is a highly political process involving the power relationships of the parties and is hence subject to the influence of differing political objectives; the Soviets are determined to achieve strategic and political parity with the United States, which is determined to resist or at least to delay this as long as possible. Nor is this by any means the end of the story. It can be argued with considerable cogency that military innovation through new technology is in certain cases positively desirable.[13] The most obvious case is where one side enjoys advantages in numbers, equipment or geography; in these cases technical innovation may very well reduce the dangers of conflict by maintaining a military equilibrium. The NATO–Warsaw Pact example is a case in point. Secondly, the deployment of less vulnerable weapons may significantly increase the stability of deterrence by reducing the dangers of surprise attack. An example here would be the deployment of nuclear submarines in the 1960s. Again, the development of accurate delivery systems clearly reduces the collateral damage of weapons and hence the destructiveness of war if it should occur. If such a process went far enough, conventional weapons might significantly reduce the pressure to resort to the use of nuclear weapons. Thirdly, constant military innovation introduces complicated calculations as to the performance of military forces and hence inhibits the confidence necessary for aggressive action.

But once all these reasons have been given, it still needs to be said that military innovation can and does have effects which are costly and dangerous and which are not attended by proportionate benefits. Some technical developments may increase damage, not limit it. Some may widen sharply the geographical boundaries of conflict. New weapons may make the problem of balancing forces in a negotiation much more difficult by creating significant asymmetries in military capabilities. If such a process goes far enough, arms control negotiations may be interrupted until the parties have reached a new level of rough equality. In the latter case governments are in effect being forced to choose between new additions which may be useful to offset an opponent's advantage (or attain an advantage of one's own) and the benefits which might or might not be achieved by continuing negotiations. In short, some technical advances should on balance be supported for both ethical and political reasons, because they help stabilize nuclear deterrence or reduce the dangers of conflict escalation; but others should on balance be rejected for directly opposite reasons. What is needed, therefore, is some way to discriminate between the two, not a blind assumption that military innovation is always politically and ethically desirable or on the other hand that it is always a victory of expediency over morality.

The issue is that new technologies exist which, if deployed, would "seriously erode the second-strike capability of land-based missiles".[14] This means that nuclear stability will be threatened, a stability which has effectively eliminated the occurrence of general war between the superpowers. A number of extremely accurate guidance systems – the *Tercom*, which matches terrain contours, the *AIRS* system, which is being developed for the new U.S. mobile missile called the MX, and a new programme for the undersea missile Poseidon – will reduce current circular error probabilities (CEP) to estimates which range from 200 to 1000 feet. New small engines weighing 100 to 150 pounds have been developed which will power missiles over ranges up to 2000 miles. A variety of new conventional warheads has been produced which, combined with the small cruise missile and the Tercom system, could be used against targets which can now be destroyed only by nuclear weapons. Developments in communications involving satellites, over-the-horizon radar, data-processing and re-targeting capabilities have increased the ability of the U.S. and the U.S.S.R. to launch limited, selective nuclear strikes. Finally, interceptor satellites are being tested and large research efforts are going into the detection of submarines and into ballistic missile defences. The suggestion has been made that these developments have called into question the future viability of fixed-site land-based missiles and have raised the spectre that the powers might be tempted to fight a limited nuclear war. In particular, it is argued that these developments have increased the dangers of a pre-emptive strike against opposing missiles in a grave crisis.[15] The conclusion is drawn that the vulnerability of land-based missiles should be reduced by making them mobile (at enormous expense) or by a strategy of launching missiles when the full scale of an attack becomes clear.

But one can and probably should question the likelihood of an attempt to destroy either of the superpowers' land-based force; for such an attack would not only pose immense problems of coordination, but have unknown effects upon one's own incoming missiles (the so-called fratricide problem). The huge uncertainties of an opponent's response would make such an attack an enormous gamble. It is estimated, for example, that a Soviet attack on the American ICBM force would produce a range of casualties extending from 10 to 25 millions, and it would be reasonable for them to fear that no American government would tolerate such enormous losses without retaliation. Moreover, by the time these new technologies make such a counterforce strike a theoretical possibility, the United States will have an estimated 6000–10,000 warheads capable of surviving a pre-emptive strike, in the shape of submarine-launched missiles, bombers and cruise missiles. This is a formidable force and it is hard to imagine a rational Soviet government ignoring this potentially devastating capability.

These arguments, while cogent, have apparently not been persuasive enough to prevent the development of the MX missile at an estimated cost of over thirty billion dollars. In part, this is a price which the Carter administration has had to pay for Senate ratification of the SALT II agreements. It is a sorry example of how the competition in arms produces a spiralling effect difficult to resist. The United States is not prepared to accept the strategic and political consequences which might flow from having its Minuteman force vulnerable even though its counter-response in the shape of the MX system could threaten Soviet missiles with a first-strike and hence produce a further Soviet effort, leaving both parties worse off. In this case, research and development on the MX may be justified, but its deployment should not be undertaken without serious efforts to protect the Minuteman force through negotiations and Soviet reductions. We do not believe that it is right to go ahead and ignore the huge waste of resources and the long-range destabilizing effects of deployment.

It does seem that it would be sensible to attempt to control the deployment, if not the development, of anti-satellite technologies. Since both sides may have achieved reasonable equivalence in this area, some hope exists of success in such negotiations. The same cannot be said of efforts to slow down anti-submarine warfare technology. Here, despite the heavy curtain of secrecy, the United States apparently has quite a substantial lead. This lead, together with the geographical problems posed for the Soviet navy by its four fleet areas and restricted access ways to the world's oceans, gives the United States a significant advantage which will not be lightly surrendered. This advantage is almost the exact equivalent, strategically speaking, of the geographic advantage held by the powerful Soviet land forces in Central Europe. And it is not a mere coincidence that attempts to negotiate away these advantages have been met, in the Vienna discussions on mutually-balanced force reductions, with a Soviet refusal.

Two rather special examples of technological innovation remain to be discussed: the cruise missile and the neutron bomb. The former weapon can be armed with either nuclear or conventional warheads. Cheap to produce and extremely accurate, it could substitute for small nuclear weapons against some types of targets. It is, therefore, clearly preferable to nuclear weapons from an ethical point of view on the grounds that it significantly reduces collateral damage to lives and property. Its opponents argue that it would lower the threshold at which escalation to nuclear war occurred and, therefore, should not be deployed. Clearly, it also complicates considerably the problems of inspection since it could, as has been said, be armed with either nuclear or conventional warheads. On the other hand, the Soviet Union has significant advantages over the Western allies by reason of its very large numbers of intermediate range ballistic missiles (the SS-20).[16] It is true, of course, that the Soviet Union has, for more than two decades, used its superiority in the medium- and intermediate-range delivery systems to compensate for American strategic superiority. This threat was real enough in that in some sense Europe was a hostage to the good behaviour of the United States but it was a threat which was tolerated because a large American strategic lead offered a counter-balancing effect. In addition, the older Soviet missiles (the SS-4 and the SS-5) were slow-reacting and relatively inaccurate.

The new situation is vastly different for several reasons. The new SS-20 is mobile, highly accurate, and has a cluster of warheads such that it poses a first-strike threat to a wide variety of European and NATO retaliatory forces. When this fact is combined with the achievement of over-all strategic parity by the Soviet Union, the distinct possibility arises that these new Soviet forces might be used in a conflict or their use threatened in a crisis without producing a U.S. reaction. In short, a kind of deterrent gap has been created in the European area with the result that the regional balance is in danger of being decoupled from the central balance. The situation is further complicated by the fact that the SS-20 can be easily and quickly converted to a long-range missile (the SS-16) thus posing serious verification problems for any arms control agreement covering these two weapons. Anyhow, to include these weapons in future SALT III negotiations would threaten NATO cohesion and would probably not achieve results since the Soviet advantage is so very great that only a large reduction of the SS-20 would prove meaningful.[17] Early Soviet diplomatic moves hinted at marginal reductions in the obvious hope that this would delay a NATO counter-buildup.[18]

The technical details of this general problem are quite complicated but the fundamental issues are clear. The United States must not allow the full range of deterrence to be undermined. This means the regional balance in Europe must be maintained in a way which closes the gap in deterrence opened by the SS-20. Whether the correct military response is the deployment of a limited force of cruise missiles or a new version of the Pershing II with a range capable of reaching the Soviet Union is a matter which cannot be competently discussed by these authors. But some response must be made and unless it is clear that European states are willing to accept the political costs of deploying some counter-weapons and the United States demonstrates its determination to proceed, there is little hope of Soviet agreement on major reductions.

There is, therefore, an *initial* ethical case for an effort to maintain the full spectrum of deterrence, preferably by negotiation but, if necessary, by the deployment of offsetting weapons. If it is true that the cruise missile poses special dangers of eroding the SALT agreements (and its versatility clearly poses such dangers), this is also true of the SS-20 because it has both a regional and a potential intercontinental role with a configuration which makes adequate satellite inspection difficult. Thus, the powers are clearly at an important crossroads in their arms control relationship and the consequences could be an upward turn in the arms race and a further blow to détente. A balance must be struck therefore before further progress can be made towards cooperation. If the Soviets prove adamant and cling to their superiority, a new NATO force would be justified. If a reasonable solution could emerge by agreement, then this would be preferable if it provided security and at the same time preserved the integrity of the SALT process. Alas, in this case, stabilized nuclear deterrence in Europe and a strengthened SALT may turn out to be mutually exclusive alternatives. If this is the case, whether one chooses the risks of a weakened deterrent in Europe in the hope of preserving the SALT process or the reverse, becomes to a large extent a matter of judgement as to Soviet future behaviour. It is easy, therefore, to differ on how to proceed. What is reasonably clear is that a large and continuing Soviet military buildup not only poses threats to the stability of deterrence in its many aspects but threatens détente itself. Indeed, one can argue that the Soviet Union is in danger of creating a hostile coalition against itself composed of the United States, Europe and China. Such a self-imposed threat of encirclement could prove a long-run danger to peace. It should be the central task of Western diplomacy to avoid this if at all possible.

Because of its special characteristics, the neutron bomb poses special ethical problems for decision-makers. It is a tactical nuclear warhead which maximizes radiation and minimizes heat and blast effects. Tank crews are vulnerable to intense radiation so that the neutron weapon is thought to be an extremely effective weapon against large-scale tank attacks. At the same time, the weapon would reduce the massive collateral damage which has been hitherto associated with tactical nuclear weapons. As with the cruise missile, fears have been widely expressed that such a weapon would lower the nuclear threshold. This seems a dubious argument. After all, the neutron bomb *is* a nuclear weapon and its use in a conflict would pose clearly the risks of escalation. In addition, its potential for blunting or stopping a major Soviet armoured thrust and thus eroding the commanding Russian lead in tanks is reasonably clear. It would at the very least create another level of uncertainty about what the response would be to an attack.

The moral issues raised by the neutron bomb do not end here.[19] The use of the bomb may violate the prohibition discussed in Chapter 3 on the avoidable killing of innocent people, or the principle of non-escalation discussed in Chapter 5. In relation to the first, it is clear that all persons in a target area not protected against radiation would suffer those effects so that the weapon does not discriminate between non-combatants and attackers. Because of its lower blast damage, the neutron bomb would, however, be a lesser evil than existing tactical weapons and also conventional bombs which, if used in large numbers, produce enormous casualties from blast and fire. There would, of course, be some long-term radiation effects from the use of neutron weapons and hence these effects would have to be calculated in any moral summation. In relation to non-escalation, the evaluation of the neutron bomb would vary with the numbers and the scale of the attack. It might, for example, be a moderate response to the crossing of the nuclear "firebreak" by an opponent. If the ideal is to keep at a minimum the damage of war to civilization, it is difficult not to agree with a current writer that the neutron warhead "represents movement toward such a goal when we make the comparison with the other weapons of contemporary warfare it is designed to replace".[20]

In sum, then, recent and potential technologies form a very mixed ethical bag indeed. Some new non-nuclear technologies (the cruise missile armed with conventional warheads) can substitute for nuclear weapons. This has the morally desirable effect of reducing destruction and at the same time widens the important threshold between nuclear and non-nuclear choices.[21] It also has significant moral gains on the political side. NATO faces a powerful opponent against which the alliance can now act effectively without threatening to commit suicide. It seems undeniable that political decisions to resist attack would be much more likely to be taken if such actions would result in reduced civilian damage. Finally, really powerful weapons which can be used with great accuracy put aggressors at a disadvantage. If, for example, the aggressor's strategy is to concentrate large forces in order to launch a "blitzkrieg" attack in Europe, these forces will be particularly vulnerable to this kind of weapon.

INTERVENTION

The second *prima facie* principle concerns the practice of unilateral and competitive intervention. Intervention has been defined by a leading authority as "forcible interference, short of declaring war, by one or more powers in the affairs of another power".[22] That is to say intervention involves the notion of "coercion short of war".[23] It always involves the use or threat of force, whether in the internal or external affairs of another state. It may be invited or not and it may involve a desire to change or to preserve the existing distribution of power. In short, the term "intervention" covers a vast array of very different sorts of political action and no simple moral principle can cover them all. We will suggest at the end of this section that a set of principles can be stated rather similar to those we discussed in connection with just war theory in Chapter 3.

The moral analyst gets very little help from international law. This is partly because intervention involves a conflict of two basic principles – the right of self-defence and the right of self-government. All nations recognize that intervention is "unlawful" but they do not agree "on what is this intervention that is unlawful".[24] This disagreement began to take its modern form following the end of the

Napoleonic wars when Austria and France intervened in 1821 and 1823 in Italy and Spain, respectively, to prevent revolution in these states, when the United States proclaimed the Monroe Doctrine to preserve the independence of the rebellious Spanish colonies and when the great powers intervened on various occasions to protect, on grounds of humanity, the inhabitants of the Ottoman empire. Disagreements were even sharper when political change was involved, for example in a rebellion or civil war, and it was controversial at what stage support for one side or the other was "justified". Whether consent of an existing government does or does not excuse intervention is still a matter of dispute, with the positions depending upon whether or not the government in question is held to represent the free choice of the people.[25] In despair, one authority concludes that the only clear line is to hold to the view that Article 2 (4) of the United Nations Charter prohibits cases of "direct, overt aggression capable of objective and persuasive proof".[26]

The legal result is to leave the problem in a kind of limbo. If agreed-upon legal norms existed, great moral weight could be attached to their maintenance or violation; but where, as here, this is not the case, moral analysis is left to appraise the issues involved with precious little support from the legal writers.

Before attempting an analysis of a range of cases, some general considerations can be advanced. In the first place *not* to intervene may have as serious consequences as actually to intervene. The case of the civil war in Spain is an example, where the Western powers refused to act and thereby aided the victory of the rebels under Franco. This case exemplifies the famous comment of Talleyrand that "non-intervention is a term of political metaphysics signifying almost the same thing as intervention". It could also be argued that in the case of intervention against a great power which is already involved in a country the burden of moral proof lies on the intervening state, since great powers are clearly likely to resist intervention by force.[27] While this criterion by itself would not *justify* the successive U.S. interventions in Central America, it would render them less objectionable simply because less risky. It is also true that collective intervention by the great powers poses fewer dangers to the general peace than unilateral intervention. Such collective undertakings assume agreement on rules of behaviour which would in effect be a return to the concert system of the nineteenth century. A pattern of this sort could emerge over time and would be an immense improvement over present great power behaviour which relies on unilateral action and sometimes accepts the risks of competitive intervention through the use of proxies. It should be pointed out, however, that the concert system systematically ignored demands for justice by the smaller powers. To the extent that these powers have gained in influence their demands will be harder to ignore.

Beyond this point the moral problems become more difficult and it is often hard to discover clear guidelines. The key general issue, however, revolves around one's view of the importance of the balance of power as a general force for order, stability and peace. If, as a matter of empirical fact, a stable balance tends to reduce the chances of war, then intervention to maintain such a state of affairs would have considerable moral merit; though this is not a point of view which would find much support in "revolutionary" capitals. But even disregarding the balance, it is not true that revolutionary regimes always make conditions better for their people, or always make them worse, and each case of intervention therefore has to be judged on its own merits. If this is objected to by visceral anti-communists, it should be pointed out that it might well be desirable for the Western powers to intervene temporarily in order to prevent cases of gross injustice or to undercut those regimes, whether communist or not, which clearly present an active threat to the peace of the region. Thus intervention to bring down a barbaric regime like Amin's in Uganda was met with wide moral acceptance.

In general, a test which might survive moral scrutiny would be this: If intervention threatens to change permanently the existing territorial balance of power, it should be ruled out as too dangerous. For such radical shifts threaten to produce counter-action and hence pose considerable dangers of wider conflict. It is an empirical fact, borne out by many examples, that "attempts to preserve the status quo, even if accompanied by measures of the utmost brutality, appear to be viewed with greater tolerance by the opposite camp than forcible efforts towards a change in the world balance".[28] This is a political fact with moral implications. The main point is that a balance of power is highly dynamic and that strong measures will be taken to prevent serious reductions in the power of one's own side and to counter increases in the power of the other. This kind of behaviour by states has been reduced by one leading scholar to three rules:

1. States inside one's own camp must, if at all possible, be prevented from leaving the fold; 2. States on the 'wrong side' of the world fence must, if possible, be induced to change sides or, at

least, to join the ranks of the non-committed countries; and 3. Non-committed countries which cannot be persuaded to join one's own camp must be kept in this position and be prevented from joining the opposite camp[29]

Sceptics who doubt that these general rules do describe the behaviour of states would do well to contemplate examples ranging from the Soviet suppression of the Hungarian Revolution in 1956 to U.S. interventions in Guatemala (1954) and Lebanon (1958), and the tactics of Castro to maintain the non-aligned front in the Havana Conference of 1979.

At this point we should like to examine a range of cases which involve other aspects of the moral dilemmas posed by intervention: in particular, the moral issues involved in political assassination as a form of intervention, the cases of U.S. intervention in Chile, Zaire and Angola, and the use of arms aid as an instrument of policy.

Political assassination – the murder of a public figure for political purposes – has been known since ancient times and is much commoner than is usually supposed. One list, prepared for the National Commission on the Causes and Prevention of Violence, found some 1500 in the period 1918–1968.[30] This list is obviously unreliable; many assassinations are not reported in the press, and on the other hand some political figures are murdered for personal, not political, reasons. If one confines the list to successful and attempted assassinations of chief executives for the same fifty-year period, the number is approximately 220.[31] There is some evidence that assassination is more frequently resorted to during and immediately after periods of war; but since the period covered is so short, one cannot be very confident of this generalization. For similar reasons, indications that the Middle East and Latin America have been more prone to this kind of violence are suggestive but not in any way conclusive. Assassination in totalitarian states tends to be relatively rare except when the government itself engages in the practice. It is equally difficult to generalize about the effects of assassination. If a regime was weak and fragmented by tensions, the death of a leader sometimes led to the end of the regime.[32] But in cases where the government has the stability which stems from popular support and recognized constitutional processes, the political impact can be minor.

When all of this has been said, it came as a great shock to the American people to learn that their own government, under several

Presidents, had been involved in attempts to remove by assassination or by *coup d'état* several foreign leaders, namely Patrice Lumumba, Fidel Castro, Rafael Trujillo and Premier Diem.[33] The official Senate report presents a difficult problem for the objective observer. There were obvious efforts to see that no one administration was singled out for blame, and participants often "lost" their ability to remember at key points. Moreover efforts had been made to protect Presidents by the use of indirect orders and vague euphemisms for the ugly word "murder", and so on. Nevertheless, some key conclusions did emerge: two cases (Lumumba and Castro) were instigated by U.S. officials; two involved coups in which the U.S. knew that killing was likely (Trujillo and Diem); an assassination capability was created and that fact made known to the President's National Security Advisor; agents of organized crime were involved in one plot; the Director of the C.I.A. (Helms) testified to his belief that the organization had been authorized to kill Castro[34] and that a Special Group had been set up to shield the President in case things went wrong.

One Senator, commenting about the nature of the evidence, said that on balance the likelihood that Presidents knew of the assassination plots was greater than the likelihood that they did not. This is a modest conclusion. Ordinary people, confronted with the stories of commands given, however obliquely, of weapons supplied to dissident groups, and so on, would have little doubt that agents of the U.S. government engaged in political murder with the sanction of the highest authorities in that government. Moreover, these campaigns of violence extended over a very long period of time and they were all directed at countries which were tiny and posed no direct threat to the security of the United States.

It is very difficult to see how such activities can be justified on moral grounds. By what reasonable doctrines can it be said that the United States or any other country should engage in activities of this nature? It is surely no defence to argue that the agents of the Soviet Union – the notorious KGB – have undoubtedly engaged in such practices. The Senate rejected the view that democratic states could justify their actions by the standards of totalitarians. They pointed out that the standards of free states "must be higher and this difference is what the struggle is all about".[35] Suppose it is true that one's adversary defends himself by political and judicial murder without feeling a need to abide by the rule of law or by any consideration of humanity. Still a government which operates under legal or moral rules must be restrained by those rules. If the government commits murder, it undermines the rule of law in its own jurisdiction. Abroad, it helps break down restraint and invites retaliation. It breeds in the minds of government leaders a vicious cycle of compromises undertaken in the mistaken belief that the end of supporting favourable regimes can justify almost any means which would otherwise be wrong.

U.S. intervention in Chile began under President Kennedy, continued under President Johnson and concluded under President Nixon.[36] It started with the supply of covert funds to support the election of a Christian Democrat, Eduardo Frei, in an effort to prevent the coming to office of a Marxist, Salvador Allende. A total of nearly four million dollars was spent on fifteen covert action projects including funds for political parties, propaganda of all sorts and the organizing of slum dwellers. The effort was successful. In 1965 funds were used to help elect nine pro-American candidates in congressional races and to defeat thirteen pro-Allende candidates. As new elections approached, the efforts continued. In addition, during the 1970 elections about $700,000 of funds from International Telephone and Telegraph and other businesses were earmarked for anti-Allende forces. A National Intelligence estimate at the time stated that, if Allende won, harsh measures would be taken against U.S. business interests, Cuba would be recognized, and a Chilean version of an East European communist state would be established. Despite U.S. efforts, Allende won a small plurality of the votes. Since a majority was needed, the Chilean Congress had to choose between the two top candidates. The special intelligence group in the White House, known as the Forty Committee, decided to bribe Chilean congressmen to vote against Allende. But this time the United States went further. President Nixon ordered the C.I.A. to organize a military coup to prevent Allende's succession. This was done despite a C.I.A. assessment of the impact of an Allende government on U.S. national interests which denied its importance.[37] Specifically, the C.I.A. declared that the U.S. had no vital national interests within Chile and that the world military balance would not be significantly altered by an Allende government. But it did conclude that hemispheric solidarity would be threatened and that an Allende victory would represent a psychological setback for the United States and an advance for Marxist ideas.

So the covert campaign was stepped up. One phase involved cutting off all bilateral credits to Chile, using the U.S. position in international financial institutions to dry up the flow of credit, and so on. The other phase involved contacts with key military figures to organize a coup. Part of this latter plot involved the kidnapping of the chief of staff who was a supporter of constitutional processes. In the course of the abduction, the chief of staff was killed. It is important to recognize that the concern of the Nixon administration was not basically related to Allende's plans to nationalize the copper mines of Chile but rather was undertaken to prevent the establishment of another Cuban-type state which might, in the end, opt for Soviet military connections. The strategy was successful in that the Chilean economy was reduced to desperate straits and, in the end, a military coup toppled Allende, in the course of which he apparently committed suicide. In his place a brutal military dictatorship was established, and extreme oppression resulted.

This is a truly appalling story when it is remembered that what the United States did was to interfere in the political processes of a country which had a long record of constitutional government. It is an example of the unscrupulous exercise of economic, political and military power in order to fend off a very uncertain future evil. We do not see anything that can be said to justify it.

The story of Chile could be duplicated in its methods, if not in its results, by an examination of U.S. intervention in Zaire and Angola.[38] The techniques are the same: propaganda, subsidization of political parties, assassination plots, the organization of coups, etc. There were of course differences, but the similarities to Chile far outweigh them. True, one can argue that in the case of the Congo (Zaire) U.S. action was taken at least in part in support of United Nations' objectives, and that it perhaps prevented a Soviet effort to exploit secessionist movements; but this is a thin cover for what was essentially a U.S. effort to establish and stabilize a pro-Western regime. The proof of this is that after the U.N. operation was phased out after 1964 the C.I.A. conducted a major military campaign against rebellions for another four years. In Angola there was in fact a struggle between factions, one supported by the United States and another supported by the Soviet Union and Cuba. The U.S. effort in Angola was small, ill-chosen and ineffective. The Soviet–Cuban effort was large, well-chosen and "successful" in that their clients succeeded in gaining temporary (?) political power. The fact is that a guerrilla war goes on, waged by a third group representing the largest tribe in the country; and by recent accounts it is gaining ground against the Cuban-supported government.[39] Meanwhile, the United States has moved on the diplomatic front to begin normalizing relations with its erstwhile opponents.

It is the conclusion of a specialist in the matter that U.S. "fears of a massive, long-term foreign communist influence" in Zaire and Angola were mistaken.[40] His reasons are that the left-wing groups were strongly nationalist and, therefore, jealous of their independence. U.S. efforts to sponsor moderate regimes dedicated to economic growth and representative government have turned out to be founded on fantasy. What has happened is that evidence of C.I.A. activity has contributed to the growth of anti-American sentiment and accentuated divisions between African states. In short, covert action in the African case looks more and more to have been counter-productive in terms of long-term American interests. As for the Soviet Union, it has very little to show for its pains. Nearly 19,000 Cubans are tied down in Angola without much prospect of eventual victory, and the government of that war-torn country remains dependent on its revenues from the off-shore operations of the Gulf Oil Company.[41] A repressive and incompetent regime remains in power in Zaire with the aid of Belgian, French and U.S. assistance.

This analysis has concentrated on describing U.S. covert activities, and has made passing references to the practices of the Soviet Union and Cuba. There is a temptation to forget that other states regularly engage in a wide range of covert (though not necessarily illicit) actions.

Saudi Arabia, for example, using loans and grants amounting to billions of dollars, "brought King Hassan II to condemn the Egyptian–Israeli peace treaty, which he had helped to bring about; in Lebanon, they imposed a truce on the Syrians and the Moslem–Palestinian leftist forces in October 1976; they bought Somalia out of the Soviet camp; they made northern Yemen renounce its radical programmes; they are putting pressure on Persian Gulf states to follow Islamic law more scrupulously; they support ... a religious party in Turkey; their aid to Pakistan and Bangladesh implied religious conditions ...; and they have offered the Filipino government aid that would follow solution of the Moslem problem on Mindanao to Saudi satisfaction".[42] Colonel Qaddafi of Libya has aided coup attempts and separatist movements, and has engaged in running guns and kidnapping. "He has helped Moslems fight Israelis and fight non-Moslems in the Spanish Sahara, Chad, Ethiopia, Lebanon, Thailand and the Philippines; he has worked to overthrow governments in Morocco, Tunisia, Egypt, the Sudan, Jordan, Turkey,

Iran, Afghanistan and Oman; he has funded and armed Moslem fanatics in Egypt, Turkey and Indonesia; ... and he has acquired a major role in the internal affairs of the Central African Empire, Uganda and Pakistan."[43]

This is quite an impressive list by anyone's standards and one wonders, in fact, whether it could be matched by the two superpowers or whether, given the flow of oil money and the Moslem world as an arena, it is ever likely to be. That being said, the question must be asked and answered: is intervention in the Third World ever justified and if so, on what principle? One seems to stand out: The Western powers should "respect the integrity of the political process" in such nations and "act only in defence of that process".[44] In short, there is a justified right of intervention only if some other country acts to impose or depose governments by force or by subversion and if the evidence for such intervention is clear.

By this criterion the U.S. intervention in Chile would be ruled out, whereas the intervention in Angola probably would not. Actual decisions would have to take into account a number of prudential considerations such as whether one's national interests were seriously involved, whether opinion in the region was favourable to the intervention and whether in any case the intervention could be successful. It is a fact and not a theory that many, if not most, of the political changes which are taking place in the Third World have local causes and have little or no connection with the global military balance. This is not to deny that a substantial increase in Soviet intervention capability has occurred. This capability has already been used effectively, and it does increase the risks and dangers of confrontation and potential miscalculation. Nor should one blind oneself to the possible effects of a series of Soviet successes which might, in the end, produce a dangerous shift in the global balance. But we are nowhere near that point as yet, certainly neither in Latin America nor in Africa. Large-scale Russian intervention in the Persian Gulf would be another matter entirely, for obvious strategic reasons; but that very fact must induce caution in Soviet governing circles. Anyhow, undue concentration on the use of force produces a distorted view of the issues. The immediate dangers in the Third World are those posed by Western apathy and cynicism resulting in a failure to apply vital economic aid and technical assistance to the basic problems in this area. It would be immoral to fail to act by these means and then later to rely on force when changes occurred which posed radical political threats to Western interests.

We could sum up by stating a theory reminiscent of the "just" or justified war theory which we discussed in Chapter 3. Unilateral and coercive intervention can be justified if it is (1) a response to intervention by one's opponents; (2) a defence of the integrity of the internal political process; (3) a means to re-establish the balance, not to destabilize it; (4) a venture with a reasonable chance of success; (5) a last resort, following humane and constructive efforts to deal with the fundamental problems; (6) an undertaking proportional in its means to the value of its end; (7) not a violation of basic moral principles such as the proscription on murder. As with the principles of just war theory, these principles should be regarded as overridable in unusual situations. But these situations must be unusual, and the principles should be very widely applicable.

Traditionally, arms aid has been used by states to build up allies and substitute arms for the use of one's own forces, to influence the balance of power in an area of the world where important interests were involved, to maintain or overthrow the status quo inside other states and for reasons of profit.[45] In the present era of growing nationalism the trade in arms is viewed as a substitute for traditional intervention as a means of influencing government elites. Exact data for the trade in arms is not available for many countries and for many kinds of equipment. We have no idea, for example, of the volume of rifles and machine guns shipped annually to recipients by communist countries; and so far efforts by the United Nations to secure disclosure of military expenditures have not been notably successful.[46] This introduces a note of caution into any discussion of the moral problems involved, particularly proposals to secure limitations on the trade in arms.

What can be said in general terms is that the world's trade in conventional arms continues to rise, reaching the 13 billion dollar mark in 1976, an increase of sixty per cent in the 1967–76 period, the last decade for which figures are available.[47] The chief suppliers are the United States (39 per cent), the Soviet Union (28 per cent), the United Kingdom and West Germany (5 per cent each), and France (6 per cent). Other developed countries total 11 per cent, with developing states contributing a growing proportion (6 per cent). It should be noted that these figures can be misleading, for the Soviet Union puts an extremely low price on all its equipment and the totals given do not include sums for training, service and construction. The range of error therefore can be said to be very great; for example, at least a 25 per cent addition should be made for training and service functions, and perhaps as much as 50 per cent in the case of Soviet activities. The real totals could then well approach the 19–20 billion dollar mark. The trends are also interesting. In 1950, when the United States began its programme of military assistance, it supplied arms to fourteen countries. Today it supplies about seventy. Developing nations now take six to eight billions worth of arms each year, and the increase is growing at a rate of about seventeen per cent annually. Moreover, the trade is shifting to sophisticated weapons. In 1965 only fourteen countries in the Third World had supersonic jets and only eight had ground-to-air missiles. By 1976 these numbers had risen to forty-four and twenty-six, respectively. There has also been a great expansion of defence industries in Argentina, Brazil, India, Israel, South Africa and Taiwan.[48] Indeed, the market in the Third World has grown so large that many new weapons are being built just for these countries. The overall result is a significant proliferation of conventional arms, the development of a buyer's market (in OPEC's case aided by huge oil revenues), the ability of many states to act militarily independently from the great powers and increasing difficulties of control by the latter.

The motives of the buyer nations are as complex as those of the suppliers; they include real or imagined security needs, old and new rivalries of power, the need to be an independent agent, prestige, internal security, and the feeling that sophisticated training in modern weapons has a spillover effect on one's economy. In short, the motives of both buyers and suppliers go deep into the political values of the parties.

Appraisals (whether moral or political) are therefore bound to be difficult. Some argue that selling purely for profit is a cynical, callous and invidious business; others that multilateral restraint has failed and that unilateral restraint by one nation (however powerful) is unlikely to be very effective since the evidence suggests that others will always be prepared to step forward.[49] But the claim that the arms sale business is necessary to drive the U.S. economy forward is weakened by the fact that only half of one per cent of the labour force is involved.[50] The claim that multilateral restraint has failed is undermined by the fact that the United States has only recently engaged in serious talks with its own allies on the subject, let alone with its chief rivals.

Having said this, it is important to recognize that the chief motive for exporting arms is the international struggle for power itself. Unless this can be modified, there is very little hope that the trade can be curtailed. The examples of the United States in Iran and the Soviet Union in Ethiopia illustrate the point nicely. In the case of Iran the United States sold that country massive amounts of arms and helped for many years to maintain a repressive regime in power in the hope of promoting stability in the Gulf area and thus maintaining access to oil. The Soviet Union for its own strategic reasons in the Horn of Africa has used arms and Cuban troops to preserve an unpopular regime in Ethiopia and that nation's empire.[51] Local injustices – however extreme – are preferred to strategic disadvantages. This may be defensible on some calculation of lesser evils, but it is becoming less easy to do as two things happen – as arms sales mount and local conflicts become more bloody and as it becomes apparent that a combination of nationalism, ethnic and religious fervour, and social change produced by modernization cannot be contained by local elites using imported arms.[52] In effect, this means that a prudent, wise and moral foreign policy will begin to switch its emphasis from arms to aid, from repression to economic growth and fuller political participation by the peoples concerned.

DIRECT CONFRONTATION

If one looks at the practice of the two superpowers, it would seem that they have evolved a tacit rule to the effect that they should avoid direct confrontation at almost any cost. Even in terms of covert action, they have tried to avoid killing each other's agents. It is true that this rule was breached in the Cuban missile crisis (the most notable exception) and certainly came very close to being breached in the Berlin crises. But nevertheless, it has proved to be a general rule of conduct which has helped to limit the danger of war. Since the competition between the two giants is so severe, ways have been found to sidestep this rule, to wit the use of proxy forces by both sides (Cuban troops in Angola, and other parts of Africa, and French forces in Zaire, to name but two examples). These breaches of the principle do add to tension but are of course much less dangerous than the direct combat of Russian and American troops.

JUSTICE, HUMAN RIGHTS AND THE DISTRIBUTION OF RESOURCES

In this section we will look at the fourth principle, that justice requires a more equal distribution of the world's resources. The discussion of justice and of world order belong together because no theory of world order can be satisfactory without showing how demands made in the name of justice can be accommodated, and a theory of international justice can only be useful if it shows what kinds of international structure or structures it requires for its implementation. To say, however, that these two values should be treated together is not to imply that they are easy to attain together. The opposite is probably the case. It has been claimed, for example, that "whereas the Western Powers, in the justifications they offer of their policies, show themselves to be primarily concerned with order, the states of the Third World are primarily concerned with the achievement of justice in the world community, even at the price of disorder".[53]

In the first chapter of this book we gave a brief account of the connection between theories of justice and the consequentialist principle that the rightness or wrongness of actions is determined by the goodness or badness of their consequences. Our conclusion was that we need to distinguish two questions, "What does our conception of justice tell us to do in this situation?" and "What should our conception of justice be?". It will often be true that the first question should be answered at the intuitive level of moral thinking and the second at the critical level. If we are unable to move to the critical level, we will have to stay with the intuitions we already have. This is what characterizes much of the discussion of human rights, which takes for granted that some particular intuition about what counts as a *just* arrangement is universally shared. But there are in fact many conceptions of justice, and it is often in the disputes between nations that these conceptions come into conflict. It is not surprising, as one writer has said, "that 'human rights' tend to become a cause of action only in the minds of people who have the historical consciousness through which to understand their local meaning".[54] For it is within a community with shared intuitions about justice and especially with a shared ideology that the demand for "human rights" can clearly be given a more than formal content. It is true that the second paragraph of the Preamble to the United Nations Charter is an undertaking "to reaffirm faith in fundamental human rights", and that in 1948 the General Assembly adopted the Universal Declaration of Human

Rights. But the Soviet bloc and Saudi Arabia and South Africa all abstained, at least partly because of diverse ideological suspicions about talk of such human rights as that of private property and that of freedom of opinion, expression and assembly. What is wrong is not to say that people should have these rights, but to suppose that we can determine this simply by asking what is demanded by *justice*. For this term means different things to different people.

The question "what should our conception of justice be?" will be answered, on our view, by looking at the general acceptance utilities of rival theories of justice. The rival theories will justify different degrees and different sorts of inequality. For a consequentialist the best theory will be the one which if generally accepted will make people happiest.[55] It is often difficult to know what makes a person happiest, especially if he or she is very different from oneself. Indeed the difficulty is probably proportional to the dissimilarity. But we gave three general sorts of reasons for supposing that more equal distributions are likely to make people happier; and that therefore a distribution which does not promote equality must be supported by some overriding moral consideration if it is to be shown to be justified.

Either nations or individuals can be said to be the bearers of rights in any of the three senses distinguished in the first chapter, and either nations or individuals can be said to have the correlative obligations. If there are such things as human rights, these will impose obligations on individuals or nations to give assistance at least to those who are in what might be called "basic need". Examples of basic needs might be the need for enough food to live on and for shelter from the elements. To say that there are *human* rights to these things is to say that humans are entitled to them simply by virtue of being human. One strong tradition in philosophy, within which we would want to stand, would say that every human being *qua* human being has a right to equal concern and respect. The requirement of formal justice can be interpreted consistently with this as stating that every human being counts equally in a moral decision. The need, for example, of any one person for enough food to live on makes as much demand on our moral consideration, other things being equal, as the same need of any other person. It is perhaps possible to derive human rights from formal justice alone if we confine ourselves to the right to the necessities of life. For it is difficult to see how it is possible to care for someone, whatever one's ideology, and not to care that he be alive rather than dead. It may be that there are other more generous human rights; but even if we restrict our attention to the human right to equal concern, we can raise the main question about justice that we want to discuss at this point.

According to the United Nations Food and Agriculture Organization, about 15,000 people die every day of malnutrition.[56] How can the rich nations and the rich individuals within them claim that they are fulfilling in their consumption patterns the moral requirements of equal concern? To give moral consideration to the starving requires that their need for enough food to live on be met, in the absence of an overriding moral reason. We will be discussing what such overriding reasons might be. It is questionable whether any ideologically neutral account can be given of any human rights that are *not* tied to the necessities of life itself. This is one reason for the unease with which President Carter's Human Rights policy was greeted by America's European allies.[57] The need for food is only one of a number of needs that we might have mentioned; the same sorts of arguments as those we shall make shortly could be made about the need for raw materials, for energy, for technology and for education. But in these cases, it is more difficult to spell out what the "human right" is without begging ideological questions. Because of limitations of space, we will deal only with world hunger, and we will discuss the arguments in a very compressed way. But hopefully it will not be hard to expand them, and generalize from them to basic needs as a whole.

We will first propose a thesis, and then consider a number of objections to it, some of them having considerable weight. The thesis is that the wealth of a rich individual or a rich nation should be given away until the point where personal or domestic need is as great as that of the people to whom the money or food might be sent. We will call this "the obligation of radical sacrifice".[58] The initial justification for this thesis is that if each person in the world counts as one, and nobody as more than one, in the moral calculation, then the resources should be used where they can meet the greatest need. The owner of the resources is not allowed morally to give his own happiness more weight just because it is his.[59] (We will assume this as a part of consequentialism for the rest of this chapter.) However this is only the beginning of the discussion. Indeed the thesis has seemed to some so outrageous that the fact that it is apparently implied by some consequentialist points of view has been used as an objection against them (see objection five). But from the fact that the thesis is contrary to received opinion it does not follow that it is wrong. What we need to look at is whether or not the consequentialist position *does* generate this conclusion. If it does, then within the ethical framework of this book we are committed to accepting it.

Before going on to the moral argument, it is worth pointing out that there are several prudential reasons that a wealthy nation might have for trying to alleviate world hunger. First, the flow in natural resources is not in one direction only. This is one characteristic weakness of the lifeboat analogy (see objection seven). Garrett Hardin imagines America as a lifeboat adequately provisioned, with drowning swimmers all round it trying to get in.[60] But the analogy breaks down if we see that just as other nations depend on America for their grain, so America depends on others for its oil, its tin, etc. America could not in fact maintain its present standard of living in isolation from the rest of the world, and the same is true of the other developed countries. There is an increasing prospect of cooperation between the developing countries which export the needed commodities, and a correspondingly growing need for the importing countries to avoid the risk of international boycott. Second, the wealthy nations are vulnerable to sabotage and terrorism, and the motivation for these is likely to increase as the gap between rich and poor nations continues to widen. Third, the reputation for open-handed generosity has proved politically useful in the struggle for international influence. But it is likely to be counter-productive if the generosity is seen as motivated entirely by national interest. More important than any of the reasons given so far is the necessity in a nuclear age of trying to work together towards a just world peace. Disarmament by itself will not be of much avail, even if it is possible, if it is not accompanied by some attempt to lessen the resentment and hostility which is caused by the disparity between nations in wealth.

These are all prudential concerns, and they are perhaps not likely to be sufficient to cause the wealthier countries to reduce their standard of living to the point of parity with the rest of the world. This is especially so because there are short-term prudential reasons on the other side. For example, grain-producing nations have an incentive to raise grain prices until they can balance their trade deficits, and to use their surplus as a political bargaining tool. But the decision about the distribution and export of national resources cannot be a merely prudential one. For any decision which affects the interests of others is in one sense a moral decision, even though those interests are not in fact considered in the decision-making process. It is a moral decision in the sense that moral considerations are *relevant* to it, whether or not they are taken into account.

The first objection to the thesis that rich nations and individuals have a moral obligation of radical sacrifice is that most of the likely recipients of foreign aid are too distant to allow us to consider them morally. Are we not supposed in a moral decision to be able to imagine what it is like to be the person or persons affected by what we do? How can a wealthy individual in a wealthy country imagine what it is like to be a poor individual in a poor country? Is it not as fruitless as asking a biologist to imagine what it is like to be the frog in his research laboratory? The answer to this is probably that it is all a question of degree. The more different a person is from oneself the harder it is to imagine oneself in his position.[61] Modern techniques of communication have made the task easier for the imagination than it was even thirty years ago. The fact that we are not likely to be very successful if the dissimilarity is very great does not remove the obligation to try. It is hard enough for a person to imagine what he himself will be like in five (let alone fifty) years' time. But that does not mean that he should not try to think it through. Besides there is every reason to suppose that starving to death is just as unpleasant for a poor human being as it is for a rich one.

The objection about distance can be put in a different way. It might be said that we have more of an obligation to those we know than to those we do not. Since we know those close to us, and on the whole we do not know those far away, we should therefore use our resources for the benefit of those close to home. As stated, this objection can be interpreted in two ways. Does it mean that we have more of an obligation to those we are acquainted with, or that our obligation is stronger if we are able to identify who it is that will receive the benefit? These claims are different, for it is possible to identify some particular person as the beneficiary without knowing him in the sense of being acquainted with him. But it is not clear that the claim is justified on either interpretation. On the first interpretation we will consider it under the objection about special relations (see objection ten). The second is implausible on its face.[62] Why should my obligation to one person be weaker than to another because I am told beforehand that the second person is to benefit from my action, but I am not told about the first? Some reason for differentiating our obligations in this way would have to be given, and it is not clear what this would be.

The second objection to the obligation of radical sacrifice is that there are enough potential contributors in the wealthy countries so that no particular individual or particular country need feel so heavy a burden of responsibility. Perhaps world hunger could be ended if every person with an income more than sufficient to cover his basic needs gave one per cent of it to famine relief (though we have not yet given a definition of "basic need"). If so, then why should any one person in this category feel guilty about not giving more than one per cent? This same point could probably be made at the level of the state, although the figures would be different. This is an argument for an obligation of minimal sacrifice, not for no obligation at all.

The problem is that there is a very low probability that every person or nation in the relevant category *will* give what would be required on this plan. There is a general question that arises here about universalizability. Suppose that we grant that every moral prescription has to be prescribed not only for the agent but for every person in a position like that of the agent in the morally relevant respects. Does it make any difference if the agent knows in advance that it is highly unlikely that those in his position will act as he is now prescribing? Some families have a system of FHB (family hold back) if there is not enough food for family and guests to have full helpings. Is a child justified in taking a large helping on the grounds that he knows his brothers and sisters will comply with the FHB order, and so there will be enough to go round? Or is he justified on the grounds that he knows that he is the only one in the family who is really hungry? Or is he justified, finally, on the grounds that he knows his siblings are not going to comply, and he does not see why he should be left out? If he argues in this third way, he is putting fairness between siblings above the obligations of hospitality.

There are similar reasons that might be given for not contributing to famine relief, but here the situation is more complicated. The question is whether we are committed to giving whatever is necessary to end world famine, or only to what would be sufficient to end world famine if everyone who could afford it gave the same. If we choose the latter, we might then renege on our commitment on the grounds that we can be sure that everyone else will be faithful, and there will be enough to go round without our contribution. But if we do this, we will have to explain why faithfulness is not morally as much required of us as of the others, and how we know that everyone else will be faithful. Secondly, we might claim that we cannot afford even a small amount. Like the child's claim to be the only one of the family who is really hungry, this claim would be a good one if it were backed by sufficient evidence. But in this case the position is complicated by the difficulty of saying what counts as not being able to afford more. This is like the difficulty in defining basic needs (see objections five and eleven). Thirdly, we might complain about others' lack of generosity, and refuse to give what is needed ourselves. But if we were to refuse on these grounds, it would be because we judged preserving the lives of those who are starving less important than preserving the parity of contribution by those who could afford it. It is like the overriding value placed by the child on fairness between siblings. But why should it be so important that everyone give the same, when the need for relief however financed is so great? Finally, if it *is* true that radical sacrifice is unnecessary for the relief of world hunger because enough people will contribute a lesser amount, this is a good objection to the thesis that the rich nations and the rich individuals within them have this radical obligation.

There are two objections that are often made against any suggestion that there are moral obligations involved in international relations. We have met both of them before. They are that morality is not relevant or appropriate in the relations between states, and that there is no international society to give such a morality a meaningful context. The first of these can be stated either as the view that states are never in fact influenced by ethical considerations in their relationships with one another, or that they never ought to be so influenced. The second chapter of this book attempts to deal with both these claims. The fourth objection relies on the claim that morality is a social institution, relying for its origins and its effectiveness upon social sanctions. Suppose we accept this view. The question whether there is an international society, even at an embryonic stage of development, could only be answered if we knew what would count as such a society. Presumably it would be characterized by a certain level of cooperation, or collective action in the pursuit of goals that the individual countries could not achieve by themselves. Now it is possible to believe that there is an international society in this sense without believing in the possibility of national altruism or even national benevolence. For it is hard to say that modern states never combine to overcome the limits of what they can achieve by themselves.

Perhaps we cannot speak of a world society before most of the countries of the world are involved in cooperation on some sorts of projects. But again there are indications that many of the problems facing individual nations cannot any longer be overcome by nations individually. There is already some cooperation to meet these problems, and there will in all probability be more. The continued existence of the United Nations organization has demonstrated the development of something like a world society in the above sense. The extent to which it has in fact led nations to transcend their national interest is controversial. Certainly this has been the aim.[63]

We have considered four objections so far. The fifth is more problematic than any of them, and we will discuss it at greater length. It has already been referred to as the suggestion that consequentialism must be wrong if it generates the conclusion that wealthy individuals and nations ought to give away their wealth to the point where they need it as much as anyone else to whom they could give it. We might call this the objection from received opinion. The trouble with it is that it might be that the rich do have the obligation of radical sacrifice even if most people in the rich countries do not think they do. Any moral insight of the general public surely deserves respect. But it is not clear that we could ever determine whether a view was that of the general public rather than of some influential and self-interested group within society. Even if a view is that of the general public, and we know that it is, it is still possible that it is dictated by self-interest rather than moral insight. The general public of a wealthy country is as much a privileged class from the standpoint of the rest of the world as the wealthier citizens are within a country. The preservation of a country's relatively high standard of living can be a vital concern for the majority of its people.

However, the objection can be stated more subtly. It can be said that the demand for such radical redistribution of resources is counterproductive. For it will seem so extreme to most of the people who are being asked to sacrifice that it will be rejected out of hand. A less ambitious demand will, on this argument, produce a fairer distribution in the end because it will be more likely to be accepted. One way to reduce the demand would be to say that the rich are obliged only to give away their *excess* resources. But this would leave open the determination of what was excess. It is true that most people do distinguish between what is essential and what is a luxury, but they draw the distinction in very different places. If the determination were left up to the individual, it is conceivable that some people would justify hair transplants or even gold bathtubs as essential. For many people draw the distinction in terms of the life plan they have chosen; they think something is essential if it contributes to the fulfilling of this plan, and thus to long-term happiness. They think that it is a luxury if it does not. Thus if someone is a cellist, a good cello (good enough to enable him to play in a good orchestra) is not a luxury. If someone is a senator, he may think that a hair transplant is necessary for re-election, and therefore for the sound governance of the country. Moreover the more materialistic a person is, the less he would be required to give by this standard, since his life plan will require an abundance of material goods.

But can excess be delimited by common consent? Perhaps there are certain needs which most people would agree have to be met first, such as the need for enough food to live on, for shelter and clothing. But far more than this is covered by the United Nations declaration, which gives to everybody "the right to a standard of living adequate for the health and well-being of himself and his family". The term "well-being" is central here, for "health" itself is defined by the World Health Organisation as "a state of complete physical, mental, and social well-being".[64] But "well-being" is an evaluative term, and it is therefore necessary to ask who is to do the evaluating. If it is the individual person or nation, we are in the same difficulty as before. What one would count as well-being another would count as severe deprivation. The situation is complicated by the almost universal "revolution of rising expectations", which means that "well-being" cannot be taken as a static reference point.[65] It is unlikely that nations could agree on how much is included in the list of "basic" or "essential" needs.

Another way to reduce the demand is to appeal to the distinction between obligation or duty on the one hand and acts of charity or supererogation on the other. The distinction is that a person is praised for performing an obligation or duty, and blamed for not performing it; whereas he is praised for doing a work of charity or supererogation, but *not* blamed for not doing it. If contributing to the relief of world hunger is a work of charity, the demand that we do so is much weaker than it is if contribution is an obligation, and we may be correspondingly more ready to accept it. In order to evaluate the usefulness of this distinction, we need to refer back to another distinction, that made in the first chapter between intuitive and critical thinking. A fairly strong argument can be made for bringing people up to accept on the intuitive level that contributing to famine relief is a work of charity. For suppose, on the contrary, the attempt were made to bring someone up to think that he was blameworthy for not reducing his standard of living to the point where he needs what he has as much as anybody else to whom it could be given. It seems quite possible that he would come to think that if that is what morality demands, so much the worse for morality. The argument continues that this might have a seriously damaging effect on his commitment to other moral standards he was brought up to, and thus lead, if generalized to the population at large, to a weakening of the moral commitment of society as a whole.

There is something artificial about this argument, For it suggests that people can hand on to their children any moral standards they choose. The truth is probably that moral standards are passed on more by practice than by precept. It is not clear that parents who enjoyed their comparative wealth could teach their children that morality demands radical sacrifice. Their children might come to feel this in reaction against their parents' way of life, but then again they might not. Children might be exposed to the demand for radical sacrifice by the media or by their schools. But the main point of the argument is untouched by this artificiality, and by the question of how the demand might be internalized. The point is that to try to internalize it in any way is likely to be counterproductive. It is true that the argument relies on a premise about people's hardness of heart which is open to dispute. It assumes that if faced with a choice between the demand of conscience and the pressure to maintain a high standard of living, large numbers of people would choose the latter. But if this is granted, the argument is a strong one.

However it does not rule out the possibility that it might be appropriate to consider at the *critical* level that contributing to famine relief is an obligation or duty. For the critical level is employed both to decide which principles it is good to live by at the intuitive level, and to adjudicate in particular cases of conflict between intuitions. One of the principles that a person is likely to have internalized is that he ought to try to prevent some harm from occurring if he can without undue sacrifice.[66] The present technology of communications makes it increasingly difficult to be oblivious to the sufferings of those in the rest of world with too little food. When this is brought to his attention, he will be faced with a conflict. On the one hand he will feel that here is a harm which he could help to prevent without sacrificing anything of equally significant value. On the other hand he will feel, if he has accepted the distinction between obligation and charity, that he is not bound to do anything about it, for contributing would be an act of charity. He will have to adjudicate at the critical level between these intuitions. All the objections that we are now considering to the view that he has an obligation of radical sacifice will need to be considered. If the argument of this chapter is correct, one or two of them have considerable force. But when he has done this, he may still conclude that on this occasion radical sacrifice or at least very extensive sacrifice is appropriate.

What is being suggested here is that the fairest distribution of resources is likely to be achieved if those in the developed countries who can afford to contribute to famine relief accept as a general background theory that their contribution is an act of charity; but that they should be reminded sufficiently often of people's sufferings elsewhere so that on those occasions they will override the background theory, and give at a much higher level of generosity. If they merely think that their giving is an act of charity, they will contribute to some extent, perhaps roughly what they do now. But the present level is not enough to alleviate world hunger substantially. In addition, therefore, it would be desirable for people to be moved to override the intuition that their contributions are supererogatory. The question of how often it should be overridden is a question of balance. For the intuition itself is a valuable one, if the previous argument is correct. But people also need to be fed and clothed and housed. The intuition should be overriden as often as it takes to meet these basic needs without destroying the intuition itself. For no intuition can survive being continually overriden. There is also the opposite danger that too frequent exposure to pictures and stories of famine leads only to indifference.

This discussion has been focused at the level of the individual. What a nation should contribute is even more difficult to assess. But perhaps it is appropriate for a nation's aid budget to proceed from the same sort of balance as that just described. The most serious objection to radical sacrifice at the national level arises from the special status of domestic needs. This is an objective we will be looking at later (see objection ten).

The sixth objection arises out of the distinction between acts and omissions, or, as it is sometimes expressed, between acts of omission and acts of commission. It was argued in the first chapter that this is a distinction with some moral significance. Thus in the case of the decisions which doctors characteristically describe in terms of this distinction, the consequences of the act of commission are often either worse than those of the act of omission, or have a higher probability of being equally bad. To kill is an act of commission. It is, roughly, to intervene in a chain of cause and effect that would otherwise not have resulted in a person's dying at a particular time, with the effect that the person dies. To refrain from sending money or food to a starving country is to allow to die; to send poisoned food is to kill.[67] The sixth objection is that we do not need to feel the obligation of radical sacrifice because in not contributing we are omitting not committing, and omissions are not serious enough to warrant drastic measures.

The merit of this objection is somewhat like the merit of the previous one. The intuition that allowing to die is more excusable than killing is sometimes a valuable one. But its significance needs to be evaluated at the critical level on those occasions where it conflicts with the intuition that a harm should be prevented if it can be without undue sacrifice. Again a balance needs to be struck between securing sufficient contributions to meet basic needs and not causing the moral demand to be so burdensome that the whole institution of morality is seriously weakened. It is clear that there are many people in the world who have basic needs that are not being met. It is also probably true that most people in the developed countries could give substantially more than they now do without interfering very much with their life plans. But it is an empirical question, and one that is extraordinarily hard to answer, how far those who can afford to contribute can be pushed before they turn around and reject the whole demand that is being placed upon them.

The seventh objection arises from a perception of what would in fact happen if an obligation of radical sacrifice were accepted and acted upon. We can call it "the lifeboat objection" after one feature of Hardin's comparison of rich nations to lifeboats. The objection is that we will in the end harm the countries we are trying to help if we send them food; for this will only encourage their population to grow and thus the total misery to increase. The objection might also be called "neo-Malthusian", for Malthus argued in 1798 that population tends to increase faster, in a geometric ratio, than the means of production provide food.[68]

It is not our intention to get involved in the debate about the figures themselves. But there are two important respects in which the lifeboat analogy seems to be misleading. First, the dependence of the poorer nations in food and high technology is balanced, as we have seen, by the dependence of the richer nations in raw materials. The suggestion of the analogy is that those in the lifeboat have no need of those outside it.[69] Second, the situation of scarcity is produced in part by the consumption and production patterns of the richer nations. Some examples of this are energy use, waste of reusable resources (including food), and high meat consumption. In the analogy the scarcity is a given, and the resources in the lifeboat are used as effectively as possible for the saving of life. But beef production is not the most efficient use of the available protein, nor is throwing away in the garbage ten per cent of the family's food.[70]

It is not enough, however, for opponents of the lifeboat analogy to point to these defects. For this leaves the essential point of the analogy untouched, that giving away the food will not help those outside the boat in the long run; for in the absence of another *boat* they will drown anyway, and their miseries will merely be increased. Is it true that the resources distributed by famine relief or general foreign aid are bound to be swallowed up by increased population? Again, we cannot get into the figures here. But one plausible view is that lower birth rates can be achieved by certain kinds of improvement in socio-economic conditions.[71] Such factors may be cited as illiteracy, high infant mortality, extremely unjust income distribution, lack of governmental social security systems, underemployment, poor agricultural productivity and the low status of women. There is clearly a very complex inter-relationship between all these. No one knows for certain exactly why population changes occur. But the evidence from such places as Sri Lanka and Korea does suggest that a decline in infant mortality rate is followed by a decline in the fertility rate. Much progress can be achieved by fairly simple programmes of better basic health services in rural areas, better hygiene and attention to better nutrition. Better education changes human aspirations, particularly those of women, and this leads in turn to lower fertility rates. Two-thirds of the world's 800 million illiterates are women. They are mainly undernourished, with the result that they produce unhealthy children. This in turn leads to more pregnancies. Since the status of women is low, sons are desired, not daughters, and a failure to produce sons leads to larger and larger families. Hence more education and better economic opportunities for women are central to any large-scale reduction in fertility rates. Family planning over the 1965–75 decade has produced 20 per cent reductions in crude birth rates in countries with strong development programmes. Economic factors are clearly integrally involved. The World Bank has initiated 210 rural development projects, doubling farm income and leading to better health and living standards. But economic growth has not produced a drop in fertility rates as effectively as it would if income were more equitably distributed. In the less developed world as a whole, the upper 20 per cent of the population receives 55 per cent of the national income, whereas the poorest 40 per cent receives only 10–15 per cent.[72]

It is true that more is needed to overcome the lifeboat objection than a mere fertility decline. For if the decline is not fast enough, it may still be the case that famine relief and general foreign aid does more harm than good in the long run. World hunger must therefore not be tackled in isolation from the other social problems of which it is both cause and effect. The same is true of family planning programmes.[73]. There is an accummulating body of evidence that it is not inevitable that birth rate grows when enough food is provided, as long as the food is accompanied by efforts to improve education, medical services, appropriate agricultural technology, etc. The lifeboat objection cannot be sustained against all proposals for famine relief, but only those which fail to link it with immediate aid in other areas of development.

The eighth objection is that the less developed countries do not deserve aid. It may be said that they have brought their troubles upon themselves, or that money which is sent to relieve hunger usually ends up in administrators' pockets. There are after all innumerable stories of corruption and bureaucratic mismanagement, and it is an important question whether states do in fact pass along transfers of resources to their poor people or simply permit such wealth to go to the already well-to-do.[74] If a state does not practise in its domestic affairs what it preaches to the more developed countries, the force of its moral demand for an international transfer of resources is weakened. But it would be difficult to show that the failure to send money where it is needed is inevitable, or even general, in countries that are the recipients of foreign aid. The matter can be complicated by genuine disagreements about what most needs to be done. It is not reasonable to expect that aid will be acceptable if it is accompanied by too many restrictions on how it is to be used.

It is a controversial question, for example, whether aid should be made contingent upon the successful implementation of a plan by the receiving nation to curtail its population growth. On the one hand it is surely wrong "to take advantage of their hunger to compel them to do what they do not yet believe to be right"; on the other hand, this sort of coercion may be the most effective way to prevent famine in the future.[75] It has been argued that restricted aid of this sort is not coercive, as no country is forced to accept it. But this is too narrow a view of coercion, for there is at least tremendous pressure to accept the aid whatever the restrictions. What seem to be in conflict here are the values of respecting national autonomy and reducing future starvation. The answer does not seem clear. But a consequentialist of the sort described in the first chapter would have to weigh heavily the long-term disadvantage of the poorer nations being made to feel that the richer nations are using famine as an excuse for intervening in their internal affairs.

The argument from merit works both ways. It may be said that economic exploitation in the past by the rich nations has produced present disparities of income, and that therefore reparation should be made. This claim implies demonstration of some kind of wrong done in the past and involves, if such a wrong can be established, some principle of redistribution. In the case of former colonies, it would be difficult to demonstrate economic injury.[76] Colonial investment yields were about the same as domestic investment except for investment in railways. Profits in the latter were higher, but this was true whether the railways were located in Latin America or the United States.[77] The former colonies suffered from severe poverty before the Western powers arrived. It is true that poverty still exists despite Western inputs of capital and technology, but this is probably due not so much to colonial oppression as to increased population growth and cultural conditions which impede education and the status of women.[78] Even if some injury did occur in the past, just how far back should one go and how would such claims be distributed? Should a poor country – for example, Spain – be assessed for the depredations of the conquistadores when Argentina's present GNP is only slightly below that of Spain? Do the present Arab oil sheikhs owe all Christians a share of their revenues due to the Muslim conquests? This kind of moral accounting is mind-boggling and leads nowhere.

The argument might be made alternatively from present injury. For the wealth of the richer nations relies to some extent upon overseas investment, and therefore upon the possibly unjust business practices of overseas companies.[79] The extent to which companies misbehave abroad is controversial. But it is clear that stockholders in these companies have a moral obligation, which for the most part they do not fulfill, to complain about any unethical business policies which come to their attention. If a company continues to pay starvation wages, or to disrupt the ecology of its host country, or if one could demonstrate that above-normal profits persist, the claim for reparations could properly be made.[80] In fact, claims of this sort migh well work in more than one direction. The 1974 increase in oil price certainly produced abnormal profits by any standard, profits which not only added to inflation world-wide, but which affected poorer nations more seriously than richer ones.[81] Nor do multinationa companies show overall rates of profit which differ in significan degree from domestic investment.[82]

It is sometimes said that the richer nations are under no obligatior to give to the poorer, because the poorer would not give to the richer i the roles were reversed.[83] This is an application of what Michael Slote has called the "brazen rule", "It is not wrong to omit doing for others what others would have omitted doing for you, if your positions had been appropriately reversed." The brazen rule has a certain intuitive appeal. It is a lower standard than the golden rule, which says that it is wrong not to be as generous to others as you would want them to be to you, however unlikely it is that they would in fact show such generosity if the roles were reversed. But it is not easy to see how the brazen rule could be justified morally, which is our present concern. Moreover it is unlikely in the case of international obligations that we could know how a poorer country would behave if it became rich. Any hypothesis would be largely speculative.

In general it does not seem that merit is a helpful basis on which to assert either the presence or the absence of an obligation of radical sacrifice.

There are three important objections which we have not yet mentioned which belong together. They are that we have a right to dispose of our own property as we see fit, that the government of a country has the obligation to care first for the needy of its own population, and that there is intrinsic value in the lifestyle of a rich country even though it is expensive to maintain.

The first of these is likely to occur to anyone who takes a libertarian political view. The objection arises out of the notion that if a person has acquired property legitimately (made it, received it by free gift, found it when it was not previously owned, or bought it), then no one else has any right to the disposal of it. This principle operates also at the level of states, and is implied in the United Nations Charter, "Every state has and shall freely exercise full permanent sovereignty, including possession, use and disposal over all its wealth, natural resources, and economic activities." In particular, it may be thought that the starving people of other countries do not have a right to the legitimately acquired wealth of the richer countries, and in addition that the governments of those richer countries do not have a right to tax legitimately acquired wealth in order to redistribute it on humanitarian grounds.[84]

In the first chapter of this book, three ways were distinguished of translating talk about rights into talk about obligations. The libertarian is saying, in the first sense of "right", that it is not wrong for him to keep his money, since it is his property; he does not have any obligation to give it away. In the second sense, he is saying that it would be wrong for any individual or any government to take it away from him. Libertarians do not generally believe in rights of the third and strongest kind. If this translation is accepted, we can see that the question of whether rich individuals and nations have a right to their wealth, in the first sense of "right", is the question whether or not they have an obligation to give it away. This is exactly what we have been discussing all along. To object that they have this right is not to give a *reason* why they do not have the obligation of radical sacrifice, but it is merely to deny the obligation in other terms. In the same way, to object that they have the right in the second sense is merely to state in other terms that it is wrong for governments or anyone else to take their wealth away.

Some form of libertarian position may be defensible from a consequentialist viewpoint. This might involve supposing that ownership plays a very large part in what makes most people happy. But it is difficult to suppose that a given resource gives more happiness to its owner, merely because he keeps the disposal of it, than it would to someone who was on the point of starvation. The issues here are extremely complex, far beyond the scope of this chapter. The consequentialist would have to examine, for example, the general acceptance utility of the principles of private ownership. Perhaps we may be allowed to say that in our opinion the ownership of a resource gives a *prima facie* right in the first sense to keep it, but that this can be overridden by competing obligations. For example, I may have legitimately acquired a seat on the bus. But when an old person comes on board in obvious distress, I may have an overriding obligation to get up. If by saying "I have a right to stay sitting", I mean "I have no obligation to get up", I may be mistaken. This is true even though there may be thirty-five other people also sitting on the bus who could equally easily sacrifice their seats. The fact that a starving Vietnamese is far away geographically makes almost no difference morally, if the previous argument in this chapter was correct. The mere fact of our ownership constitutes a preliminary objection to the suggestion that we have an obligation of radical sacrifice. But the moral, not the legal, rights of ownership can be overridden by the existence of overwhelming need.

It is claimed that a country should feed its own hungry first; that the relationship between a government and its people is a special one, analogous to that between parents and their children; and that just as it is right for a parent to save his own child first from drowning, so it is right for a government to devote its revenues first to relief programmes at home, even if this means that other people in other countries starve. This point can be made at the level of the individual family and at that of the state. The consequentialist justification is that children are best looked after in general if their parents feel this sort of special obligation, and similarly with people and their governments.

The first question that needs to be asked about this claim is how much it is supposed to justify. Does it cover only domestic *famine relief* projects, or does it include programmes for recreation and the enjoyment of leisure? It is not clear whether the domestic standard of living whose maintenance is to be justified on this argument is equal to or higher than bare subsistence. Part of the discussion of this can be deferred to the consideration of the next objection. But let us assume that the claim is supposed to justify not luxury, but a higher standard of living than that enjoyed by other countries who could be helped by the available resources. What merit does the claim have?

It might be said that the government has been elected *in order to* improve the lot of the people of the country, and that it would be dishonest of political leaders not to carry out this mandate. It is surely true that elected politicians have a *prima facie* obligation to keep their promises just as anyone else does. But it is also possible that we elect representatives partly to be more generous in heart than we are ourselves. This is a venerable debate. There is probably a balance for any politician between doing what his constituents have said they wanted, or doing what he judges they would want if they had fuller knowledge of the facts, and doing what he judges they ought to want. In any case it is not clear that his function is merely to transmit the wishes of those who voted for him into policy without any independent judgement.[85]

It was said that the government of a country is more likely to have the interests of its own people at heart than are the governments of any other countries. In the same way the parents of a child are likely to be more concerned for his welfare than any body else's parents. In both cases this assumption can be rebutted. Abused children can legally and morally be removed from their homes by the courts, and we do not always object morally when tyrannical governments are overthrown by the help of foreigners sympathetic to the people's plight. In general, though, the assumption may be correct. But what follows from this is only that we can justify the decision of a government to make domestic distribution of national resources a priority; that in the choice between supporting a certain standard of living abroad and maintaining the same standard at home, it should choose the latter. But this is not sufficient to justify maintaining at home a far higher standard than that which could be supported by the same resources abroad.

Ten years ago the United Nations Commission of International Development met under the chairmanship of Lester Pearson and put the problem this way, "The war against poverty and deprivation begins at home but it must not end there. Both wars must be won. Both problems must be solved." But if this second war is to be won, it may require a radical sacrifice in living standards by the wealthier nations. One of Rawl's famous principles of justice is that any deviations from equality can only be just if they work to the benefit of the least favoured.[86] If applied internationally, this might have exactly the effect of requiring this sort of sacrifice. On the consequentialist view, the favoured status given to its own citizens by a government would be hard to justify if it resulted in gross inequalities between peoples. These inequalities would not maximise total happiness because of such factors as diminishing marginal utility, the promotion of envy and hatred, and the discouragement of self-respect and mutuality.

It might be argued that a government knows its own people best and, therefore, has the clearest perception of the people's needs and the best way to meet them; that it is therefore most efficient for each country to look after its own needs, so as to reduce the number of times that inappropriate aid is given. This argument is a good one. But what it shows is not that the richer nations should not give aid to the poorer, but that they should leave the management of it to a great extent up to foreign nationals. The argument would work against all foreign aid only if it showed that one country could not clearly see the desperate need of another.

This leaves the final objection, which is that there are things which wealth makes possible which are good in themselves, and that it is therefore wrong to destroy them by encouraging people to give away their wealth to relieve starvation. The sort of thing in question here might be a symphony orchestra. It is incredibly expensive to maintain an orchestra of any calibre. Part of the expense is due to extraneous factors such as the cost of travel or the desire of businessmen to invest in rare instruments. But some of the expense is essential to any attempt to make beautiful orchestral music. It is bound to take many years to train the musicians, and they are bound to need good instruments. Other examples could easily be found, such as the preservation of large areas of wilderness for hiking and camping, when these acres could be used for lumbering, perhaps mining, and when cleared, for producing food. No doubt there are many features of life in wealthier countries which could be sacrificed without too much real loss. Different people will have different lists, but such things might appear as plastic wishing wells and gold bathtubs. But what about good music and wilderness? Narveson says, "Either we literally do everything we can: which, in the case of many of us, would mean not ten dollars or two or three per cent of our incomes, but probably sixty or seventy per cent. Or we make a judgement that the importance of the kind of life we have set out to live is greater than the amount of suffering preventable by depriving ourselves of the means to live it."[87]

But there are replies to this point. It can be said that the gold bathtubs should go first. Perhaps it is possible to preserve the ultimately valuable things and still meet our obligations to the rest of the world. It can also be argued that the beauty of our music and our unspoilt country is a heritage that can be shared somehow with other peoples. There will be uniquely valuable things that each civilization can contribute to humanity, and it is foolish to destroy them in the name of the general good. This point is obscured by an exclusive concentration on people's material needs. It is true that this argument can be self-serving, but it does not need to be. There is a serious difficulty in trying to select what these uniquely valuable things are, for there may be as many opinions about this as there are people. This is the sort of question that we may have to settle by experience rather than by speculation. For decisions of this sort will in fact have to be made by most of the wealthier nations and have already been made to some extent in countries like the United Kingdom whose wealth has declined in comparision with the rest of the world. It is not yet clear whether anything of fundamental value to humanity has been lost in this process.

These eleven objections do not exhaust the field and they have been dealt with in summary form. But some of them have been seen to have more weight than others; and we can conclude, chiefly from the last three objections and objection five, that it is appropriate to decide at the critical level that the obligation of radical sacrifice is not something we should embrace for day-to-day living. "Such a life", as Aristotle would say, "would be too high for man", although there will be some saints and heroes who can live up to it. But the relegation of famine relief and world aid to the category of charity has not in the past led the richer individuals and nations to contribute at a high enough level of generosity. It is, therefore, also appropriate to decide at the critical level that it is on occasion wrong not to give sacrificially. There is something apparently paradoxical about this conclusion. For it seems to imply self-deception. Surely we cannot both blame and justify the neglect of radical sacrifice. But ideals function best like spurs on a horse; continual use would be counterproductive. The element of self-deception comes in because the suggestion is that a person should use spurs, so to speak, on himself. But the point is that we are on some occasions capable of greater generosity than on others, for a multitude of reasons. This is true at the level of the individual and at the level of the state.[88] We may be inspired by someone else's example or by a vivid picture of the sufferings we might help to alleviate. It is rational and consistent to accept the principle that we should try to multiply these occasions and use them to the full.

INTERNATIONAL INSTITUTIONS

The argument so far is that a relatively stable military balance of power is now necessary for world order because it presents a would-be aggressor with potentially high (perhaps absolute) costs if expansion is pursued and it discourages coercive intervention engaged in without any restraint. This is not to deny that *some* competition at *some* level may be found attractive. A very large number of possible relationships exists given the premises stated in Section 1. We may exclude a cessation of the competition altogether, and we may hope to avoid unrestrained struggle. Between these two extremes many different outcomes are possible. For example restraint could develop to the point where nuclear-free zones are created, entire areas are neutralized from superpower activities, and a new form of the concert system is developed. Intermediate possibilities exist; nuclear weapons could be excluded from an area by agreement, conventional arms levels could be reduced and competition between the great powers could be carried on by economic and diplomatic means with very little growth in more cooperative behaviour.

There is also a wide range of possible outcomes of the efforts to strengthen existing international institutions or to create new institutional relationships. This is so for two reasons: (1) the costs and benefits of these organizations fall unequally on states and (2) their capacities to affect or be affected by such arrangements vary quite dramatically. These considerations apply whether the issue is extended control over nuclear proliferation or the use of oceanic resources (to name only two). The results are roughly the same as in the security area – a wide range of behaviour which reflects the very different capabilities of the parties, and the different costs and benefits to them. For these reasons negotiated agreements on rules and institutions will not be permanent, but will reflect the changing relationships among the participants. In other words, the institutional dimension of world order must be viewed as part of the political process.

This process will determine which issues are likely to produce large-scale mutual benefits and lower costs for which states under which institutional arrangements. United States' and Soviet technical capabilities indicate cooperation in the area of global monitoring of the physical environment but not a regime for the controlled exploitation of the sea bed. New international monetary arrangements to replace the older Bretton Woods regime seem to be a vital interest of the great trading states and OPEC but not the Soviet Union or China. Even in the case of the two former groups of states, the form of the new rules will result from a long and intense process of bargaining.

The point of these examples is to illustrate the fact that we face an extremely complex situation in which many international regimes may be developed, some of which will endure while others will not. The process will be long-term but in the course of these experiences a massive reshaping of values will inevitably take place. It is simply not possible to know the end result or even to indicate the general direction these shifts and compromises will take. It follows, therefore, that it is not possible to predict the kind of world community consensus which may develop.

One could make a case for certain general propositions. National policies which emphasize the importance of respecting local autonomy and indigenous cultures will likely have a head start in competition with policies choosing the opposite. Policies which look ahead to severe population dilemmas and their amelioration will almost certainly be required. Whether the energy dilemma can be combined with new monetary arrangements to produce a new regime is unclear. This does not mean such an effort should not be made but only that preliminary indications do not make the prospects a hopeful one. There is in fact a pattern which explains why the outlook for such new regimes is bleak. It is that such regimes are established and maintained by the most powerful states, for example Britain before the First World War and the United States after the Second World War. When the economic position of the leading state declined then the international regime declined with it. In short, if the leading state or states lack the power to make their policies prevail, the rules are challenged by weaker states and the institution grows unstable; for the costs and benefits change for the parties and new negotiations take place which then result in new rules and a less effective regime.

Our conclusion is that international institutions will not push us despite ourselves into a world community. As with arms control, and for many of the same reasons, progress will only come as the powers perceive this to be in their national interest, weighing the costs and benefits in terms of their own frameworks of value. World society, the *civitas maxima*, is not likely to overtake them unawares. But, as we argued in Chapter 2, it may be in the national interest not to ask repeatedly whether a policy is in the national interest. Moreover it is quite possible that *individuals* will come to share the goal of transcending the national interest. We saw some cases in Chapter 4. Lord Selbourne, P. J. Grigg, General Richard McCreary, Field Marshal Alexander and General Eisenhower all opposed the return of the Russian prisoners to their almost certain death. Alexander said that such treatment was "quite out of keeping with the principles of democracy and justice as we know them". All five of them linked considerations of prudence and morality as did Eden. But one receives a strong impression from reading what they said that Eden used morality (the Russians' behaviour had "often been revolting") as a support for what he perceived as British interests; whereas the others used political arguments ("public opinion" will find the return "revolting") as a support for their moral convictions. It is interesting that it was often those who had to implement the policies, the military, who raised the moral objections. It is no doubt easier for statesmen to forget the human realities which their policies create.

This is why General Marshall gave President Roosevelt the casualty figures every morning with his breakfast. Stimson, too, was deeply moved by the plight of the men he visited who had returned from the Pacific, and he was also committed to the idea of limits on warfare. Again there is a mixture of prudence and morality. But one receives the impression from what he wrote that he went through a genuine moral struggle, and made a sincere attempt to find some other way to end the war than atomic bombs on Japanese cities. The moral commitment of political and military leaders can make a difference in policy-making. It would be foolish to deny this of Gandhi, for example, or Dag Hammarskjold. It is therefore of very great importance that this commitment be nurtured and sustained.

There are two ways which can be almost guaranteed to prevent this. The first is to label morality "moralism" and declare it out-of-bounds for hard-headed or "realistic" statecraft. The second is to embrace an all-or-nothing idealism which will end up with nothing because it cannot get all. We have commented before (as Reinhold Niebuhr did, but paradoxically) that these two positions are equivalent in practice. What we hope to have illustrated in various ways throughout the book is that there can be a movement in both directions between firm general principles and the hopefully impartial and informed consideration of consequences, and that political leaders, like all other moral agents, have to know how and when to make the move. We have tried consistently to give general rules, for example about intervention and deterrence; but we have also given examples of where these rules need to be broken. The point is that to break rules is not to eliminate them. If they are good rules, and we think we have given good ones, they will continue to be useful in practice and to give an account of what those who subscribe to them are in *fact* aiming at in international affairs.

Notes

1. The theoretical framework presented in this chapter owes much to the work of R. M. Hare, although he would not always agree with the position we have taken, and should not be held responsible for our mistakes.

2. But the words "legalistic" and "neurotic" themselves imply value judgements, and it is hard not to beg the question about the value of the training by weighting the words used to describe it in such a way as to secure the eventual verdict one way or another.

3. We are using the term "consequentialism" rather than "utilitarianism" because the latter term has been used for a number of views which we do not hold.

4. John C. Ford, "The Morality of Obliteration Bombing". Reprinted in Richard Wasserstrom, *War and Morality* (Belmont, 1970) esp. p. 31. See the discussion of the doctrine of double effect on pp. 22–3.

5. For a discussion of some of the problems here, see Anthony Kenny, "Divine Foreknowledge and Human Freedom", in Anthony Kenny (ed.), *Aquinas: A Collection of Critical Essays* (New York, 1969).

6. *Nicomachean Ethics*, book V, ch. 1.

7. Cf. Wesley Hohfeld, for a classic statement of the differences between kinds of rights, in "Fundamental Legal Conceptions as Applied to Judicial Reasoning". Partly reprinted in Edward A. Kent (ed.), *Law and Philosophy* (New York, 1970) pp. 127–42.

8. Cf. Nicholas Rescher, *Unselfishness* (Pittsburgh, 1975) esp. ch. 5.

9. Cf. Aristotle, *Nicomachean Ethics*, book IX, ch. 8.

10. Cf. Joseph Butler, *Five Sermons* (New York: Liberal Arts Press, 1949). Butler's views are summarized in William Frankena, *Ethics* (Englewood Cliffs, N.J., 1973) esp. pp. 17–23.

11. Cf. Michael Walzer, *Just and Unjust Wars* (New York, 1977) esp. pp. 19–20.

12. Robert E. Osgood, *Ideals and Self-Interest In America's Foreign Relations* (Chicago, 1953) esp. pp. 17–20.

13. Cf. Melvin Richter, *The Politics of Conscience* (Cambridge, Mass.: Harvard University Press, 1964).

14. Jonathan Glover, *Causing Death and Saving Lives* (London: Penguin, 1977) ch. 6. Glover wants to rule out the consistency of making a moral distinction between acts of omission and commission with his version of utilitarianism. But he does not consider the point that professional use of the distinction between acts and

omissions may be systematically misleading.
15. John C. Ford, "The Morality of Obliteration Bombing", reprinted in Wasserstrom, op. cit., p. 27.
16. Thomas Aquinas, *Summa Theologica*, II–III, Q. 64, art. 7.
17. For a discussion of the legal difficulties, see H. L. A. Hart and A. M. Honore, *Causation in the Law* (Oxford, 1959) esp. pp. 59–78.

CHAPTER 2   THE POLITICAL REALISTS

1. G. B. Kerferd, "The Doctrine of Thrasymachus in Plato's Republic", *Durham University Journal* (1947–48).
2. Plato, *Republic*, 338c.
3. Ibid., 351b.
4. Thucydides, *History of the War Between Athens and Sparta*, book V, ch. 17.
5. Werner Jaeger, *Paideia: The Ideals of Greek Culture*, vol. I, book II (Oxford, 1945) ch. 6.
6. Michael Walzer, *Just and Unjust Wars* (New York, 1977) pp. 4–13.
7. For example, that man has a function in the same sense of "function" in which a pruning hook has a function, and that any art or skill is restricted in essence to promoting the well-being of a single class of objects.
8. We will consider this argument further at the end of this chapter.
9. Plato, *Gorgias*, 483.
10. Thucydides, op. cit., book III, chapters 82 and 83.
11. Cf. Aristotle *Nicomachean Ethics*, book II, ch. 6, 1107a10.
12. See John Plamenatz, *Man and Society*, vol. I (New York, 1963) p. 28.
13. Niccolo Machiavelli, *The Prince*, ch. 18.
14. Ibid., ch. 15.
15. For a concise definition of psychological egoism, see William Frankena, *Ethics* (Englewood Cliffs, N.J., 1963), pp. 20–3.
16. Thomas Hobbes, *Leviathan*, part I, ch. 6.
17. Hans J. Morgenthau, *Scientific Man vs. Power Politics* (Chicago, 1946) p. 154 (henceforth referred to as *SMPP*).
18. Plato, *Gorgias*, 484–5.
19. Hans J. Morgenthau, *Politics Among Nations*, 1st edn (New York, 1950) p. 315, (henceforth referred to as *PN*).
20. Morgenthau, *SMPP*, p. 196.
21. Soren Kierkegaard, *Works of Love*, trans. Howard and Edna Hong (New York, 1962) p. 68.
22. Anders Nygren, *Agape and Eros*, trans. Philip Watson (New York, 1969) p. 732.
23. Werke: Kritische Gesamtausgabe (Weimarer Ausgabe) Weimar (Hermann Böhlaus Nachfolger, 1883) pp. 652, 654 ff.
24. Reinhold Niebuhr, *The Nature and Destiny of Man*, part II, (New York, 1941–3) p. 72.
25. Reinhold Niebuhr, *Moral Man and Immoral Society* (New York, 1932) p. 258 (henceforth referred to as *MMIS*).
26. Aristotle, *Nicomachean Ethics*, book V, ch. 1.
27. Harry David and Robert E. Good (eds), *Reinhold Niebuhr on Politics* (New York, 1960) p. 136.

28. Niebuhr, *MMIS*, p. 57. The following quotations in this paragraph are from the same work: on Gandhi, pp. 242–4; on the ideal of justice, p. 80; on the conflict of ethics and politics, p. 257; on national self-interest, p. 237.

29. Ibid., p. 58. The following quotations in this paragraph are from the same work: on the illusion of perfect justice, p. 277; on religious truth, p. 81; on the possibility of a just society, p. xx and *passim*.

30. Reinhold Niebuhr, *The Nature and Destiny of Man*, op. cit., part II, p. 290.

31. Niebuhr, *MMIS*, op. cit., p. 270.

32. Ibid., p. xxiv. The following quotations in this paragraph are from the same work: on the Marxists, p. 195; on the advice to statesmen, p. 267.

33. Cf. David Hume, *Essays, Moral and Political* part I, essay 6 (1977).

34. Cf. also Niebuhr, *Faith and History* (New York, 1949) pp. 185–7.

35. Niebuhr, *MMIS*, op. cit., p. 91.

36. Ibid., p. 93.

37. The analysis here, and throughout this section, is indebted to Gene Outka, *Agape, An Ethical Analysis* (New Haven, Conn.: Yale University Press, 1972).

38. Matthew 22, 37–40. But it is not clear whether the command is to love one's neighbour as one *is to* love oneself, or as one *in fact* loves oneself. If it is the latter, the passage cannot be used to establish that self-love is prescribed in the New Testament.

39. Niebuhr, *MMIS*, op. cit., p. 69.

40. Paul Ramsey, *Deeds and Rules in Christian Ethics* (New York, 1967) p. 187.

41. J. O. Urmson, "Saints and Heroes", in Joel Feinberg (ed.), *Moral Concepts* (Oxford, 1969) p. 70.

42. Niebuhr, *MMIS*, op. cit., p. 260.

43. Ibid., p. 263.

44. Morgenthau, *SMPP*, op. cit., p. 196.

45. Ibid., on appalling results, p. 188; on conflicting duties, p. 190; on inter-personal measure, p. 183; on ends and means, pp. 181 and 185; on self-sacrifice, p. 192; on reason as a slave, pp. 154 ff and 209.

46. Frankena, *Ethics*, op. cit., pp. 9–11.

47. See Paul Ramsey, *The Patient as Person* (New Haven, Conn.: Yale University Press, 1970). ch. 7, for some medical examples.

48. Walzer, *Just and Unjust Wars*, op. cit., p. 111.

49. Herbert Feis, *The Road to Pearl Harbor* (Princeton University Press, 1950), pp. 326–40.

50. Morgenthau, *SMPP*, p. 8.

51. Kennan also produces examples of this sort, such as American disillusionment with China; see *American Diplomacy, 1900–1950* (Chicago, 1951) chapter III. For a more recent view of the same period, see Michael Schaller, *The U.S. Crusade in China, 1938–1945* (New York, 1979).

52. Morgenthau, *SMPP*, p. 42.

53. Morgenthau, *PN*, p. 68. The other references in this paragraph are to the same work: on definition, p. 315; on the *animus dominandi*, p. 12.

54. The references to *PN* in this paragraph are as follows: on the voluntary surrender of power, p. 22; on international military force, p. 263; on collective security, p. 334; on shared culture, p. 408; on poison gas, p. 329; on politically empty territory, p. 278; on the world community, pp. 191 and 205.

55. Thucydides, op. cit., book III, ch. 9. See Walzer, op. cit., ch. 1.

56. The references to *PN* in this paragraph are as follows: on moral consensus, pp. 165 and 172; on the art of diplomacy, p. 139; on crusades, pp. 181 ff.

57. The references to *PN* in this paragraph are as follows: on the urgency of peace, p. 265; on freeing diplomacy from constraint, p. 419; on the brilliance of diplomats, pp. 106–108, 368, 429; on their not committing errors, p. 445; on diplomatic brains, p. 105; on Hitler's mind, p. 107; on the need for morality in diplomacy,.p. 444.

58. The references to *PN* in this paragraph are as follows: on the Peloponnesian war, p. 174; on genocide, p. 177; on not breaking the enemy's will, p. 443; on morale and power, p. 100.

59. The references to Burke are to Edmund Burke, *Reflections on the Revolution in France* (1790), ed. Mahoney (New York, 1955); on pretext, p. 162; on the sentiments which soften society, p. 86; on the yoke of moderation and virtue, p. 115; on the present opinion in Paris, p. 197.

60. George Kennan, *American Diplomacy, 1900–1950* (Chicago, 1951) p. 182 (henceforth referred to as *AD*). The other references in this paragraph are to *AD*, p. 100 and to *Realities of American Foreign Policy* (Princeton University Press, 1954) pp. 47–48 (henceforth referred to as *RAFP*).

61. *RAFP*, pp. 47–8.

62. *AD*, p. 98. The other quotations in this paragraph are from *AD*, pp. 40 and 42 about China, and *The Cloud of Danger, Current Realities in American Foreign Policy* (Atlantic Monthly Press Book, 1977) p. 41, about democracy.

63. *AD*, p. 136.

64. *AD*, p. 138 and *RAFP*, p. 96.

65. Kennan has perhaps been misled by the analogy between morality and law. If law is seen as typified by a written constitution, the analogy might suggest that morality is too abstract or too inflexible for international use. But there are other models of law, and the analogy is in any case a weak one.

66. *The Cloud of Danger*, op. cit., p. 25, and *Russia, the Atom and the West* (New York, 1957) p. 13.

67. *The Cloud of Danger*, op. cit., pp. 19 ff.

68. *RAFP*, p. 120, emphasis added.

69. Kennan, "Foreign Policy and Christian Conscience", *Atlantic Monthly*, CCIII, no. 5 (May 1959) 44–9.

70. Quoted in Zbigniew Brzezinski, *The Soviet Bloc* (Cambridge, Mass.: Harvard University Press, 1967) p. 485.

71. Henry Kissinger, *The Necessity for Choice* (New York, 1960) pp. 328–9.

72. Robert C. Good, "National Interest and Moral Theory: The 'Debate' Among Contemporary Political Realists" in Roger Hilsman and Robert C. Good (eds), *Foreign Policy in the Sixties: The Issues and the Instruments* (Baltimore, 1965) pp. 271–92.

73. George Kennan, "Ethics and Foreign Policy: An Approach to the Problem" in Theodore M. Hesburgh and Louis J. Halle, *Foreign Policy and Morality, Framework for a Moral Audit* (New York, 1979) pp. 42–4.
    There is a recent collection of essays by ethicists which reflects in three ways the realist tradition we have been considering: first in a reaction against the "optimism" of classical utilitarianism, second in the espousal of a sort of "frank dualism" between private and public morality, and third in the distaste for "the finely calculated more and less" which consequentialists of most sorts find

fundamental to morality. See especially the essays by Stuart Hampshire, Bernard Williams and Thomas Nagel in Stuart Hampshire (ed.) *Public and Private Morality* (Cambridge, 1978).
74. Kennan, "Overdue Changes in Our Foreign Policy", Harpers, CCXIII (August 1956), e.g., p. 33, "learning, and helping others to learn, how man can live in fruitful harmony."
75. Morgenthau, *In Defense of the National Interest* (New York, 1951) p. 242.
76. S. I. Benn and R. S. Peters, *Principles of Political Thought* (New York, 1953) pp. 42 ff.
77. *In Defense of the National Interest*, op. cit., pp. 15–16.
78. Robert Osgood, *Ideals and Self-Interest in America's Foreign Relations* (Chicago, 1953).
79. Arnold Wolfers makes a similar point in *Discord and Collaboration: Essays on International Politics* (Baltimore, 1962), e.g., pp. 58–60.

CHAPTER 3   ETHICS AND WAR

1. The position that war in particular or politics in general are outside the scope of moral evaluation is the position of the realists, and we discussed it in the previous chapter. If the claim is factual, that political decisions about war are never influenced by moral considerations, it can be shown to be false by an examination of the historical record. If it is itself a moral claim, that these decisions *ought* not to be taken on moral grounds, it has to rely on the very dubious premise that the world would be better off if every country pursued its own national interest, by war if necessary, without considering the interests of other nations except as they impinged on its own.
2. Ruth F. Benedict, "Anthropology and the Abnormal", *Journal of General Psychology*, X (1934) 59–80.
3. John H. Yoder, *Nevertheless* (Scottdale, Pennsylvania, 1971) distinguishes eighteen types of pacifism.
4. The argument that pacifism is inconsistent has been made by Jan Narveson, "Pacifism: A Philosophical Analysis", *Ethics*, 75 (1965) 259–71.
5. For a theory of non-violent strategies of national defence, see Gene Sharp, *The Politics of Non-Violent Action* (Boston, 1973); and Mahadevan, Roberts and Sharp (eds), *Civilian Defense: An Introduction* (Gandhi Peace Foundation: New Delhi, 1967).
    There is a tendency by many writers on war to dismiss the pacifist strategy of unarmed defence on the grounds that no successful strategies of this kind have been worked out. These writers fail to engage in any effort to work out such a strategy themselves, but there is no demonstration they can rely on which shows that no such strategy *could* be developed.
6. See Reinhold Niebuhr, *Moral Man and Immoral Society*, op. cit., pp. 241–5.
7. Paul Lehmann, *Ethics in Christian Context* (New York, 1963) pp. 142–3. For a critique, see Paul Ramsey, *Deeds and Rules in Christian Ethics* (New York, 1967) p. 94.
8. Barrie Paskins and Michael Dockrill, *The Ethics of War* (Minnesota, 1979) pp. 112–15.
9. W. K. Clifford, "Lectures and Essays" (1879), reprinted in Baruch A. Brody

(ed.), *Readings in the Philosophy of Religion* (Englewood Cliffs, New Jersey, 1974) pp. 241–7.

10. William James, "The Will to Believe", (1896), reprinted in Brody, op. cit., p. 257.

11. Paskins and Dockrill, op. cit., pp. 122–6.

12. This question will be dealt with at much greater length in ch. 6.

13. John Rawls, *A Theory of Justice* (Cambridge, Mass.: Harvard University Press, 1971) sect. 58.

14. Michael Howard, "Temperamenta Belli: Can War Be Controlled?", in Michael Howard (ed.), *Restraints on War* (Oxford, 1979) pp. 1–2.

15. Quincy Wright, *A Study of War*, 2 vols. (Chicago, 1942). See also Walter Millis, *A World Without War*, (Santa Barbara, 1961) pp. 9–15; and Hedley Bull, "War and International Order", in Alan James (ed.), *The Bases of International Order* (London, 1973); also the short but brilliant lecture by Martin Wight, "War and International Politics", *Listener*, 13 Oct. 1955, pp. 584–5.

16. G. I. A. D. Draper, "Wars of National Liberation and War Criminality", in Howard, op. cit., p. 136.

17. Richard L. Purtill, "On the Just War", *Social Theory and Practice*, vol. I (Spring 1971) 97–102. Reprinted in Tom L. Beauchamp (ed.), *Ethics and Public Policy* (Englewood Cliffs, N.J., 1975). He is modifying the criteria of Joseph McKenna, "Ethics and War: A Catholic View", *American Political Science Review* (Sept. 1960) 647–58.

18. Julius Stone, *Aggression and World Order* (University of California, 1958). It is too soon to tell whether the recent definition by the United Nations General Assembly Resolution 3314 (xxx), December 1974, can overcome this objection. See Julius Stone, "Hopes and Loopholes in the 1974 Definition of Aggression", *American Journal of International Law*, LXXI, no. 2, (Apr. 1977) 224–46.

19. *Aggression and World Order*, p. 182.

20. Michael Walzer, *Just and Unjust Wars* (New York Basic Books, 1977). A penetrating critique is given by Gerald Doppelt, "Walzer's Theory of Morality in International Relations", *Philosophy and Public Affairs*, vol., VIII, no. 1 (Fall 1978) 1–26.

21. Walzer, op. cit., pp. 101–6.

22. Ibid., p. 94.

23. Hedley Bull, *The Anarchical Society* (London, 1977) pp. 16–17.

24. Ibid., pp. 86–93.

25. Paul Ramsey, *War and the Christian Conscience* (Durham, N.C.: Duke University Press, 1961) p. 115.

26. Article 2, Hague Regulations 1907. Article 4A (6), Geneva (P.O.W.) Convention, 1949.

27 Hedley Bull, *The Anarchical Society* (London, 1977) p. 268.

28. Draper, op. cit., p. 144.

29. Paskins and Dockrill, op. cit., pp. 90–6.

30. Walzer, op. cit., pp. 201 ff.

31. Bowyer Bell, *A Time of Terror* (New York, 1978) and Jan Schreiber, *The Ultimate Weapon: Terrorists and World Order* (New York, 1978). On the other hand, Conor Cruise O'Brien sees terrorism as essentially a moral phenomenon, in *Herod: Reflections on Political Violence* (London, 1978).

32. Herrs Buback, Pronto and Schleyer, *The Annual Register* (1977), pp. 130–1.

33. See R. V. Samson, *Tolstoy: The Discovery of Peace* (London, 1973).
34. Donald V. Wells, "How Much Can 'the Just War' Justify?" *Journal of Philosophy*, vol. LXVI no. 23 (4 December 1969).
35. R. B. Brandt, "Utilitarianism and the Rules of War," in Marshal Cohen, Thomas Nagel and Thomas Scanlon (eds), *War and Moral Responsibility* (Princeton, N.J., 1974) p. 37.
36. The consequentialist principle is discussed in ch. 1.
37. Carey B. Joynt and Percy E. Corbett, *Theory and Reality in World Politics* (London, 1978)p.15.
38. Draper, op. cit., p. 155.
39. John C. Ford, "The Morality of Obliteration Bombing", reprinted in Richard Wasserstrom (ed.), *War and Morality* (Belmont, California, 1970) p. 21.
40. *Shimoda–v.–Japan*, 355 Hanrei Jiho 17 (Tokyo Dist. Ct., 7 Dec. 1963), see Marshall Cohen, "War and Its Crimes", in Virginia Held, Sidney Morgenbesser and Thomas Nagel (eds), *Philosophy, Morality, and International Affairs* (Oxford, 1974) p. 80.
41. Sir Solly Zuckerman, *From Apes to Warlords* (New York, 1978) p. 405.
42. Quoted in Walzer, op. cit., p. 256.
43. Zuckerman, op. cit., p. 224.
44. Quoted in Draper, op. cit., p. 159.
45. J. R. Hale, "International Relations in the West: Diplomacy and War", in *The New Cambridge Modern History*, vol. 1 (Cambridge, 1951) p. 259.
46. L. Oppenheim, *International Law*, 6th edn, revised and edited by H. Lauterpacht (London, 1944) pp. 144–5.
47. F. H. Hinsley, in a lecture at Cambridge, Apr. 1975.
48. Donald Cameron Watt, "Restraints on War in the Air Before 1945", in Howard, op. cit., pp. 57–77.
49. Article 232 of the Versailles Treaty.
50. Ibid., article 227.
51. See the contrasting views of P. R. Corbett, *Law and Society in the Relations of States* (New York, 1951) pp. 224–37, where the trials are viewed as the application of *ex post facto* law, and Julius Stone, *Legal Controls of International Conflict* (New York, 1954) who heralds the trials as "an important judicial contribution to the pre-existing evidence of the growth by custom of an international criminal law".
52. D. P. O'Connell, "Limited War at Sea Since 1945", in Howard, op. cit., pp. 123–34, esp. pp. 127–9.
53. P. R. Corbett, op. cit., p. 224; and Alistair Horne, *A Savage War of Peace, Algeria 1954–1962* (New York, 1977); and William Colby, *Honorable Men* (New York, 1978), esp. p. 230. Thus in the Algerian War, torture led to an escalation of brutality; intelligence services were faced with a huge amount of false information since the victims either told the torturer what they wanted to hear or kept quiet anticipating death at the end of their ordeal. (This was also true in Vietnam.) Torture drove into the enemy camp innocent people who were wrongly tortured; it tended to eliminate any moderates who were inclined to compromise and, finally, it demoralized those who inflicted the torture.
54. Quoted in R. B. Brandt, op. cit., p. 27.
55. See Richard Wasserstrom, "The Responsibility of the Individual for War Crimes", in Virginia Held, op. cit., esp. pp. 50–2.

56. Richard Wasserstrom, "The Law of War", *Monist*, 56, vol. 1, (1972) 1–19.
57. Telford Taylor, *Nuremberg and Vietnam: An American Tragedy* (New York, 1970 p. 36; quoted in Wasserstrom, "The Responsibility of the Individual for War Crimes", op. cit., p. 50.
58. Marshall Cohen, "War and Its Crimes", in Virginia Held, op. cit., p. 77.
59. Michael Walzer, "Political Action: The Problem of Dirty Hands", in Marshall Cohen *et al.* (eds), *War and Moral Responsibility* (Princeton University Press, 1974) pp. 62–82.
60. Joel J. Kupperman, "Inhibition", *Oxford Review of Education*, IV 3 (1978); and J. J. C. Smart, "Benevolence as an Overriding Attitude", *Australian Journal of Philosophy*, LV (1977); and Robert Nozick, "Moral Complications and Moral Structures", *Natural Law Forum* XII (1968) 1–50, especially his references to "moral traces".
61. Walzer, *Just and Unjust Wars*, p. 323.
62. Quoted in Walzer, "Political Action: The Problem of Dirty Hands", p. 69.
63. Wasserstrom, "The Laws of War", see note 56. Reprinted in *War and Morality*, see note 39.
64. Marshall Cohen, "War and Its Crimes", pp. 85–6.
65. Alfred Vagts, *Defense and Diplomacy* (New York, 1956) ch. 8.
66. Walzer, *Just and Unjust Wars*, ch. 5, esp. p. 85.
67. W. S. Churchill, *The Gathering Storm* (Cambridge, 1948) p. 320.
68. Lord Beaverbrook, *Politicians and the War* (London, 1948) p. 35.
69. Alfred F. Pribram, *Austrian Foreign Policy 1908–1918* (London, 1923).
70. A. Gentile, *De Iure Belli, Libri Tres*, trans. J. C. Rolfe, vol. II, (Oxford, 1933) book I, ch. 14; Francis Bacon, *Essays*, "Of Empire".
71. Vagtd, op. cit., p. 271.

CHAPTER 4   THREE HARD CHOICES

1. Nicholas Bethell, *The Last Secret* (New York, 1974) p. ix.
2. *American Diplomacy*, op. cit., p. 18.
3. For a discussion of the notion of an ideal observer, see ch. 1, pp. 13–20.
4. Bethell, op. cit., p. 2.
5. Ibid., p. 22.
6. Ibid., p. 77.
7. Ibid., p. 38.
8. Ibid., p. 155.
9. Ibid., p. 185.
10. See Martin J. Sherwin, *A World Destroyed: The Atomic Bomb and the Grand Alliance* (New York, 1975) p. 273. Also Robert J. C. Butow, *Japan's Decision to Surrender* (Stanford, Ca., 1954); Herbert Feis, *Japan Subdued* (Princeton, New Jersey, 1961); Robert Batchelder, *The Irreversible Decision, 1939–1950* (Boston, Mass., 1962).
11. Feis, op. cit., p. 80. The leading U.S. naval historian, Samuel Eliot Morison, gives a figure of 5350 aircraft left with perhaps 7000 more in reserve (*Atlantic Monthly*, Oct. 1960).
12. Batchelder says the losses would have been twice as high, op. cit., p. 150.
13. Butow, op. cit., p. 231.

14. Batchelder, op. cit., pp. 121, 90.
15. Stimson, in "The Atomic Bomb and the Surrender of Japan" in Edwin Fogelman (ed.), *Hiroshima: The Decision to Use the A-Bomb* (New York, 1964) p. 13.
16. Batchelder, op. cit., p. 37.
17. Ibid., p. 38.
18. Walzer, *Just and Unjust Wars*, p. 256. See also, in this book, pp. 65–6.
19. Sir Solly Zuckerman, *From Apes to Warlords*, esp. ch. 15.
20. Batchelder, op. cit., p. 187.
21. Ibid., pp. 209, 265. Sherwin, op. cit., p. 111.
22. Walzer, op. cit., p. 264.
23. Harold Urey, in Batchelder, op. cit., p. 156.
24. Sherwin, op. cit., p. 230.
25. Batchelder, op. cit., p. 214.
26. E.g. P. M. S. Blackett, *Fear, War and the Bomb: Military and Political Consequences of Atomic Energy* (New York, 1948) p. 139; "So we may conclude that the dropping of the atomic bombs was not so much the last military act of the Second World War, as the first major operation of the cold diplomatic war with Russia now in progress."
27. Szilard used this argument in 1944, though he changed his mind later and so did Conant, Compton, Oppenheimer and Teller. Sherwin, op. cit., pp. 118, 200, 213 and 218.
28. Batchelder, op. cit., pp. 69 and 217.
29. Paul Ramsey, *War and the Christian Conscience* (Durham, 1961) pp. 65–6.
30. Walzer, op. cit., p. 268.
31. There is a very large literature on the subject. Vehemently opposed are J. F. C. Fuller, *The Second World War: 1939–45* (New York, 1948); Liddell Hart, *The Defense of the West* (New York, 1950); Chester Wilmot, *The Struggle For Europe* (New York, 1952). Sir John Slessor, *The Central Blue* (New York, 1957) is less emphatic. Later scholars are divided: Anne Armstrong, *Unconditional Surrender* (Rutgers, N.J., 1961) condemns the policy whereas Paul Kecskemeti, *Strategic Surrender* (Stanford, Cal., 1959), presents a more mixed evaluation.
32. See Bradley F. Smith and Elina Agarossi, *Operation Sunrise: The Secret Surrender* (New York, 1979).
33. Kecskemeti, op. cit., p. 239.
34. Ibid., p. 206.
35. For different appraisals see the following works: A. J. P. Taylor, *The Origins of the Second World War*, 2nd edn, (New York, 1963); Christopher Thorne, *The Approach of War 1938–39* (London, 1968); E. M. Robertson, *Hitler's Pre-War Policy* (London, 1963); Sir John W. Wheeler-Bennett, *Munich: Prologue to Tragedy* (London, 1964); Laurence Thompson, *The Greatest Treason* (New York, 1968); Sir Keith Feiling, *The Life of Neville Chamberlain* (London, 1946).
36. Thompson, op. cit., p. 52.
37. Ibid., pp. 230, 258 and 265.

CHAPTER 5   DETERRENCE

1. Quoted in Michael Walzer, *Just and Unjust Wars*, op. cit., p. 275; from George Kennan, "A Conversation with George F. Kennan", *Encounter* XLVII 3:37 (Sept. 1976).
2. Webster's International Dictionary.
3. Michael Walzer, *Just and Unjust Wars*, especially chapter 17; and Barrie Paskins and Michael Dockrill, *The Ethics of War*, especially pp. 236–44.
4. Walzer, op. cit., p. 272.
5. Herman Kahn denied this thesis in *On Thermonuclear War* (Princeton, N.J., 1960). His point of view is attacked in Paul Ramsey, *War and the Christian Conscience* (Durham, 1961), especially pp. 244–72.
6. This analysis of the word "bluff" is consistent with the dictionaries, but it is not vital for the argument of the chapter. For whether or not we *call* "bluff" the making of a threat before forming the intention to carry it out or not to carry it out, this will remain a morally significant category of threats.
7. *The Ethics of War*, p. 211.
8. Cf. Paul Ramsey, "A Political Ethics Context for Strategic Thinking" in Morton A. Kaplan (ed.), *Strategic Thinking and Its Moral Implications* (Chicago, 1973) pp. 134–5.
9. *The Ethics of War*, p. 238.
10. It is also possible that the authors are talking about "moral luck" in the sense which they define later in the book. One relies on moral luck, in their sense, if one risks "intrinsic failure"; the failure not just of some particular moral effort but of one's whole value structure at once. The notion of moral luck itself needs discussion. But it will not in any case help with our present difficulty. For what is apparently needed is a conception of luck which is independent of an assessment of probabilities. But what differentiates moral luck is not an independence from probabilities but the nature of what is risked.
11. Aristotle, *Nicomachean Ethics*, III 5. Under the law of Pittacus, the penalty was doubled for offences committed under the influence of alcohol.
12. An excuse, not a justification, cf. J. L. Austin, "A Plea for Excuses", in his *Philosophical Papers* (Oxford, 1970) pp. 175 ff.
13. One suggestion of T. C. Schelling, *The Strategy of Conflict* (Cambridge, Mass.: Harvard University Press, 1960) pp. 261 ff.
14. The objector might appeal to one of Kant's formulations of the categorical imperative and say that such a strategy uses the members of the armed forces as "means" rather than "ends" by failing to recognize their dignity as moral agents. See H. J. Paton, *The Moral Law* (London, 1948) p. 91.
15. There is an objection to this response that might be made from an analogy with the willing accomplice of a pathological killer. When the accomplice hands the killer the gun, he does not *know* that the gun will be used. But this does not excuse his action either legally or morally. If the bombardier is a killer, are not the pilot and the navigator (e.g. of the Enola Gay) in the position of willing accomplices? The answer is that it is a question of the degree of information available. The willing accomplice of a pathological killer is not a good example for most of the thousands of people involved in the development, maintenance and even targeting of the nuclear weapons. For these people have good general reason to suppose that those in high command are neither insane nor vicious;

they can believe both that massive retaliation would not be justified and that their commanders would not in fact set it in motion. But those, if there are any, who have good reason to suppose that they are *not* engaged in mere bluff cannot appeal to this argument. The original objection was that even if the president and his advisers have not formed the intention to use the weapons, they must rely on some members of the armed forces to form the intention to obey the order to use them. If this is correct, the only response is that the wrong done to these members of the rank and file is still the lesser of two evils. We are indebted to Prof. Ralph Lingdren in the discussion of this point.

16. It is not just their moral anguish that is relevant here. For if the president had hired pathological killers to do the job, they would still be wronged by being commanded to do it.
17. F. H. Hinsley, in a lecture at Cambridge University (Apr. 1975).
18. Sissela Bok, *Lying* (New York, 1978), pp. 141 ff.
19. Cf. Philip Green, *Deadly Logic* (Ohio, 1966) p. 299; "By 'escalation' we mean the transgression on (sic) an implicitly or explicitly established limit by one side in a military conflict."
20. We considered the case of the attack on Hiroshima in Ch. 4.
21. General war is not limited geographically, total war is not limited in level of force; but the terms are not precise. There is a distinction between the principle that one should not be the first to use nuclear weapons and the principle that one should not escalate levels once the first principle has been broken by oneself or one's opponent. But the distinction is one of degree not of kind. At each point the risk of a failure at the present level of conflict has to be weighed against the risk of unlimited war if the step is taken to the next highest level. But we do *not* suppose that failure at any given level is inevitable. It would be inconsistent to believe both in the desirability of graduated response and in the claim that the *only* thing that makes graduated response effective is the threat of unlimited war.
22. Ch. 3, p. 64.
23. *The Military Balance, 1978–79*, p. 113.
24. Ibid., p. 108.
25. We will discuss this question further in the final chapter.
26. Carey B. Joynt, "The Anatomy of Crises", *The Year Book of World Affairs, 1974* vol. 28 (London, 1974), 15–22.
27. We can call "landslide" stakes those which pose the danger of a hierarchical shift in the international system; marginal stakes are those which pose the possibility of gains and losses but which do not involve a hierarchical shift. For the concept of a hierarchical ranking, see G. Schwarzenberger, *Power Politics* (1951) chs. 6 and 7.
28. See Hedley Bull, *The Anarchical Society* (New York, 1977) pp. 124–6.
29. F. H. Hinsley, *Power and the Pursuit of Peace* (Cambridge, 1963) pp. 76–9 and p. 355.
30. Convenient sources for the nuclear proliferation issues are: John Maddox, *Prospects for Nuclear Proliferation*, Adelphi Papers 113 (London, 1975); Ted Greenwood, George W. Rathjens and Jack Ruina, *Nuclear Power and Weapons Proliferation*, Adelphi Papers 130 (London, 1976); Ted Greenwood, "The Proliferation of Nuclear Weapons", in *The Diffusion of Power*, Adelphi Papers 133 (London, 1977) 24–32; Albert Wohlstetter, "Spreading the Bomb Without Quite Breaking the Rules", *Foreign Policy*, 25 (Winter 1976/77) 88–96 and

145–79; Thomas Halsted, "Why No End to Nuclear Testing", *Survival* (Mar./ Apr. 1977) 60–6; L. A. Dunn, M. Brennert and J. S. Nye, Jr., "Proliferation Watch", *Foreign Policy* 36 (Fall 1979) 71–104.

31. Wohlstetter, op. cit., p. 96.
32. Halsted, op cit., p. 65.
33. Maddox, op. cit., pp. 3–4.
34. *New York Times* 4 Nov. 1979. Wohlstetter, op. cit., pp. 149–50, indicates three conditions in which plutonium could be produced from nuclear electric generating plants: (1) from irradiated or "spent" uranium fuel; (2) in fresh mixed plutonium oxide fuel rods; (3) at the output end of a separation plant or the input end of facilities that make mixed plutonium and uranium fuel rods.
35. John R. Larmarch in the *New York Times*, 24 Nov. 1979.
36. Greenwood, *Adelphi Papers* 133, p. 25.
37. Here we follow Greenwood, ibid., pp. 25 ff. We have not discussed either the Threshold Test Ban Treaty of 1976 by which the Soviet Union and the United States stopped testing above 150 kilotons or the Treaty of Underground Explosion for Peaceful Purposes. The reason for this is that they *do not* prevent the superpowers from continuing weapons tests (Halsted, op. cit., p. 65).

CHAPTER 6   ARMS CONTROL AND DISARMAMENT

The literature on these matters is enormous, much of it propagandistic or utopian in nature. What follows is a selection to indicate some of the enduring features of the problems involved and the main lines of argument utilized by different schools of thought. The single best treatment is Hedley Bull, *The Control of the Arms Race* (London, 1961 and 1965). A good short analysis of technical problems is R. J. Barnet and R. A. Falk (eds), *Security in Disarmament* (Princeton, 1965).

1. Rolland A. Chaput, *Disarmament in British Foreign Policy* (London, 1935) p. 17.
2. Merze Tate, *The Disarmament Illusion* (New York, 1942) p. 346. Martin Wight, *Power Politics* (London, 1978) p. 274.
3. Tate, op. cit., p. 347; Wight, ibid., p. 277 argues that "the relation between disarmament and security is more fundamental than the relation between disarmament and international change...."
4. Tate, op. cit., p. 348.
5. William L. Langer, *The Diplomacy of Imperialism, 1890–1902*, 2nd edn (New York, 1951).
6. Tate, op. cit., p. 348.
7. Ibid., p. 348.
8. See, for example, Sir Winston Churchill's speech of 30 Mar. 1954, *House of Commons — Debates*, cols. 1839–1842.
9. *New York Times*, 1 Sept. 1957.
10. Sir Herbert Richmond, *Statesmen and Sea Power* (Oxford, 1946); E. L. Woodward, *Great Britain and the German Navy* (Oxford, 1935) pp. 455–73.
11. Chaput, op. cit., p. 30.
12. W. S. Churchill, *The Gathering Storm* (London, 1948) p. 115.
13. W. M. Jordan, *Great Britain, France, and the German Problem 1918–1939* (London, 1943) p. 160; Chaput, *Disarmament in British Foreign Policy*, pp. 160 ff. This issue

became paramount at the Geneva Naval Conference of 1927. For a brilliant analysis, see John W. Wheeler-Bennett, *Disarmament and Security Since Locarno 1925–1931* (New York, 1932) pp. 122 ff.

14. Salvador De Madariaga, *Disarmament* (New York, 1929); for a slightly different version, see W. S. Churchill, *Arms and the Covenant* (London, 1938) p. 17. Marion W. Boggs, "Atttempts to Define and Limit Aggressive Armament in Diplomacy and Strategy", *University of Missouri Studies*, vol. 16 (Columbia, Mont., 1941).

15. John W. Wheeler-Bennett, *The Pipe Dream of Peace* (New York, 1935) chs. 1, 5 and 9. The English edition is entitled *The Disarmament Deadlock* (London, 1934).

16. U.S. Congress, Senate Committee on Foreign Relations, Sub-committee on Disarmament: Control and Reduction of Armaments. A Decade of Negotiations, 1946–1956. 84th Congress, 2nd Sess. (Washington, 1956) 4. Hereinafter referred to as *Decade of Negotiations*.

17. Woodward, *Great Britain and the German Navy*, ch. 5.

18. *New York Times*, 26 Aug. 1957.

19. Woodward, *Great Britain and the German Navy*, pp. 15, 33, 67 ff, 141 ff, and 431. If weapons changes occur rapidly, no long-range planning is possible. J. Stone, *Containing the Arms Race* (London, 1966) p. 158. Also, Richard Burt, "Technology and Arms Control", *International Affairs* (Jan. 1977) 54.

20. Aristotle, *Politics*, v, 11. 1313 B28; Quincy Wright, *A Study of War* (Chicago, 1942) vol. 2, 760.

21. *New York Times*, 8 July 1957.

22. *Decade of Negotiations*, p. 20. After another decade's experience, the same conclusion is reached in Thomas B. Larson, *Disarmament and Soviet Policy, 1964–1968* (Englewood Cliffs, N.J., 1969), p. 194.

23. Chaput, op. cit., pp. 42–3.

24. Ibid., p. 44.

25. But see Erich Fromm, "The Case for Unilateral Disarmament", in D. G. Brennan, *Arms Control and Disarmament* (London, 1961) pp. 187–97.

26. For one of the first arguments that nuclear war can be kept limited, see Henry A. Kissinger, *Nuclear Weapons and Foreign Policy* (New York, 1957) pp. 222–36.

27. See, for example, Bertrand Russell, "Values in the Atomic Age" in *The Atomic Age*, Sir Halley Stewart Lectures, 1948 (London, 1949) pp. 81–104; Gilbert McAllister (ed.), *The Bomb, Challenge and Answer* (London, 1955) pp. 13–47; Jules Moch, *Human Folly, To Disarm or Perish?* (London, 1955) pp. 61–134.

28. Moch, op. cit., pp. 50–3.

29. Alexander Haddow, "The Problem Before Mankind", in *The Bomb, Challenge and Answer*, p. 18.

30. See the literature cited by Professor Haddow, op. cit., pp. 19–31.

31. *Decade of Negotiations*, p. 11.

32. Wight, *Power Politics*, pp. 286–8. A short analysis of the proliferation problem is in Leonard Beaton, *Must the Bomb Spread* (London, 1966). A disappointing treatment is Ted Greenwood (et al.), *Nuclear Proliferation* (New York, 1977).

33. The point is made by J. I. Coffey, "Threat, Reassurance and Nuclear Proliferation", in B. Boskey and M. Willrich, *Nuclear Proliferation: Prospects for Control* (New York, 1970) p. 132.

34. J. S. Nye, "Nonproliferation: A Long-Term Strategy", *Foreign Affairs* (Apr. 1978) 611. Nye chaired the Carter Administration's National Security Council

group on the problem. His suggestions on the security and prestige aspects of the problem are nebulous in the extreme. The role of U.S. carelessness in spreading the bomb is described in A. Wohlstetter, "Spreading the Bomb Without Quite Breaking the Rules", *Foreign Policy* (Winter 1976/77) p. 88 ff.

35. For a neutral's critical analysis, see Alva Myrdal, *The Game of Disarmament* (New York, 1976) pp. 103–8. The following articles will be cited: *Strategic Survey for 1974, 1975* and *1976*; Colin S. Gray "SALT II and the Strategic Balance", *British Journal of International Studies*, vol. 1 (1975) 183–208; M. Leitenberg, "The SALT II Ceilings and Why They are So High", *British Journal of International Studies*, vol. 2 (1976) pp. 149–63; S. Lodgaard, "The Functions of SALT", *Journal of Peace Research*, vol. 14, no. 1 (1977) pp. 1–22; Paul H. Nitze, "Assuring Strategic Stability in an Era of Détente", *Foreign Affairs*, vol. 54 (Jan. 1976) 207–32; Alton Frye, "Strategic Restraint, Mutual and Assured", *Foreign Policy* (Summer 1977) pp. 3–24; Richard Burt, "The Scope and Limits of SALT", *Foreign Affairs*, vol. 56 (July, 1978) pp. 751–70. A short review of arms sales is Leslie H. Gelb, "Arms Sales", *Foreign Policy* (Winter 1976/77) pp. 3–23.

36. Leitenberg, op. cit., p. 151.

37. Lodgaard, op. cit., p. 6.

38. See Nitze, op. cit. p. 228.

39. Burt, op. cit., p. 760.

40. Frye, op. cit., p. 7.

41. Following S. Sienkiewicz, "SALT and Soviet Nuclear Doctrine", *International Security* (Spring 1978) pp. 94 ff.

42. Trevor Taylor, "President Nixon's Arms Supply Policies", *The Year Book of World Affairs 1972* (London, 1972) pp. 65–80. *Strategic Survey 1976*, p. 24. See also, in this book, Ch. 7, pp. 160–162.

43. Iran, the British Chieftain 1200 tank and the "Rapier" missile; Saudi Arabia, the "Maverick" missile. The Israelis sold arms in 1977 to the tune of about half a billion dollars. In 1976 five Third World countries produced a large range of equipment. (*Strategic Survey, 1976*, p. 21).

44. *Strategic Survey 1976*, p. 26.

45. Martin Wight, *Power Politics* (London, 1978) p. 288. Possibilities for an integrated Western approach to the European area are in Richard Burt, "Technology and East–West Arms Control", *International Affairs*, vol. 53 (Jan. 1977) pp. 51–72. No clear path ahead is seen by Neville Brown, *The Future Global Challenge: A Predictive Study of World Security, 1977–1990* (London, 1978) ch. 25.

46. A recent study – Robert Ranger, *Arms and Politics 1958–1978: Arms Control in a Changing Political Context* (Toronto, 1979) – criticizes severely U.S. policy on arms control. The burden of Ranger's complaint is that the United States has treated threats to stability as primarily technical in nature whereas in fact the dangers arise from political differences between the superpowers.

The directly opposite view – that it is the technologist who is at the heart of the arms race and, in effect, has made captives of governments by a series of ever new weapons – is held by a distinguished British scientist, Lord Zuckerman. (See *The Times*, 21 Jan. 1980).

Our argument is that both technical and political problems exist and that they are inextricably intertwined.

47. For other suggestions, see Franklin Griffiths and John C. Polanyi (eds), *The

Dangers of Nuclear War (Toronto, 1979) particularly ch. 5.
48. Ethical issues involving new weapons technologies will be discussed in the final chapter.

CHAPTER 7   THE PROBLEMS OF WORLD ORDER

1. Hans J. Morgenthau, *Politics Among Nations* (New York, 1950) pp. 80–108.
2. Martin Wight, "The Balance of Power and International Order" in Alan James (ed.), *The Bases of International Order* (London, 1973) p. 104.
3. Here we rely on a consensus of expert opinion. See, *New Conventional Weapons and East–West Security, Adelphi Papers* no. 144 and 145 (London, International Institute for Strategic Studies, 1978).
4. Christoph Bertram in *Adelphi Papers* no. 144, pp. 1–2.
5. Christopher Harvie, ibid., p. 12. See also the discussion in Chapter 6, Section 2.
6. For example, G. W. Rathjens, *The Future of the Arms Race* (1969).
7. See C. S. Gray, "The Arms Race Phenomenon", *World Politics*, vol. 24 (1971) pp. 39–79; and A. Wohlstetter, "Is There a Strategic Arms Race?" *Foreign Policy*, vol. 15 (1974) pp. 3–20; and controversy in succeeding issues. For an analysis arguing that arms races can be conceived of in terms of an equilibrium process, see C. B. Joynt, "Arms Races and the Problem of Equilibrium", *The Year Book of World Affairs 1964* (London, 1964).
8. A recent provocative analysis is Robin Ranger, "Arms Control in Theory and Practice", *The Year Book of World Affairs 1977* (London, 1977) pp. 112–37. This chapter follows Ranger's broad conclusions with the addition of Richard Burt "Implications for Arms Control", in *Adelphi Papers*, no. 145, pp. 16 ff.
9. Some of the more prominent thinkers were: Bernard Brodie, *The Absolute Weapon* (1946); Henry A. Kissinger, *Nuclear Weapons and Foreign Policy* (1957); R. E. Osgood, *Limited War* (1957); M. H. Halperin, *Limited War in the Nuclear Age* (1963); Herman Kahn, *On Thermonuclear War* (1960); Klaus Knorr and Thornton Read (eds), *Limited Strategic War* (1962); T. C. Schelling, *The Strategy of Conflict* (1960); Albert Wohlstetter, "The Delicate Balance of Terror", *Foreign Affairs*, vol. 37 (1959) pp. 209–34. See also D. G. Brennan (ed.), *Arms Control, Disarmament and National Security* (1961); and the classic, Hedley Bull, *The Control of the Arms Race* (1961). One should also consult the annual volumes of the Stockholm Peace Research Institute on the subject.
10. Ranger, op. cit., p. 119.
11. For a cogent argument to this effect, see Milton Leitenberg, "The SALT II Ceilings and Why They are so High", *British Journal of International Studies*, vol. 2 (1976) pp. 149–63.
12. Ibid., p. 155.
13. The following is based on Burt, *Adelphi Papers*, no. 145, pp. 16–19.
14. See the short but powerful exposition in *Strategic Survey 1977*, The International Institute for Strategic Studies (London, 1977).
15. Ibid., p. 116.
16. The U.S.S.R. deploys about 620 of these, mostly west of the Urals. See, *The Military Balance, 1977–1978*, p. 8. The new Soviet backfire bomber adds to the danger. See L. Ruehl, "The Grey-Area Problem", *Beyond Salt II, Adelphi Papers*, no. 141 (London, 1978) p. 28.

17. *Strategic Survey 1978* (London, 1979) p. 109.
18. *New York Times*, 6 Nov. 1979.
19. For a thorough discussion, see James T. Johnson, "The Cruise Missile and the Neutron Bomb: Some Moral Reflections", *Worldview* (December 1977), pp. 20 ff. A response by Paul Ramsey is in the following issue. We have not considered here the vexing question of whether the *threat* to use a morally objectionable weapon differs ethically from its actual use. We have argued in Chapter 5 that it does so.
20. Johnson, op. cit., p. 26.
21. Henry Rowen in *Adelphi Papers*, no. 145, p. 4.
22. Martin Wight, *Power Politics* (New York, 1978) p. 191.
23. Ibid., p. 191.
24. Louis Henkin, "Force, Intervention and Neutrality in Contemporary International Law", *Proceedings of the American Society of International Law* (1963) p. 154.
25. A typical treatment is Charles G. Fenwick, *International Law* (New York, 1948) p. 243.
26. Henkin, op. cit., p. 158.
27. Wight, op. cit., p. 192.
28. George Schwarzenberger, "Hegemonial Intervention", in *The Year Book of World Affairs 1959* (London, 1959) p. 262.
29. Ibid., p. 262.
30. M. C. Havens et al., *Assassination and Terrorism: Their Modern Dimensions* (Manchaca, Texas, 1975) p. 22.
31. Ibid., Appendix A. See also W. J. Crotty (ed.), *Assassinations and the Political Order* (New York, 1971).
32. For example, the Congo and the Dominican Republic following the assassinations of Lumumba and Trujillo.
33. Details can be found in Senate Report, no. 94-465. *Alleged Assassination Plots Involving Foreign Leaders* (Washington, 1975). Referred to hereafter as *Senate Report on Assassination Plots*. There were probably other attempts than those investigated, including Sukarno of Indonesia and Duvalier of Haiti. A summary of the Senate report can be found in the *New York Times* (21 Nov. 1975).
34. See *Senate Report on Assassination Plots*, esp. pp. 121 and 149-150.
35. *New York Times*, 21 Nov. 1975.
36. Basic details on the Chile operation are contained in *Senate Report on Assassination Plots*, pp. 225-254. Tad Szulc, *The Illusion of Peace* (New York, 1978) pp. 353-69, 480-6 and 643-7 contains a somewhat longer version.
37. *Senate Report on Assassination Plots*, p. 229.
38. A short but careful account is Stephen R. Weissman, "CIA Covert Action in Zaire and Angola: Patterns and Consequences", *Political Science Quarterly*, vol. 95 (Summer 1979) pp. 263-86.
39. *New York Times*, 9 Nov. 1979.
40. Weissman, op. cit., p. 264.
41. *The Annual Register* (1978) p. 241. News reports indicate the Cubans have taken several thousand Angolan children to Cuba for communist indoctrination against their will. (*New York Times*, 8 Nov. 1979).
42. Daniel Pipes in the *New York Times*, 8 Nov. 1979.
43. Pipes, op. cit.

44. William P. Bundy, "Who Lost Patagonia? Foreign Policy in the 1980 Campaign", *Foreign Affairs*, vol. 58 (Fall 1979) p. 22.
45. See the discussion of nuclear proliferation in Ch. 5, pp. 121–4, and of arms sales in Ch. 6, pp. 135–6. The following sources have been used for the problems of arms sales: *World Military Expenditures and Arms Transfers 1967–1976*, U.S. Arms Control and Disarmament Agency (Washington, D.C., 1978); David W. Moore, "United States Aid and the Arms Trade", *Current History* (July–Aug., 1979) pp. 5–8, 34–5; Leslie H. Gelb, "Arms Sales", *Foreign Policy*, no. 25 (Winter 1976–1977) pp. 3–23; Ian Bellamy, "The Acquisition of Arms by Poor States", *The Year Book of World Affairs, 1976*, vol. 30 (London, 1976) pp. 174–89; Trevor Taylor, "President Nixon's Arms Supply Policies", *The Year Book of World Affairs, 1972*, vol. 26 (London, 1972) pp. 65–80.
46. *World Military Expenditures*, p. 15.
47. Ibid., p. 7.
48. For an extensive treatment of this aspect of the problem, see Michael Moodie, "Sovereignty, Security, and Arms", *The Washington Papers*, no. 67 (London, 1979).
49. For over a decade the U.S. only supplied small amounts to Latin America. European states simply moved in as suppliers.
50. Moore, op. cit., p. 8.
51. A succinct article is Mohammed Ayoob, "The Super-Powers and Regional 'Stability': Parallel Responses to the Gulf and the Horn", *The World Today* (May 1979) pp. 197–205.
52. The same argument is made in Ernst B. Haas, "Why Collaborate? Issue–Linkage and International Regimes", *World Politics*, vol. 32 (Apr. 1980) p. 387.
53. Hedley Bull, *The Anarchical Society*.
54. Roger Scruton, Viewpoint, *Times Literary Supplement*, 14 (1980) p. 291.
55. We have not tried to discuss the merits of 'classical' as opposed to 'average' utilitarianism, but in a more detailed treatment, especially of problems within population policy, this would need to be done.
56. James Rachels, "Vegetarianism" and "The Other Weight Problem", in William Aiken and Hugh LaFollette (eds), *World Hunger and Moral Obligation* (Englewood Cliffs, N.J., 1977) p. 91. We have benefited a great deal from this volume.
57. See Evan Luard, "Putting the world to rights", *Manchester Guardian Weekly*, 7 May 1978.
58. Peter Singer, "Famine, Affluence and Morality", *Philosophy and Public Affairs*, I, 3, (1972) 229–243, reprinted in Aiken, op. cit., pp. 22–36.
59. This feature of moral judgement was discussed in Chapter 1, Section 1.
60. Garrett Hardin, "Lifeboat Ethics, The Case Against Helping the Poor", *Psychology Today* VIII (September 1974) 38–143, 123–26, reprinted in Aiken, op. cit., pp. 12–21. See also Hardin, "Carrying Capacity as an Ethical Concept", in G. R. Lucas, Jr. and T. W. Ogletree (eds), *Lifeboat Ethics* (New York, 1976) pp. 120–137.
61. We will not discuss here the question of whether our moral obligations extend to animals.
62. Jonathan Glover, *Causing Death and Saving Lives* (London: Penguin, 1977) pp. 100–102.

63. See, for example, the U.N. Declaration of Human Rights, part of which is quoted in William K. Frankena, "Moral Philosophy and World Hunger", in Aiken, op. cit., pp. 67–84.

64. Preamble to the Constitution of the World Health Organization, in *World Health Organization: Basic Documents*, 26th ed., Geneva: World Health Organization (1976) p. 1.

65. Ervin Lazlo (ed.), *Goals for Mankind. A Report of the Club of Rome on the New Horizons of Global Community* (New York, 1977). See also John G. Sommer, *Beyond Charity: U.S. Voluntary Aid for a Changing Third World* (New York, 1977).

66. Singer, op. cit., p. 24.

67. Philippa Foot, "The Problem of Abortion and the Doctrine of the Double Effect", *The Oxford Review* (1967) quoted in Glover, op. cit., p. 93.

68. Joseph Fletcher, "Give If It Helps, But Not If It Hurts", in Aiken, op. cit., pp. 104–14, esp. p. 107.

69. See M. S. Sorous, "The Commons and Lifeboat as Guides for International Ecological Policy", *International Studies Quarterly*, XXI(December 1977) 647–74.

70. Rachels, op. cit., esp. p. 184.

71. There is an enormous literature on the problem. See Arthur J. Dyck, "Assessing the Population Debate", *The Monist* (January 1977) and "The Bucharest World Plan of Action", reprinted in an appendix to "A Report on Bucharest", *Studies in Family Planning* V 12 (New York, December 1974).

72. For a short impressive analysis along these lines, see Robert S. McNamara, "Population and International Security", *International Security*, vol. 2 (Fall 1977) 25 ff. Longer works include John W. Sewell (ed.), *The U.S. and World Development Agenda 1977* (New York, 1977); Denis Goviet, *The Uncertain Promise. Value Conflicts in Technology Transfer* (New York, 1977).

73. Michael S. Teitelbaum, "Population and Development: Is a Consensus Possible?", *Foreign Affairs* (July 1974).

74. Robert W. Tucker, "Egalitarianism and International Politics", *Commentary* (Sept. 1975).

75. Frankena, op. cit., and Singer, op. cit., argue for opposite positions on this question.

76. David K. Fieldhouse, *Economics and Empire, 1830–1914* (London, 1973).

77. Michael Edelstein, "Realized Rates of Return on U.K. Home and Overseas Portfolio Investment in the Age of High Imperialism", *Explorations in Economic History* (July 1976) pp. 283–9, quoted in Richard N. Cooper, "A New International Economic Order for Mutual Gain", *Foreign Policy* (Spring 1977) pp. 66–120, esp. p. 88.

78. McNamara, op. cit.

79. Michael A. Slote, "The Morality of Wealth" in Aiken, op. cit., pp. 124–47.

80. Cooper, op. cit., p. 82.

81. Ibid., p. 90. For a large-scale study, see Richard N. Cooper, *The Economics of Interdependence* (New York, 1968).

82. Ibid., pp. 117–120.

83. Slote, op. cit., pp. 135–9.

84. A now famous account of one form of the libertarian position is Robert Nozick, *Anarchy, State and Utopia* (New York, 1974). Nozick's position is related to world hunger by Jan Narveson, "Morality and Starvation", in Aiken, op. cit., pp. 49–65.

85. See the remarks of George Kennan on this subject, quoted in Ch. 2, pp. 42–3.
86. John Rawls, *A Theory of Justice* (Cambridge, 1971) pp. 75 ff.
87. Jan Narveson, "Aesthetics, Charity, Utility, and Distributive Justice", *Monist* (1972) p. 530.
88. Robert Endicott Osgood, *Ideals and Self-Interest in America's Foreign Relations*, (Chicago, 1953). Especially pp. 441–52.

Index